Matthew Syed   makes au   *Newsnight* and regularly appears on CNN International and World Service TV. After graduating from Oxford University with a prize-winning First in Politics, Philosophy and Economics, Matthew was the   nd table te.....   ...   ...st a decade, three times ......onweal.. Champion...   ne twice rep......nted Great Britain in the Olympic Games.

Matthew Syed's first book, *Bounce: The Myth of Talent and the Power of Practice*, was shortlisted for the William Hill Sports Book of the Year and became a UK bestseller.

Praise for *Black Box Thinking*

'Matthew Syed has issued a stirring call to revolutionise how we think about success – by changing our attitude to failure. Failure shouldn't be shameful and stigmatising, but exciting and enlightening. Full of well-crafted stories and keenly deployed scientific insights, *Black Box Thinking* will forever change the way you think about screwing up' Daniel Pink, author of *Drive* and *To Sell Is Human*

'Retrieval was Matthew Syed's forte when he was England's number one table tennis player. You couldn't get anything past him. And retrieval is the subject of this extraordinarily wide-ranging book. Retrieval of hope, retrieval of experience – not just a true sportsman's determination to retrieve success from the lessons of failure, but a true humanitarian's too. A book that dares us to do better' Howard Jacobson, Winner of the Man Booker Prize

'Excellent . . . Together with his previous book it adds up to a persuasive account of human accomplishment . . . This book is a sustained argument about the damage done by the growth of blame culture in Britain and America . . . Syed's lively book is a powerful warning of the damage such a culture can do' *The Times*

'I think Matthew Syed is on to something. As a former England table tennis champion with a starred first in PPE, he has moved effortlessly on to a writing and broadcasting career of some distinction. Few people are better qualified to write about success . . . Syed's book is soundly constructed, well argued and highly persuasive. And his stories stick in the mind' *Daily Mail*

Also by Matthew Syed

Bounce: The Myth of Talent and the Power of Practice

Black Box Thinking

Marginal Gains and the Secrets of High Performance

MATTHEW SYED

JOHN MURRAY

First published in Great Britain in 2015 by John Murray (Publishers)
An Hachette UK company

First published in paperback in 2016

1

Copyright © Matthew Syed 2015

A CIP catalogue record for this title is available from the British Library

ISBN 978-1-47361-380-5
Ebook ISBN 978-1-47361-379-9

Typeset in Warnock Light by Hewer Text UK Ltd, Edinburgh

Printed and bound by Clays Ltd, St Ives plc

Hodder & Stoughton policy is to use papers that are natural, renewable
and recyclable products and made from wood grown in sustainable
forests. The logging and manufacturing processes are expected to
conform to the environmental regulations of the country of origin.

John Murray (Publishers)
Carmelite House
50 Victoria Embankment
London EC4Y 0DZ

www.johnmurray.co.uk

For Kathy

Contents

Part 6: Creating a Growth Culture

PART 1

The Logic of Failure

1

A Routine Operation

I

On 29 March 2005, Martin Bromiley woke up at 6.15 a.m. and made his way to the bedrooms of his two young children, Victoria and Adam, to get them ready for the day. It was a rainy spring morning, a few days after Easter, and the kids were in high spirits as they sprinted downstairs for breakfast. A few minutes later, they were joined by Elaine, their mum, who had snatched a few extra minutes in bed.

Elaine, a vivacious thirty-seven-year-old who had worked in the travel industry before becoming a full-time mother, had a big day ahead: she was due in hospital. She had been suffering from sinus problems for a couple of years and had been advised that it would be sensible to have an operation to deal with the issue once and for all. 'Don't worry,' the doctor had told her. 'The risks are tiny. It is a routine operation.'[1]

Elaine and Martin had been married for fifteen years. They met at a country dance through a close friend, had fallen in love, and eventually moved in together in a house in North Marston, a cosy village in the heart of rural Buckinghamshire, thirty miles north-west of London. Victoria had arrived in 1999 and Adam two years later, in 2001.

Life was, as for many young families, hectic, but it was also tremendous fun. They had been in an aeroplane for the first time as a family the previous Thursday and had gone to a friend's wedding on the Saturday. Elaine wanted to get her operation out of the way so she could enjoy a few days' break.

At 7.15 a.m., they left home. The kids chatted in the car as they made the short journey to the hospital. Martin and Elaine were relaxed about the operation. The ear, nose and throat (ENT) surgeon, Dr Edwards, had more than thirty years of experience, and was well regarded. The anaesthetist, Dr Anderton, had sixteen years of experience.* The hospital had excellent facilities. All was set fair.

When they arrived they were shown to a room where Elaine was put into a blue gown for her operation. 'How do I look in this?' she asked Adam, who giggled. Victoria climbed up onto the bed so that her mother could read to her. Martin smiled as he listened to a plot that was, by now, familiar. On the windowsill, Adam played with his toy cars.

At one point Dr Anderton came in to ask a couple of standard questions. He was chatty and in fine humour. Like any good doctor, he understood the importance of setting a relaxed tone.

Just before 8.30 a.m., Jane, the head nurse, arrived to wheel Elaine into the operating theatre. 'Are you ready?' she asked with a smile. Victoria and Adam walked alongside the trolley as it rolled down the corridor. They told their mum how much they were looking forward to seeing her in the afternoon, after the operation. As they reached a junction in the corridor, Martin ushered his children to the left as Elaine was wheeled to the right.

She leaned up, smiled, and cheerily said: 'Byeeee!'

As Martin and the kids were walking into the car park – they were going to the supermarket to do the weekly shop and buy a treat for Elaine (cookies) – Elaine's trolley was being wheeled into the pre-operating room. This room, adjacent to the operating theatre, is where last-minute checks are made and the general anaesthetic administered.

Dr Anderton was with her: a familiar and reassuring face. He inserted a straw-shaped tube called a cannula into a vein in the back of her hand, which would deliver the anaesthetic directly into her bloodstream.

'Nice and gently,' Dr Anderton said. 'Here you go . . . into a deep sleep.' It was now 8.35 a.m.

Anaesthetics are powerful drugs. They don't just send a patient to sleep, they also disable many of the body's vital functions, which have to be managed artificially. Breathing is often assisted using a

---

* All names of medical staff have been changed to protect anonymity.

device called a laryngeal mask. This is an inflatable pouch that is inserted into the mouth and sits just above the airway. Oxygen is then pumped into the airway, and down into the lungs.

But there was a problem. Dr Anderton couldn't get the mask into Elaine's mouth: her jaw muscles had tightened, a familiar problem during anaesthesia. He delivered an additional dose of drugs to loosen the muscles, then tried a couple of smaller laryngeal masks but, again, couldn't insert them.

At 8.37, two minutes after being put under, Elaine was beginning to turn blue. Her oxygen saturation had fallen to 75 per cent (anything below 90 per cent is 'significantly low'). At 8.39 Dr Anderton responded by trying an oxygen facemask, which sits over the mouth and nose. He still couldn't get air into her lungs.

At 8.41 he switched to a tried-and-tested technique called tracheal intubation. This is standard protocol when ventilation is proving impossible. He started by delivering a paralysing agent into the bloodstream to completely disable the jaw muscles, allowing the mouth to be fully opened. He then used a laryngoscope to cast a light into the back of the mouth, helping him to place a tube directly into the airway.

But he hit another snag: he couldn't see the airway at the back of the throat. Normally, this is a neat, triangular hole, with the vocal cords to either side. It is usually quite easy to push the tube into the airway and get the patient breathing. With some patients, however, the airway is obscured by the soft palate of the mouth. You just can't see it. Dr Anderton pushed on the tube again and again, hoping that he would find the target, but he couldn't get it in.

By 8.43 Elaine's oxygen saturation had dropped to 40 per cent. This was so low it represented the lower limit of the measuring device. The danger is that, without oxygen, the brain will swell, causing potentially serious damage. Elaine's heart rate had also declined, first to 69 beats-per-minute, then 50. This indicated a lack of oxygen to the heart too.

The situation was becoming critical. Dr Bannister, an anaesthetist in the adjacent operating theatre, arrived to provide assistance. Soon Dr Edwards, the ENT surgeon, had joined them too. Three nurses were on standby. The situation was not yet disastrous, but the margin for error had started to shrink. Every decision now had potentially life-and-death consequences.

Thankfully, there is a procedure that can be used in precisely this situation. It is called a tracheostomy. All the setbacks so far had been in trying to access Elaine's airway via her mouth. A tracheostomy has one huge advantage: you don't go near the mouth. Instead, a hole is cut directly into the throat and a tube inserted into the windpipe.

It is risky, and only used as a last resort. But this *was* a last resort. It was now possibly the only thing standing between Elaine and life-threatening brain damage.

At 8.47 the nurses correctly anticipated the next move. Jane, the most experienced of the three, darted out to fetch a tracheostomy kit. When she returned, she informed the three doctors who were now surrounding Elaine that the kit was ready for use.

They shot a glance back, but for some reason they didn't respond. They were continuing to try to force the tube into Elaine's concealed airway at the back of her mouth. They were absorbed in their attempts, craning their necks, talking hurriedly with each other.

Jane hesitated. As the seconds ticked by, the situation was becoming ever more critical. But she reasoned that three experienced consultants were at hand. They had surely considered the use of a tracheostomy.

If she called out again, perhaps she would distract them. Perhaps she would be culpable if something went wrong. Perhaps they had ruled out a tracheostomy for reasons she hadn't even considered. She was one of the most junior people in the room. They were the authority figures.

The doctors had, by now, significantly elevated heart rates. Perception had narrowed. This is a conventional physiological response to high stress. They continued to try to insert the tube into the airway at the back of the throat. The situation was becoming desperate.

Elaine was now a deep blue. Her heart-rate was a mere 40 beats per minute. She was starved of oxygen. Every second delayed was narrowing her chances of survival.

The doctors persisted in their increasingly frantic attempts to access the airway via the mouth. Dr Edwards tried intubation. Dr Bannister attempted to insert another laryngeal mask. Nothing seemed to work. Jane continued to agonise over whether to speak up. But her voice died in her throat.

By 8.55 it was already too late. By the time that the doctors had finally got oxygen saturation back up to 90 per cent, eight minutes had passed since the first, vain attempt at intubation; in all, she had been starved of oxygen for twenty minutes. The doctors were astounded when they looked at the clock. It didn't make sense. Where had the time gone? How could it have passed so quickly?

Elaine was transferred to intensive care. A brain scan would later reveal catastrophic damage. Normally, with a scan, it is possible to clearly make out textures and shapes. It is recognisably a picture of a human brain. For Elaine the scan was more like television static. The oxygen starvation had caused irreparable harm.

At 11 a.m. that morning, the phone rang in the living room of the Bromiley home in North Marston. Martin was asked to return to the hospital as soon as possible. He could tell that something was wrong, but nothing prepared him for the shock of seeing his wife in a coma, fighting for her life.

As the hours passed, it became clear the situation was deteriorating. Martin couldn't understand it. She had been healthy. Her two kids were at home waiting for her to return. They had bought the cookies from the supermarket for her. What on earth had gone wrong?

He was taken to one side by Dr Edwards. 'Look Martin, there were some problems during the anaesthesia,' he said. 'It is one of those things. Accidents sometimes happen. We don't know why. The anaesthetists did their very best, but it just didn't work out. It was a one-off. I am so sorry.'

There was no mention of the futile attempts at intubation. No mention of the failure to perform an emergency tracheostomy. No mention of the nurse's attempt to alert them to the growing disaster.

Martin nodded and said: 'I understand. Thank you.'

At 11.15 p.m. on 11 April 2005 Elaine Bromiley died after thirteen days in a coma. Martin, who had been at her bedside every day, was back at the hospital within minutes. When he got there Elaine was still warm. He held her hand, told her that he loved her, and said that he would look after the kids as best he could. He then kissed her goodnight.

Before returning the following day to collect her belongings, he asked the children if they wanted to see their mum one last time. To his surprise, they said 'yes'. They were led into a room and Victoria stood at the end of the bed, while Adam reached out to touch his mother and say goodbye.

Elaine was just thirty-seven.

II

This is a book about how success happens. In the coming pages, we will explore some of the most pioneering and innovative organisations in the world, including Google, Team Sky, Pixar and the Mercedes Formula One team as well as exceptional individuals like the basketball player Michael Jordan, the inventor James Dyson, and the football star David Beckham.

Progress is one of the most striking aspects of human history over the last two millennia and, in particular, the last two and a half centuries. It is not just about great businesses and sports teams, it is about science, technology and economic development. There have been big picture improvements and small picture improvements, changes that have transformed almost every facet of human life.

In these accounts we will attempt to draw the strands together. We will look beneath the surface and examine the underlying processes through which humans learn, innovate and become more creative: whether in business, politics or in our own lives. And we will find that in all these instances the explanation for success hinges, in powerful and often counter-intuitive ways, on how we react to failure.

Failure is something we all have to endure from time to time, whether it is the local football team losing a match, underperforming at a job interview, or flunking an examination. Sometimes, failure can be far more serious. For doctors and others working in safety-critical industries, getting it wrong can have deadly consequences.

And that is why a powerful way to begin this investigation, and to glimpse the inextricable connection between failure and success, is to contrast two of the most important safety critical industries in the world today: healthcare and aviation. These organisations have differences in psychology, culture and institutional change, as we shall see. But the most profound difference is in their divergent approaches to failure.

In the airline industry the attitude is striking and unusual. Every aircraft is equipped with two, almost-indestructible black boxes, one of which records instructions sent to the onboard electronic systems, and another which records the conversations and sounds in the cockpit.* If there is an accident, the boxes are opened, the data is analysed, and the reason for the accident excavated. This ensures that procedures can be changed so that the same error never happens again.

Through this method aviation has attained an impressive safety record. In 1912, eight of fourteen US Army pilots died in crashes: more than half.[2] Early fatality rates at the army aviation schools were close to 25%. At the time this didn't seem entirely surprising. Flying large chunks of wood and metal at speed through the sky in the early days of aviation was inherently dangerous.

Today, however, things are very different. In 2013, there were 36.4 million commercial flights worldwide carrying more than 3 billion passengers, according to the International Air Transport Association. Only 210 people died. For every one million flights on western-built jets there were 0.41 accidents – a rate of one accident per 2.4 million flights.[3]

In 2014, the number of fatalities increased to 641, in part because of the crash of Malaysia Airlines Flight 370, where 239 people died. Most investigators believe that this was not a conventional accident, but an act of deliberate sabotage. The search for the black box was still ongoing at the time of publication. But even if we include this in the analysis, the jet accident rate per million take-offs fell in 2014 to a historic low of 0.23.[4] For members of the International Air Transport

---

* Today the 'black' boxes are actually bright orange in colour, to improve visibility, and are often combined in a single unit.

Association, many of whom have the most robust procedures to learn from error, the rate was 0.12 (one accident for every 8.3 million take-offs).[5]

Aviation grapples with many safety issues. New challenges arise almost every week: in March 2015, the Germanwings plane crash in the French Alps brought pilot mental health into the spotlight. Industry experts accept that unforeseen contingencies may arise at any time that will push the accident rate up, perhaps sharply. But they promise that they will always strive to learn from adverse events so that failures are not repeated. After all, that is what aviation safety ultimately means.

In healthcare, however, things are very different. In 1999, the American Institute of Medicine published a landmark investigation called 'To Err is Human'. It reported that between 44,000 and 98,000 Americans die each year as a result of preventable medical errors.[6] In a separate investigation, Lucian Leape, a Harvard University professor, put the overall numbers higher. In a comprehensive study, he estimated that a million patients are injured by errors during hospital treatment and that 120,000 die each year in America alone.[7]

But these statistics, while shocking, almost certainly underestimate the true scale of the problem. In 2013 a study published in the *Journal of Patient Safety*[8] put the number of premature deaths associated with preventable harm at more than 400,000 per year. (Categories of avoidable harm include misdiagnosis, dispensing the wrong drugs, injuring the patient during surgery, operating on the wrong part of the body, improper transfusions, falls, burns, pressure ulcers and postoperative complications.) Testifying to a Senate hearing in the summer of 2014, Peter J. Pronovost, MD, professor at the Johns Hopkins University School of Medicine and one of the most respected clinicians in the world, pointed out that this is the equivalent of two jumbo jets falling out of the sky every twenty-four hours.

'What these numbers say is that every day, a 747, two of them are crashing. Every two months, 9-11 is occurring,' he said. 'We would not tolerate that degree of preventable harm in any other forum.'[9] These figures place preventable medical error in hospitals as the third biggest killer in the United States – behind only heart disease and cancer.

And yet even these numbers are incomplete. They do not include fatalities caused in nursing homes or in outpatient settings, such as pharmacies, care centres and private offices, where oversight is less rigorous. According to Joe Graedon, adjunct assistant professor in the Division of Pharmacy Practice and Experiential Education at the University of North Carolina, the full death toll due to avoidable error in American healthcare is more than half a million people per year.[10]

However, it is not just the number of deaths that should worry us; it is also the non-lethal harm caused by preventable error. In her testimony to the same Senate hearing, Joanne Disch, clinical professor at the University of Minnesota School of Nursing, referred to a woman from her neighbourhood who 'underwent a bilateral mastectomy for cancer only to find out shortly after surgery that there had been a mix up in the biopsy reports and that she didn't have cancer'.[11]

These kinds of errors are not fatal, but they can be devastating to victims and their families. The number of patients who endure serious complications is estimated to be ten times higher than the number of patients killed by medical error. As Disch put it: 'We are not only dealing with 1,000 preventable deaths per day, but 1,000 preventable deaths *and* 10,000 preventable serious complications per day . . . It affects all of us.'[12]

In the UK the numbers are also alarming. A report by the National Audit Office in 2005 estimated that up to 34,000 people are killed per year due to human error.[13] It put the overall number of patient incidents (fatal and non fatal) at 974,000. A study into acute care in hospitals found that one in every ten patients is killed or injured as a consequence of medical error or institutional shortcomings. French healthcare put the number even higher, at 14 per cent.

The problem is not a small group of crazy, homicidal, incompetent doctors going around causing havoc. Medical errors follow a normal, bell-shaped distribution.[14] They occur most often not when clinicians get bored or lazy or malign, but when they are going about their business with the diligence and concern you would expect from the medical profession.

Why, then, do so many mistakes happen? One of the problems is complexity. The World Health Organisation lists 12,420 diseases and disorders, each of which requires different protocols.[15] This complexity provides ample scope for mistakes in everything from diagnosis to treatment. Another problem is scarce resources. Doctors are often overworked and hospitals stretched; they frequently need more money. A third issue is that doctors may have to make quick decisions. With serious cases there is rarely sufficient time to consider all the alternative treatments. Sometimes procrastination is the biggest mistake of all, even if you end up with the 'right' judgement at the end of it.

But there is also something deeper and more subtle at work, something that has little to do with resources, and everything to do with culture. It turns out that many of the errors committed in hospitals (and in other areas of life) have particular trajectories, subtle but predictable patterns: what accident investigators call 'signatures'. With open reporting and honest evaluation, these errors could be spotted and reforms put in place to stop them from happening again, as happens in aviation. But, all too often, they aren't.

It sounds simple, doesn't it? Learning from failure has the status of a cliché. But it turns out that, for reasons both prosaic and profound, a failure to learn from mistakes has been one of the single greatest obstacles to human progress. Healthcare is just one strand in a long, rich story of evasion. Confronting this could not only transform healthcare, but business, politics and much else besides. A progressive attitude to failure turns out to be a cornerstone of success for any institution.

In this book we will examine how we respond to failure, as individuals, as businesses, as societies. How do we deal with it, and learn from it? How do we react when something has gone wrong, whether because of a slip, a lapse, an error of commission or omission, or a collective failure of the kind that caused the death of a healthy thirty-seven-year-old mother of two on a spring day in 2005?

All of us are aware, in our different ways, that we find it difficult to accept our own failures. Even in trivial things, like a friendly game of golf, we can become prickly when we have underperformed, and we are asked about it in the clubhouse afterwards. When failure is related to something important in our lives – our job, our role as a parent, our wider status – it is taken to a different level altogether.

When our professionalism is threatened, we are liable to put up defences. We don't want to think of ourselves as incompetent or inept. We don't want our credibility to be undermined in the eyes of our colleagues. For senior doctors, who have spent years in training and have reached the top of their profession, being open about mistakes can be almost traumatic.

Society, as a whole, has a deeply contradictory attitude to failure. Even as we find excuses for our own failings, we are quick to blame others who mess up. In the aftermath of the South Korean ferry disaster of 2014, the Korean prime minister accused the captain of 'unforgivable, murderous acts' before any investigation had even taken place.[16] She was responding to an almost frantic public demand for a culprit.

We have a deep instinct to find scapegoats. When one reads about the moments leading up to the death of Elaine Bromiley, it is easy to feel a spike of indignation. Perhaps even anger. Why didn't they attempt a tracheostomy sooner? Why didn't the nurse speak up? What were they thinking? Our empathy for the victim is, emotionally speaking, very nearly synonymous with our fury at those who caused her death.

But this has recursive effects, as we shall see. It is partly because we are so willing to blame others for their mistakes that we are so keen to conceal our own. We anticipate, with remarkable clarity, how people will react, how they will point the finger, how little time they will take to put themselves in the tough, high-pressure situation in which the error occurred. The net effect is simple: it obliterates openness and spawns cover-ups. It destroys the vital information we need in order to learn.

When we take a step back and think about failure more generally, the ironies escalate. Studies have shown that we are often so worried about failure that we create vague goals, so that nobody can point the finger when we don't achieve them. We come up with face-saving excuses, even before we have attempted anything.

We cover up mistakes, not only to protect ourselves from others, but to protect us from ourselves. Experiments have demonstrated that we all have a sophisticated ability to delete failures from memory, like editors cutting gaffes from a film reel – as we'll see. Far from learning from mistakes, we edit them out of the official autobiographies we all keep in our own heads.

This basic perspective – that failure is profoundly negative, something to be ashamed of in ourselves, and judgemental about in others – has deep cultural and psychological roots. According to Sidney Dekker, a psychologist and systems expert at Griffith University, Australia, the tendency to stigmatise errors is at least two and a half thousand years old.[17]

The purpose of this book is to offer a radically different perspective. It will argue that we need to redefine our relationship with failure, as individuals, as organisations, and as societies. This is the most important step on the road to a high-performance revolution: increasing the speed of development in human activity and transforming those areas that have been left behind. Only by redefining failure will we unleash progress, creativity and resilience.

Before moving on it is worth examining the idea of a 'closed loop', something that will recur often in the coming pages. We can get a handle on this idea by looking at the early history of medicine, where pioneers such as Galen of Pergamon (second century AD) propagated treatments like bloodletting and the use of mercury as an elixir. These treatments were devised with the best of intentions, and in line with the best knowledge available at the time.[18]

But many were ineffective, and some highly damaging. Bloodletting, in particular, weakened patients when they were at their most vulnerable. The doctors didn't know this for a simple but profound reason: they never subjected the treatment to a proper test – and so they never detected failure. If a patient recovered, the doctor would say: 'Bloodletting cured him!' And if a patient died, the doctor would say: 'He must have been very ill indeed because not even the wonder cure of bloodletting was able to save her!'

This is an archetypal closed loop. Bloodletting survived as a recognised treatment until the nineteenth century. According to Gerry

Greenstone, who wrote a history of bloodletting, Dr Benjamin Rush, who was working as late as 1810, was known to 'remove extraordinary amounts of blood and often bled patients several times'. Doctors were effectively killing patients for the better part of 1,700 years not because they lacked intelligence or compassion, but because they did not recognise the flaws in their own procedures. If they had conducted a clinical trial (an idea we will return to),* they would have spotted the defects in bloodletting: and this would have set the stage for progress.

In the two hundred years since the first use of clinical trials, medicine has progressed from the ideas of Galen to the wonders of gene therapy. Medicine has a long way to go, and suffers from many defects, as we shall see, but a willingness to test ideas and to learn from mistakes has transformed its performance. The irony is that while medicine has evolved rapidly, via an 'open loop', healthcare (i.e. the institutional question of how treatments are delivered by real people working in complex systems) has not. (The terms 'closed loop' and 'open loop' have particular meanings in engineering and formal systems theory, which are different to the way in which they are used in this book. So, just to re-emphasise, for our purposes a closed loop is where failure doesn't lead to progress because information on errors and weaknesses is misinterpreted or ignored; an open loop does lead to progress because the feedback is rationally acted upon).

Over the course of this book, we will discover closed loops throughout the modern world: in government departments, in businesses, in hospitals, and in our own lives. We will explore where they come from, the subtle ways they develop, and how otherwise smart people hold them tightly in place, going round and round in circles. We will also discover the techniques to identify them and break them down, freeing us from their grip and fostering knowledge.

---

* The first proper clinical trial, according to many historians, was conducted by James Lind, a Scottish physician, in 1747. He was trying to find a cure for scurvy and conducted a test on the efficacy of citrus fruit during a long voyage with the East India Company.

Many textbooks offer subtle distinctions between different types of failure. They talk about mistakes, slips, iterations, suboptimal outcomes, errors of omission and commission, errors of procedure, statistical errors, failures of experimentation, serendipitous failures, and so on. A detailed taxonomy would take up a book on its own, so we will try to allow the nuances to emerge naturally as the book progresses.

It is probably worth stating here that nobody wants to fail. We all want to succeed, whether we are entrepreneurs, sportsmen, politicians, scientists or parents. But at a collective level, at the level of systemic complexity, success can only happen when we admit our mistakes, learn from them, and create a climate where it is, in a certain sense, 'safe' to fail.

And if the failure is a tragedy, such as the death of Elaine Bromiley, learning from failure takes on a moral urgency.

III

Martin Bromiley has short brown hair and a medium build. He speaks in clear matter-of-fact tones, although his voice breaks when he talks about the day he switched off Elaine's life support machine.

'I asked the children if they wanted to say goodbye to Mummy,' he says when we meet on a clear spring morning in London. 'They both said "yes", so I drove them to the hospital and we stroked her hand, and said goodbye.'

He pauses to compose himself. 'They were so small back then, so innocent, and I knew how much the loss was going to affect the rest of their lives. But most of all I felt for Elaine. She was such a wonderful mother. I grieved that she wouldn't have the joy of seeing our two children growing up.'

As the days passed, Martin found himself wondering what had gone wrong. His wife had been a healthy, vital thirty-seven-year-old. She had her life in front of her. The doctors had told them it was a routine operation. How had she died?

Martin felt no anger. He knew that the doctors were experienced and had done their best. But he couldn't stop wondering whether lessons might be learned.

When he approached the head of the Intensive Care Unit with a request for an investigation into Elaine's death, however, he was instantly rebuffed. 'That is not how things work in healthcare,' he was told. 'We don't do investigations. The only time we are obliged to do so is if someone sues.'

'He didn't say it in an uncaring way, he was just being factual,' Martin tells me. 'It is not something they have historically done in healthcare. I don't think it was that they were worried about what the investigation might find. I think they just felt that Elaine's death was one of those things. A one-off. They felt it was pointless to linger over it.'

In her seminal book *After Harm*, Nancy Berlinger, a health research scholar, conducted an investigation into the way doctors talk about errors. It proved to be very eye-opening. 'Observing more senior physicians, students learn that their mentors and supervisors believe in, practice and reward the concealment of errors,' Berlinger writes. 'They learn how to talk about unanticipated outcomes until a "mistake" morphs into a "complication". Above all, they learn not to tell the patient anything.'

She also writes of: 'the depths of physicians' resistance to disclosure and the lengths to which some will go to justify the habit of nondisclosure – it was only a technical error, things just happen, the patient won't understand, the patient doesn't need to know.'[19]

Just let that sink in for a moment. Doctors and nurses are not, in general, dishonest people. They do not go into healthcare to deceive people, or to mislead them; they go into the profession to heal people. Informal studies have shown that many clinicians would willingly trade a loss of income in order to improve outcomes for patients.

And yet, deep in the culture, there is a profound tendency for evasion. This is not the kind of all-out deceit practised by conmen. Doctors do not *invent* reasons for an accident to pull the wool over the eyes of their patients. Rather, they deploy a series of euphemisms – 'technical error', 'complication', 'unanticipated outcome' – each of which contains an element of truth, but none of which provides the whole truth.

This is not just about avoiding litigation. Evidence suggests that medical negligence claims actually go down when doctors are open and honest with their patients. When the Veterans Affairs Medical Center in Lexington, Kentucky, introduced a 'disclose and compensate' policy, its legal fees fell sharply.[20] Around 40 per cent of victims say that a full explanation and apology would have persuaded them not to take legal action.[21] Other studies have revealed similar results.[22]

No, the problem is not just about the *consequences* of failure, it is also about the *attitude towards* failure. In healthcare, competence is often equated with clinical perfection. Making mistakes is considered to demonstrate ineptness. The very idea of failing is threatening.

As the physician David Hilfiker put it in a seminal article in the *New England Journal of Medicine*: 'The degree of perfection expected by patients is no doubt also a result of what we doctors have come to believe about ourselves, or better, have tried to convince ourselves about ourselves. This perfection is a grand illusion, of course, a game of mirrors that everyone plays.'[23]

Think of the language: surgeons work in a 'theatre'. This is the 'stage' where they 'perform'. How dare they fluff their lines? As James Reason, one of the world's leading thinkers on system safety, put it: 'After a very long, arduous and expensive education, you are expected to get it right. The consequence is that medical errors are marginalised and stigmatised. They are, by and large, equated to incompetence.'[24]

In these circumstances the euphemisms used by doctors to distract attention from mistakes ('technical error', 'complication', 'unanticipated outcome') begin to make sense. For the individual doctor the threat to one's ego, let alone reputation, is considerable. Think how often you have heard these euphemisms outside healthcare: by politicians when a policy has gone wrong; by a business leader when a strategy has failed; by friends and colleagues at work, for all sorts of reasons. You may have heard them coming from your own lips, from time to time. I know I have heard them coming from mine.

The scale of evasion in healthcare is most fully revealed not just in the words used by clinicians, but in hard data. Epidemiological estimates of national rates of iatrogenic injury (injuries induced inadvertently by doctors, treatments or diagnostic procedures) in the United States suggest that 44 to 66 serious injuries occur per 10,000 hospital visits. But in a study involving more than 200 American hospitals, only 1 per cent reported their rates of iatrogenic injury as within that range. Half of the hospitals were reporting fewer than 5 cases of injury per 10,000 hospital visits. If the epidemiological estimates were even close to accurate, the majority of hospitals were involved in industrial levels of evasion.[25]

Further studies on both sides of the Atlantic have revealed similar results. Investigators working for the Inspector General of the Department of Health and Human Services in the United States analysed 273 hospitalisations and found that hospitals had missed or ignored 93 per cent of events that caused harm.[26] A European study discovered that although 70 per cent of doctors accepted that they should disclose their errors, only 32 per cent actually did.[27] In a different study of 800 patient records in three leading hospitals, researchers found more than 350 medical errors. How many of these mistakes were voluntarily reported by clinicians? Only 4.[28]

Think back to the way Dr Edwards talked about the incident. 'Look Martin, there were some problems during anaesthesia,' he said. 'It is one of those things. The anaesthetists did their very best, but it just didn't work out. It was a one-off. I am so sorry.'

This was not an out-and-out lie. Indeed, he may even have believed what he was saying. After all, the doctors *were* unlucky. It *is* unusual for a patient to have tight jaw muscles. It is also unfortunate that Elaine had a blocked airway that was resistant to attempts at tracheal intubation. They had done their best, hadn't they? What more is there to say?

This kind of reasoning represents the essential anatomy of failure-denial. Self-justification, allied to a wider cultural allergy to failure, morphs into an almost insurmountable barrier to progress*.

For many patients, traumatised by the loss of a loved one, this

---

* It has been argued by some doctors that it makes sense to cover up mistakes. After all, if patients were to find out about the scale of medical error, they might refuse to accept any treatment at all, which might make the overall situation even worse. But this misses the point. The problem isn't that patients aren't finding out about mistakes; it's that doctors aren't finding out about them, either, and are therefore unable to learn from them. Besides, concealing failure rates from patients undermines their ability to make rational choices; patients have a right to know about the appropriate risks before undergoing treatment.

might have been the end of the story, particularly in the UK where doctors are rarely challenged. It is not easy for a grieving family to insist on an investigation when the experts are telling them it is not necessary.

But Martin Bromiley wouldn't give up. Why? Because he had spent his entire professional life in an industry with a different – and unusual – attitude to failure. He is a pilot. He has flown for commercial airlines for more than twenty years. He has even lectured on system safety. He didn't want the lessons from a botched operation to die along with his wife.

So he asked questions. He wrote letters. And as he discovered more about the circumstances surrounding his wife's death, he began to suspect that it wasn't a one-off. He realised that the mistake may have had a 'signature', a subtle pattern which, if acted upon, could save future lives.

The doctors in charge of the operation couldn't have known this for a simple but devastating reason: historically, healthcare institutions have not routinely collected data on how accidents happen, and so cannot detect meaningful patterns, let alone learn from them.

In aviation, on the other hand, pilots are generally open and honest about their own mistakes (crash-landings, near misses). The industry has powerful, independent bodies designed to investigate crashes. Failure is not regarded as an indictment of the specific pilot who messes up, but a precious learning opportunity for all pilots, all airlines and all regulators.

A quick example: in the 1940s the famous Boeing B-17 bomber was involved in a series of seemingly inexplicable runway accidents. The US Army Air Corps responded by commissioning Alphonse Chapanis, a psychologist with a PhD from Yale, to undertake an investigation. By studying the crashes – their chronology, dynamics, and psychological elements – Chapanis identified poor cockpit design as a contributing factor.[29]

He found that the switches controlling the flaps in B-17s were identical to the switches controlling the landing gear (the wheels), and were placed side by side. This was not a problem when the pilots were relaxed and flying conditions perfect. But under the pressure of a difficult landing, pilots were pulling the wrong lever. Instead of retracting the flaps, to reduce speed, they were retracting the wheels, causing the plane to bellyflop onto the runway, with catastrophic results.

Chapanis came up with the idea of changing the shape of the levers so that they resembled the equipment they were linked to. A small rubber wheel was attached to the landing-gear switch and a small flap shape to the flaps control. The buttons now had an intuitive meaning, easily identified under pressure. What happened? Accidents of this kind disappeared *overnight*.[30]

This method of learning from mistakes has been applied to commercial aviation now for many decades, with remarkable results.

Success in aviation has many components, of course. The speed of technological change has helped as has the fact that airlines, worried about reputational damage, competition from other providers, and insurance costs, have a strong commercial incentive to improve safety. Aviation has also benefited from the use of high-resolution simulators and effective training, as we'll see.

However, the most powerful engine of progress is to be found deep within the culture of the industry. It is an attitude that is easy to state, but whose wider application could revolutionise our attitude to progress: instead of denying failure, or spinning it, aviation learns from failure.

And yet how does this happen in practice? How is learning institutionalised in the aviation system (given that pilots, regulators, engineers and ground staff are dispersed across the world), how is an open culture created, and, most importantly of all, how can we apply the lessons beyond aviation?

To find out, we'll examine one of the most influential crashes of recent times, perhaps in the entire history of powered flight. We will see how investigators go about their business, excavate the lessons and turn tragedies into learning opportunities.

The name of the flight was United Airlines 173.

2

United Airlines 173

I

United Airlines Flight 173 took off from JFK International airport in New York on the afternoon of 28 December 1978 bound for Portland, Oregon as its final destination. The sky was clear, the flying conditions close to perfect.[1]

Malburn McBroom, a fifty-two-year-old with silver-grey hair and a clipped voice, was the captain. A veteran of the Second World War, he had more than twenty-five years of flying experience, and lived with his wife in Boyd Lake, Colorado. His ambition to become a pilot had been ignited as a child when he saw travelling barnstormers while walking with his mother. 'I'm going to fly aeroplanes, Mom,' he said.

McBroom's first officer was Rodrick Beebe, a forty-five-year-old who had been with United Airlines for thirteen years and had logged more than five thousand hours of flying time. The third person in the cockpit was Flight Engineer Forrest Mendenhall, a forty-one-year-old who had been with the airline for eleven years. He had clocked 3,900 flying hours. The passengers were in safe hands.

After a brief stopover in Denver, United Airlines 173 departed for Portland at 14.47. It was three days after Christmas and the majority of the 181 passengers were returning home after the holidays. Up in the flight deck, the crew members chatted happily as the plane reached its cruising altitude. The planned flying time was 2 hours and 26 minutes.

At around 17.10, as the plane was given clearance to descend by Air Traffic Control (ATC) at Portland Approach, McBroom pulled the lever to lower the landing gear. Normally this is followed by a smooth descent of the wheels and undercarriage, and an audible click as it locks into place. On this occasion, however, there was a loud thud, which reverberated around the aeroplane, followed by a shudder.

In the cabin the passengers looked around anxiously. They began to speculate on the cause of the noise. Up in the cockpit the crew were also perturbed. Had the landing gear locked into place? If so, what was the loud thud? One of the lights that would normally be glowing if the landing gear was safely in place hadn't illuminated. What did that mean?

The captain had no choice. He radioed to Air Traffic Control and asked them to give him some additional flying time so he could troubleshoot the problem. Portland Approach instantly came back to advise United Airlines 173 to 'turn left heading one zero zero'. In effect, the plane had been put into a holding pattern to the south of the airport, over the Portland suburbs.

The crew made various checks. They couldn't see beneath the plane to determine whether the landing gear was in place, so they made some proxy checks instead. The engineer was sent into the cabin to see whether a couple of bolts, which shoot up above the wing tips when the landing gear is lowered, were visible. They were. They also contacted the United Airlines Systems Line Maintenance Control Center in San Francisco, California. Everything seemed to indicate that the gear was safely down.

The captain was still worried, however. He couldn't be certain. He knew that landing the plane without the gear lowered carried serious risks. Statistics show that planes that attempt to land without the wheels lowered typically suffer no fatalities, but it is still dangerous. McBroom, a responsible pilot, wanted to be sure.

As the plane circled over Portland, he searched for an answer. He pondered why one of the landing gear lights had failed to turn green. He wondered if there was some way of checking the wiring. He searched his mind for other ways to troubleshoot the problem.

While he deliberated, however, another problem was looming. At first, it was just a metaphorical speck in the distance, but as United Airlines 173 continued in its holding pattern, it became ever more real. There were 46,700 lbs of fuel on board the aircraft when it departed Denver, more than enough to reach its destination. But a

DC8 burns fuel at around 210 lbs per minute. The plane could not circle indefinitely. At some point McBroom would have to bring the plane into land.

At 17.46 local time, the fuel level dropped to 5 on the dials. The situation was still within control, but the margin for error was shrinking. Time was becoming ever more critical. The engineer became agitated. He informed the pilot about the state of the fuel, warning about flashing lights in the fuel pump. The cockpit voice recording transcript reveals his growing anxiety.

But McBroom didn't respond in the way the engineer expected. The pilot is ultimately in charge of the flight. He has primary responsibility for the 189 passengers and crew. They were under his protection. He knew the dangers if he came into land without the landing gear lowered. He was adamant that wouldn't happen. He had to find out what was wrong. He had to be certain.

He continued to focus on the landing gear. Was it down? Were there any further checks they hadn't thought of? What more could they do?

At 17.50 Engineer Mendenhall tried again to alert the captain to the dwindling reserves. The captain replied that there were still 'fifteen minutes' of fuel in the tank, but he was wrong. He seemed to have lost track of time. 'Fifteen minutes?' the engineer replied, a tone of incredulity in his voice. 'Not enough . . . Fifteen minutes is gonna really run us low on fuel here.'

With each second, the reserves of fuel were diminishing. A holding pattern had now become a potential catastrophe, not just for the passengers, but also for the residents of southern Portland. A 90 tonne aircraft was circling above a city with its energy draining away.

The first officer and engineer could not understand why the pilot was not heading directly to the airport. Fuel was now the principal danger. The landing gear hardly mattered any more. But he was the authority figure. He was the boss. He had the experience and the seniority. They called him 'sir'.

At 18.06, the fuel was so low that the fourth engine flamed out. 'I think you just lost number four, buddy, you . . .' Thirty seconds later, he repeated the warning. 'We're going to lose an engine, buddy.'

Even now the pilot was oblivious to the catastrophic situation. His awareness of time had all but disintegrated. 'Why?' he replied, seemingly incredulous at the loss of an engine. 'Fuel' came the emphatic response.

United Airlines 173 was perfectly capable of landing. The landing gear, it was later established, was in fact down and secure. Even if it hadn't been, an experienced pilot could have landed the plane without loss of life. The night was crystal clear and the airport had been in sight since the initial descent had been aborted.

But now, to the horror of the crew, they were 8 miles short of the runway, over a major city, and the fuel had all but disappeared.

It was too late now. As the remaining engines flamed out, all hope vanished. The plane was losing altitude at more than 3,000 feet per minute and they were not going to make it.

McBroom strained his eyes across the horizon in a desperate search for a field or open space amid the mass of homes and apartment blocks stretching beneath the plane. Even now, he couldn't understand what had happened. Had the fuel vanished into the ether? Where had the time gone?

The last few moments of the transcript reveal their desperation as the flight careered down into suburban Portland:

1813:38 CAPTAIN: They're all going [i.e. all the engines are flaming out]

1813:41 CAPTAIN: We can't make Troutdale [another airport in Portland]

1813:43 CO-PILOT: We can't make anything

1813:46 CAPTAIN: OK, declare a mayday

1813:50 CO-PILOT (to Tower): Portland tower, United one seventy three, heavy Mayday we're . . . the engines are flaming out, we're going down, we're not going to be able to make the airport

1813:58 TOWER: United one . . .

1814:35 (impact with transmission lines)

(end of tape)

United Airlines 173 was chosen as a vehicle to explore the aviation system for two reasons. Firstly, it was a watershed event in aviation safety. That much is widely acknowledged. But for our purposes, it has an additional significance: it mirrors, in an intriguing way, the tragedy of Elaine Bromiley. While one accident happened in the skies and another in an operating theatre, they share the same basic signature.

Even on a cursory inspection the similarities are striking. Like Captain McBroom, who had become fixated on the landing gear problem, Dr Anderton had become fixated on accessing the airway via the mouth. Perception had narrowed. Like McBroom, who had lost any sense of the dwindling reserves of fuel, the doctors overseeing Elaine Bromiley had lost perspective on the absence of oxygen. While McBroom was trying to solve the landing gear problem and the doctors were frantically trying to place the tracheal tube into the airway, the real disaster was all but ignored.

Like Engineer Mendenhall, who had warned the captain but hadn't got a response, Jane, the nurse, had alerted Dr Anderton. They had both issued strong hints, had agonised about making their concerns more explicit, but had been intimidated by the sense of hierarchy. Social pressure, and the inhibiting effects of authority, had destroyed effective teamwork.

But what is important for our purposes is not the similarity between the two accidents; it is the difference in *response*. We have already seen that in healthcare, the culture is one of evasion. Accidents are described as 'one-offs' or 'one of those things'. Doctors say: 'we did the best we could'. This is the most common response to failure in the world today.

In aviation, things are radically different: learning from failure is hardwired into the system.

All airplanes must carry two black boxes, one of which records instructions sent to all on-board electronic systems. The other is a cockpit voice recorder, enabling investigators to get into the minds of the pilots in the moments leading up to an accident. Instead of concealing failure, or skirting around it, aviation has a system where failure is *data rich*.

In the event of an accident, investigators, who are independent of the airlines, the pilots union and the regulators, are given full rein to explore the wreckage and to interrogate all other evidence. Mistakes are not stigmatised, but regarded as learning opportunities. The interested parties are given every reason to cooperate since the evidence compiled by the accident investigation branch is inadmissible in court proceedings. This increases the likelihood of full disclosure.

In the aftermath of the investigation the report is made available to everyone. Airlines have a legal responsibility to implement the recommendations. Every pilot in the world has free access to the data. This enables everyone to learn from the mistake, rather than just a single crew, or a single airline, or a single nation. This turbo-charges the power of learning. As Eleanor Roosevelt put it: 'Learn from the mistakes of others. You can't live long enough to make them all yourself.'

And it is not just accidents that drive learning; so, too, do 'small' errors. When pilots experience a near-miss with another aircraft, or have been flying at the wrong altitude, they file a report. Providing that it is submitted within ten days, pilots enjoy immunity. Many planes are also fitted with data systems that automatically send reports when parameters have been exceeded. Once again, these reports are de identified by the time they proceed through the report sequence.*

In 2005, for example, a number of reports were filed in rapid succession alerting investigators to a problem with the approach to Lexington Airport in Kentucky. Just outside the airport, local authorities had installed a large mural on an empty expanse of land, as a way of brightening it up. At the top of the mural, they had placed lamps to illuminate it at night.

But the lights were playing havoc with the perception of pilots. They were mistaking the mural lights for lights on the runway. They were coming in too low. Fortunately nobody crashed, but the

---

* Awareness of small errors has vital implications for companies, too. As Amy Edmondson, a professor at Harvard Business School, puts it: 'Most large failures have multiple causes, and some of these causes are deeply embedded in organisations . . . Small failures are the early warning signs that are vital to avoiding catastrophic failure in the future.'

anonymous reports revealed a latent problem before it was given a chance to kill anyone. Shawn Pruchnicki, an aviation safety expert who attended the meeting, told me: 'We saw a whole bunch of reports in a single week. We instantly realised there was a problem, and that we had to act.'

Within minutes an email was sent out to all flights scheduled to land at Lexington warning of a potential distraction on approach. Within days the mural and its lights had been removed (this would have happened far sooner had the land been under the jurisdiction of the airport). An accident had been prevented before it had happened.

Today many prestige airlines have gone even further, creating the real-time monitoring of tens of thousands of parameters, such as altitude deviation and excessive banking, allowing continuous comparison of performance to diagnose patterns of concern. According to the Royal Aeronautical Society: 'It is the most important way to dramatically improve flight safety.'[2] The current ambition is to increase the quantity of real-time data so as to render the black boxes redundant. All the information will already have been transmitted to a central database.

Aviation, then, takes failure seriously. Any data that might demonstrate that procedures are defective, or that the design of the cockpit is inadequate, or that the pilots haven't been trained properly, is carefully extracted. These are used to lock the industry onto a safer path. And individuals are not intimidated about admitting to errors because they recognise their value.

II

What did all this mean for United Airlines 173? Within minutes of the crash an investigation team was appointed by the National Transportation Safety Board, including Alan Diehl, a psychologist, and Dennis Grossi, an experienced investigator. By the following morning they had arrived in suburban Portland to go over the evidence with a fine-tooth comb.

It is a testament to the extraordinary skill of McBroom that he kept the plane under control for as long as he did. As the aircraft was dropping he noticed an area amid the houses and apartment blocks that looked like an open space, possibly a field, and steered towards it. As he got closer, he realised that it was, in fact, a wooded suburb. He tried to steer between the trees, collided with one, ploughed through a house, and came to rest on top of another house across the street.

The first house was obliterated. Pieces of the aircraft's left wing were later found in another part of the suburb. The lower left side of the fuselage, between the fourth and sixth rows of passenger seats and below window level, was completely torn away. Miraculously, there were no fatalities on the ground; eight passengers and two crew members died. One of them was Flight Engineer Mendenhall, who had vainly attempted to warn the pilot of the dwindling fuel reserves. McBroom, the captain, survived with a broken leg, shoulder and ribs.

As the investigators probed the evidence of United Airlines 173, they could see a pattern. It was not just what they discovered amid the wreckage in Portland, it was the comparison with previous accidents. One year earlier another DC8 crashed in almost identical circumstances. The plane, destined for San Francisco from Chicago, had entered a holding pattern at night because of a problem with the landing gear, flew around trying to fix it, and then flew into a mountain killing everyone on board.[3]

A few years earlier, Eastern Airlines 401 suffered a similar fate as it was coming in to land at Miami International Airport. One of the lights in the cockpit had not illuminated, causing the crew to fear that the landing gear had failed to lower into place. As the crew focused on troubleshooting the problem (it turned out to be a faulty bulb), they failed to realise that the plane was losing altitude, despite warnings from the safety systems. It crashed into the Everglades, killing 101 people.[4]

In each case the investigators realised that crews were losing their perception of time. Attention, it turns out, is a scarce resource: if you focus on one thing, you will lose awareness of other things.

This can be seen in an experiment where students were given a series of tasks. One task was easy: reading out loud. Another task was trickier: defining difficult words. After they had completed the tasks, the students were asked to estimate how much time had passed. Those with the easy task gave accurate estimates; those with the tough task underestimated the time by as much as 40 per cent. Time had flown by.

Now think of McBroom. He didn't just have to focus on difficult words. He had to troubleshoot a landing gear problem, listen to his co-pilots, and anticipate landing under emergency conditions. Think back, too, to the doctors surrounding Elaine Bromiley. They were absorbed in trying to intubate, frantically trying to save the life of their patient. They lost track of time not because they didn't have enough focus, but because they had *too much focus*.* Back in Portland, Oregon, Diehl realised that another fundamental problem involved communication. Engineer Mendenhall had spotted the fuel problem. He had given a number of hints to the captain and, as the situation became serious, made direct references to the dwindling reserves. Diehl, listening back to the voice recorder, noted alterations in the intonation of the engineer. As the dangers spiralled he became ever more desperate to alert McBroom, but he couldn't bring himself to challenge his boss directly.

This is now a well-studied aspect of psychology. Social hierarchies inhibit assertiveness. We talk to those in authority in what is called 'mitigated language'. You wouldn't say to your boss: 'It's imperative we have a meeting on Monday morning.' But you might say: 'Don't worry if you're busy, but it might be helpful if you could spare half an hour on Monday.'[5] This deference makes sense in many situations, but it can be fatal when a 90 tonne aeroplane is running out of fuel above a major city.

The same hierarchy gradient also exists in operating theatres. Jane, the nurse, could see the solution. She had fetched the tracheostomy kit. Should she have spoken up more loudly? Didn't she care enough?

---

* In many circumstances, task-focused behaviour is actually an effective way of applying one's effort. The problem is when this focus comes at the expense of the 'bigger picture'. This is when excessive focus undermines performance and, in the case of aviation, safety.

That is precisely the wrong way to think about failure in safety critical situations. Remember that Engineer Mendenhall paid for his reticence with his life. The problem was not a lack of diligence or motivation, but a system insensitive to the limitations of human psychology.

Now let us compare the first and third person perspectives. For the doctors at the hospital near North Marston, the accident may indeed have seemed like a 'one-off'. After all, they didn't know that they had spent eight long minutes in a vain attempt at intubation. To them, they had been trying for a fraction of that time. Their subjective sense of time had all but vanished in the panic. The problem, in their minds, was with the patient. She had died far quicker than they could have possibility anticipated. In the absence of an investigation how could they have known any better?

An almost identical story can be told of United Airlines 173. When Diehl, the investigator, went to the hospital in Oregon to interview McBroom a few days after the crash, the pilot informed him that the fuel reserves had depleted 'incredibly quickly'. He offered the possibility that there had been a leak in the tanks. From his perspective, with his awareness of time obliterated by the growing crisis, this was a rational observation. To him, the fuel running out just didn't make sense.

But Diehl and his team took the trouble to double check the black box data. They looked at the reserves at the time of the decision to go into a holding pattern, checked how fast DC8s deplete fuel on average, then looked at when the fuel actually ran out. They correlated perfectly. The plane had not run out of fuel any quicker than expected. The leak was not in the tank, but in McBroom's sense of time.

Only through an investigation, from an independent perspective, did this truth come to light. In healthcare nobody recognised the underlying problem because, from a first person perspective, it didn't exist. That is one of the ways that closed loops perpetuate: when people don't interrogate errors, they sometimes don't even know they have made one (even if they suspect they may have).

When Diehl and his colleagues published the report on United Airlines 173 in June 1979, it proved to be a landmark in aviation. On the thirtieth page, in the dry language familiar in such reports, it offered the following recommendation: 'Issue an operations bulletin to all air carrier operations inspectors directing them to urge their assigned operators to ensure that their flight crews are indoctrinated in principles of flightdeck resource management, with particular emphasis on the merits of participative management for captains and assertiveness training for other cockpit crewmembers.'

Within weeks, NASA had convened a conference to explore the benefit of a new kind of training: Crew Resource Management. The primary focus was on communication. First officers were taught assertiveness procedures. The mnemonic which has been used to improve the assertiveness of junior members of the crew in aviation is called P.A.C.E. (Probe, Alert, Challenge, Emergency).* Captains, who for years had been regarded as big chiefs, were taught to listen, acknowledge instructions and clarify ambiguity. The time perception problem was tackled through a more structured division of responsibilities.

Checklists, already in operation, were expanded and improved. The checklists have been established as a means of preventing oversights in the face of complexity. But they also flatten the hierarchy. When pilots and co-pilots talk to each other, introduce themselves, go over the checklist, they open channels of communication. It makes it more likely the junior partner will speak up in an emergency. This solves the so-called 'activation problem'.

Various versions of the new training methods were immediately trialled in simulators. At each stage, the new ideas were challenged,

---

* We can see what this would look like in practice by applying it to a real-world event. This is what Jane, the head nurse, might have said if she had used this approach during the operation of Elaine Bromiley:

PROBE – 'Doctor, what other options are you considering if we can't get the tube in?'

ALERT – 'Doctor, oxygen is 40 per cent, and is still dropping, the tube is not going in, what about a tracheostomy kit?'

CHALLENGE – 'Doctor, we need to conduct a tracheostomy now or we will lose the patient.'

EMERGENCY – 'I'm alerting the resuscitation team to do the tracheostomy.'

rigorously tested, and examined at their limits. The most effective proposals were then rapidly integrated into airlines around the world. After a terrible set of accidents in the 1970s, the rate of crashes began to decline.

'United Airlines 173 was a traumatic incident, but it was also a great leap forward,' the aviation safety expert Shawn Pruchnicki says. 'It is still regarded as a watershed, the moment when we grasped the fact that "human errors" often emerge from poorly designed systems. It changed the way the industry thinks.'

Ten people died on United Airlines 173, but the learning opportunity saved many thousands more.

This, then, is what we might call 'black box thinking'.* For organisations beyond aviation, it is not about creating a literal black box; rather, it is about the willingness and tenacity to investigate the lessons that often exist when we fail, but which we rarely exploit. It is about creating systems and cultures that enable organisations to learn from errors, rather than being threatened by them.

Failure is rich in learning opportunities for a simple reason: in many of its guises, it represents a violation of expectation.[6] It is showing us that the world is in some sense different from the way we imagined it to be. The death of Elaine Bromiley, for example, revealed that operating procedures were insensitive to limitations of human psychology. The failure of United Airlines 173 revealed similar problems in cockpits.

These failures are inevitable because the world is complex and we will never fully understand its subtleties. The model, as social scientists often remind us, is not the system. Failure is thus a signpost. It reveals a feature of our world we hadn't grasped fully and offers vital clues about how to update our models, strategies and behaviours. From this perspective, the question often asked in the aftermath of an adverse event, namely 'can we afford the time to investigate

---

* 'Black box' sometimes has the connotation of an unknown and possibly inscrutable process lying between some input and its result. Here we are using it in the slightly different but related sense of the data recorder in an accident investigation.

failure?', seems the wrong way round. The real question is 'can we afford not to?'

This leads to another important conclusion. It is sometimes said that the crucial difference between aviation and healthcare is available resources: because aviation has more money at its disposal, it is able to conduct investigations and learn from mistakes. If healthcare had more resources, wouldn't it do the same? However, we can now see that this is profoundly wrongheaded. Healthcare may indeed be under-resourced, but it would *save* money by learning from mistakes. The cost of medical error has been conservatively estimated at more than $17 billion in the US alone.[7] As of March 2015 the NHS Litigation Authority had set aside £26.1 billion to cover outstanding negligence liabilities. Learning from mistakes is not a drain on resources; it is the most effective way of safeguarding resources – and lives.*

Psychologists often make a distinction between mistakes where we already know the right answer and mistakes where we don't. A medication error, for example, is a mistake of the former kind: the nurse knew she should have prescribed Medicine A but inadvertently prescribed Medicine B, perhaps because of confusing labelling, combined with pressure of time.

But sometimes mistakes are consciously made as part of a process of discovery. Drug companies test lots of different combinations of chemicals to see which have efficacy and which don't. Nobody knows in advance which will work, and which won't, but this is precisely why they test extensively, and fail often. It is integral to progress.

On the whole, we will be looking at the first type of failure in the early part of the book and the second type in the later part. But the crucial point is that in both scenarios error is indispensable to the process of discovery. In industries like healthcare, errors provide signposts about how to reform the system to make future errors less likely; in the latter case, errors drive the discovery of new medicines.

---

* As a Parliamentary Select Committee report in the UK in 2015 put it: 'resources devoted to investigating and learning to improve clinical safety will save unnecessary expense by reducing avoidable harm to patients.'

A somewhat overlapping distinction can be made between errors that occur in a practice environment and those that occur in a performance environment. Figure skaters, for example, fall over a lot in training. By stretching themselves, attempting difficult jumps, and occasionally falling onto the cold ice, they progress on to more difficult jumps, improving judgement and accuracy along the way. This is what enables them to perform so flawlessly when they arrive at a big competition.

In effect, practice is about harnessing the benefits of learning from failure while reducing its cost. It is better to fail in practice in preparation for the big stage than on the big stage itself. This is true of organisations, too, which conduct pilot schemes (and in the case of aviation and other safety critical industries test ideas in simulators) in order to learn, before rolling out new ideas or procedures. The more we can fail in practice, the more we can learn, enabling us to succeed when it really matters.

But even if we practise diligently, we will still endure real-world failure from time to time. And it is often in these circumstances, when failure is most threatening to our ego, when we need to learn most of all. Practice is not a substitute for learning from real-world failure, it is complementary to it. They are, in many ways, two sides of the same coin.

With this in mind, let us take one final example of a 'black box style investigation'. It involved the losses of bomber aircraft during the Second World War and was conducted by one of the most brilliant mathematicians of the twentieth century: Abraham Wald.

His analysis was not just a pivotal moment in a major conflict, but also an important example within the context of this book. Learning from adverse events can sometimes look easy with the benefit of hindsight. Weren't the lessons from United Airlines 173, for example, just obvious? Didn't they jump out of the data?

At the time of the investigation, however, the data can often seem far more ambiguous. The most successful investigators reveal not just a willingness to engage with the incident, but also have the analytical skills and creative insights to extract the key lessons. Indeed, many aviation experts cite the improvement in the quality and sophistication of investigations as one of the most powerful spurs to safety in recent years.[8]

But few investigations have been as ingenious as that conducted by Wald. His work was classified for decades, but the full story, and how it contributed to the defeat of Nazism, has recently been told. Most of all his investigations reveal that in order to learn from failure, you have to take into account not merely the data you can see, but also the data you can't.

III

Abraham Wald was born in Hungary in 1902 to a Jewish baker. He was educated at home by his older brother, Martin, who was a qualified engineer. Early on he developed a love for mathematics and, at the age of fourteen, geometry. According to those who knew him, little Abraham was always creating and solving puzzles.

Wald left home in 1927 to study at the University of Vienna. He had a quizzical face, dark hair and bright eyes and his sharp mind was instantly recognised by his teachers and fellow students. As one colleague put it: 'I was captivated by his great ability, his gentleness and the extraordinary strength with which he attacked his problems.'[9]

While at the university Wald was invited by Karl Menger, one of the greatest mathematicians of his generation, to join the Colloquium, a group of scholars who would meet informally to discuss maths and philosophy, and which included names that would later become legendary, such as Kurt Gödel and Alfred Tarski. Wald continued to flourish, writing a series of papers on geometry that Menger described as 'deep, beautiful and of fundamental importance.'[10]

But Wald was not able to gain a teaching post in Vienna: his Jewish background made it politically impossible. 'At that time of economic and incipient political unrest, it was out of the question for him to secure a position at the University of Vienna, although such a connection would certainly have been as profitable for the institution as for himself,' Menger would later write. 'With his characteristic modesty, Wald told me that he would be perfectly satisfied with any small private position that would enable him to continue his work with the Mathematical Colloquium.'[11]

But even this minor role would prove problematic as Europe headed towards war. In 1937, the presence of Wald within the Mathematical Colloquium was criticised by Nazi sympathisers. A year later, when Hitler marched into the Austrian capital, Wald was sacked. He remained for a few weeks after the occupation, but as the Nazis ratcheted up their persecution of the Jews, Menger, who had already fled to the United States, managed to secure him a job in America.

Wald was reluctant to leave Vienna, a city he had fallen in love with (in a letter to a friend, he wrote that it had become 'a second home'), but the decision to depart almost certainly saved his life. Eight of his nine family members would later die at the hands of the Nazis. His parents and sisters were killed in the gas chambers of Auschwitz while his beloved older brother, Martin, who had introduced him to mathematics, perished as a slave labourer in western Germany. Wald would remain unaware of these tragedies until the end of the war.

In America he was hugely relieved when he found out that he would be able to pursue his love of maths. He was ultimately offered a post with a team with the seemingly banal name of the Applied Mathematics Panel. He found himself working out of a fourth-floor apartment a few streets away from the centre of Harlem. It turned out to be a turning point in the war.[12]

The panel were a group of brilliant mathematicians. Working on behalf of the military, they were given the job of analysing a whole range of issues, such as the most effective pattern of torpedo launching and the aerodynamic efficiency of missiles. As the author David McRaney put it: 'People walking by the apartment at the time had no idea that four stories above them some of the most important work in applied mathematics was tilting the scales of a global conflict.'[13]

Much of the work was highly confidential and the papers produced by the panel remained classified for decades. But over recent years researchers have begun to piece together the contribution of these 'soldier mathematicians' and discovered that it was vital to the outcome of the war. Wald's involvement, which only came to light years later, was perhaps the most astonishing of all.

He was asked by the military to help them with a crucial issue. Bomber aircraft in Europe were being asked to take huge risks. For certain periods of the conflict, the probability of a pilot surviving a tour of duty was little better than fifty-fifty. Kevin Wilson, the military historian, described these remarkable and brave men as 'ghosts already'.[14]

The wartime leaders realised that they needed to reinforce the planes with armour. This would help protect them from gunfire, from the ground and the air. The problem is that they could not armour the entire surface area because the planes would become too heavy to fly, and lose manoeuvrability. Wald was brought in to prioritise the areas that needed armour most.

He had lots of data to work from. To their credit, the air force had taken the trouble to examine returning aircraft to assess the extent of the damage, and how they might respond to it. This was black box-style behaviour. They were examining the data from adverse events in order to work out how to improve the safety of the aircraft.

To the relief of the air-force command, the pattern seemed clear. Many of the planes were riddled with gunfire all over the wings and fuselage. But they were not being hit in the cockpit or tail. The longer the incident reporting continued, the clearer the pattern became.

You can see the pattern in the diagram below.

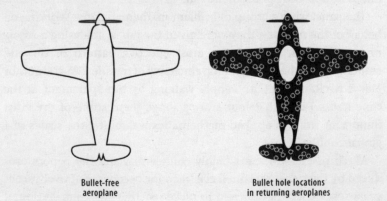

Bullet-free
aeroplane

Bullet hole locations
in returning aeroplanes

The military command came up with what seemed like the perfect plan: they would place armour on the areas of the plane where there were holes. This is where the bullets were impacting and, therefore, where the planes needed additional protection. It was plain common sense. To those in positions of military leadership, it was the best way to shield their brave airmen from enemy fire.

But Wald disagreed. He realised that the chiefs had neglected to take into account some key data. They were only considering the planes that had returned. They were not taking into account the planes that *had not* returned (i.e. the planes that had been shot down). The observable bullet holes suggested that the area around the cockpit and tail didn't need reinforcing because it was never hit. In fact, the planes that were hit in these places were crashing because this is where they were most vulnerable.

In effect, the holes in the returning aircraft represented areas where a bomber *could* take damage and still return home safely. They had survived precisely because they had not been hit in the cockpit and tail. The pattern of holes, far from indicating where the armour needed to be added to the aircraft, was actually revealing the areas where it did not.

The insight turned out to be of profound importance, not just to bomber command, but to the entire war effort.

This is a powerful example because it reveals a couple of key things. The first is that you have to take into account all the data, including the data you cannot immediately see, if you are going to learn from adverse incidents. But it also emphasises that learning from failure is not always easy, even in conceptual terms, let alone emotional terms. It takes careful thought and a willingness to pierce through the surface assumptions. Often, it means looking beyond the obvious data to glimpse the underlying lessons. This is not just true of learning in aviation, but in business, politics and beyond.

As Amy Edmondson of Harvard Business School has put it: 'Learning from failure is anything but straightforward. The attitudes and activities required to effectively detect and analyze failures are in short supply in most companies, and the need for context-specific learning strategies is underappreciated. Organizations need new and better ways to go beyond lessons that are superficial.'[15]

Wald's analysis of bullet-riddled aircraft in the Second World War saved the lives of dozens of brave airmen. His seminal paper for the military was not declassified until July 1980, but can be found today via a simple search on Google. It is entitled: 'A Method of Estimating Plane Vulnerability Based on Damage of Survivors.'[16]

It wasn't until after the war that Wald learned of the murder of eight of his nine family members at the hands of the Nazis. According to those who knew him best, the pain of the loss never left him. One of his closest friends wrote: 'even this cruel blow failed to make him embittered, although a certain sadness could be felt to be with him for the rest of his life.'[17]

In the late 1940s, he managed to organise a passage to the United States for his older brother, Hermann, the sole family member to survive the Holocaust. His friends would testify that he took 'great comfort' in the company of his brother, as well as in continuing work in mathematics at Columbia University.

One hopes that this remarkable and gentle man also took comfort from the fact that his analytical insights played a crucial role in defeating the evil ideology that murdered his loved ones.

He was a black box thinker *par excellence*.

3

The Paradox of Success

I

At 3.25 p.m. on 15 January 2009, US Airways Flight 1549 was given clearance to take off from runway 4 of New York's LaGuardia Airport.

It was a clear afternoon and up in the cockpit Captain Chesley Sullenberger and First Officer Jeffrey Skiles ran through the checklists. They were looking forward to the trip. What neither of them realised is that they were about to embark on one of the most celebrated commercial flights of modern times.[1]

Less than two minutes after take-off, a flock of Canada geese suddenly loomed into view to the right of the plane. The speed of approach was so fast that the pilots had no chance to take evasive action. Two birds flew into the right engine and at least one more into the left.

After a series of loud thuds, the plane seemed to come to a halt, followed by deathly silence. The engines had lost thrust. The pilots felt their pulses racing, their perception narrowing: the classic responses to danger. They were now 3,000 feet above New York in a 70 tonne Airbus A320 with no power.

They had to make a series of split-second decisions. They were offered a return to LaGuardia, then a rerouting to Teterboro, an airport in the New Jersey Meadowlands, a few miles away. Both options were rejected. The plane would not glide that far. It was dropping too fast.

At 3.29 p.m. Sullenberger uttered the words that would create headlines around the world: 'We're going to be in the Hudson.'

*

In the opening part of this book we have focused on failure in two safety-critical areas: aviation and healthcare. We have looked at responses, attitudes and investigations into failure. Now we will have a brief look at success, and our responses to that. By shining a light on how we get things right we will discover a little more about why we get things wrong.

Sullenberger ultimately landed the plane, all 70 tonnes of it, on the Hudson River. It was a brilliantly judged manoeuvre. The captain was diligent in the aftermath too. He walked through the cabin twice to ensure that all the passengers had exited onto the wings, lying inches above the surface of the river, before leaving his aircraft. There were no fatal injuries.

His coolness mesmerised America. The then fifty-seven-year-old received a phone call from President-Elect Obama. He was invited to the presidential inauguration. *Time Magazine* listed him second in its section of Heroes & Icons in its TIME 100 of 2009.[2] Academics hailed a new kind of authentic heroism amid a superficial celebrity culture. To the public it was an episode of sublime individualism; one man's skill and calmness under pressure saving more than a hundred lives.

But aviation experts took a different view. They glimpsed a bigger picture. They cited not just Sullenberger's individual brilliance but also the system in which he operates. Some made reference to Crew Resource Management. The division of responsibilities between Sullenberger and Skiles occurred seamlessly. Seconds after the bird strike, Sullenberger took control of the aircraft while Skiles checked the quick reference handbook.

Channels of communication were open until the very last seconds of the flight. Skiles called out airspeeds and altitudes to provide his captain as much situational awareness as possible as the aircraft dropped. With just a few seconds to go until impact they were still talking. 'Got any ideas?' Sullenberger asked. 'Actually not,' replied Skiles.

Other safety experts talked about the fly-by-wire technology (the sophisticated autopilot systems which are active in all Airbus planes), which corrected the tilt of the plane inches from contact with the water. Still others credited checklists and clever ergonomic design, both of which assisted the crew as the pressure intensified after the bird strike.

This was a fascinating discussion, which largely took place away from the watching public. But even this debate obscured the deepest truth of all. Checklists originally emerged from a series of crashes in the 1930s. Ergonomic cockpit design was born out of the disastrous series of accidents involving B-17s. Crew Resource Management emerged from the wreckage of United Airlines 173.

This is the paradox of success: it is built upon failure.

It is also instructive to examine the different public responses to McBroom and Sullenberger. McBroom, we should remember, was a brilliant pilot. His capacity to keep his nerve as the DC8 careered down, flying between trees, avoiding an apartment block, finding the minimum impact force for a 90 tonne aircraft hitting solid ground, probably saved the lives of a hundred people.

After the accident, however, he was shunned. Although the prevailing attitude within aviation was largely driven by a desire to learn from the mistake, wider society rushed to stigmatise the man who had been at the controls when the mistake was made. People were outraged at how a trained pilot had crashed a perfectly adequate plane because he had allowed it to run out of fuel.

He retired from flying shortly afterwards. He and his wife had separated within three years. At a reunion eight years before his death in 2004, he was described by Aimee Conner, a survivor of United Airlines 173, as 'a very broken man . . . He was devastated. He lost his licence. He lost his family. The rest of his life was just shattered.'

His tragedy, if you can call it that, was to fly at a time when the limitations of human attention and effective communication were not fully understood. He flew United Airlines 173 with a latent error in the system: an error waiting to happen, just like Dr Edwards and Dr Anderton, two outstanding doctors, in an operating theatre near North Marston more than twenty-five years later.

The irony is that Sullenberger, feted by presidents, might have made the precisely same mistake in the same circumstances. The fact that he didn't, and emerged a hero, was for a simple but profound reason: the industry in which he operates had learned the lessons. It is both apt and revealing that Sullenberger, a modest and self-evidently decent man, has made precisely this point. In a television interview months after the miracle landing on the Hudson, he offered this beautiful gem of wisdom:

> Everything we know in aviation, every rule in the rule book, every procedure we have, we know because someone somewhere died . . . We have purchased at great cost, lessons literally bought with blood that we have to preserve as institutional knowledge and pass on to succeeding generations. We cannot have the moral failure of forgetting these lessons and have to relearn them.

II

These words of Sullenberger are worth reflecting upon because they offer the chance to radically re-imagine failure. The idea that the successful safety record in aviation has emerged from the rubble of real-world accidents is vivid, paradoxical and profound. It is also revelatory. For if one looks closely enough it is an insight echoed across almost every branch of human endeavour.

Take science, a discipline where learning from failure is part of the method. This is a point that has been made by the philosopher Karl Popper, who suggested that science progresses through its vigilant response to its own mistakes. By making predictions that can be tested, a scientific theory is inherently vulnerable. This may seem like a weakness, but Popper realised that it is an incalculable strength.

'The history of science, like the history of all human ideas, is a history of . . . error,' Popper wrote. 'But science is one of the very few human activities – perhaps the only one – in which errors are systematically criticized and fairly often, in time, corrected. This is why we can say that, in science, we learn from our mistakes and why we can speak clearly and sensibly about making progress.'[3]

In this context, consider the experiment (which is probably apocryphal) conducted by Galileo in sixteenth-century Italy. For many centuries the physics of Aristotle had dominated the world, a bit like the ideas of Galen dominating medicine. People had faith in the Greek thinker and, to a certain extent, it was considered impertinent to challenge him. Aristotle argued, among other things, that heavy objects fall faster than lighter ones, in direct proportion to weight.

But was he right? Galileo conducted a test. He climbed the Leaning Tower of Pisa and dropped two balls of different masses. He found that the two objects fell with the same degree of acceleration and, in that moment, revealed that Aristotle's theory was flawed. To use the terminology of Popper, he had 'falsified' Aristotle's hypothesis.

This was a failure for Aristotle and a painful blow to his followers, many of whom were outraged by the experiment. But it was a profound victory for science. For if Aristotle was wrong, scientists were handed the impetus to figure out why, and come up with new theories which, in turn, could be subjected to future falsification. This is, at least in part, how science progresses.*

The same idea can be seen in relation to Einstein's Theory of Relativity. In 1919 a British scientist called Arthur Eddington travelled to Africa to test one of Relativity's most novel claims: that light is attracted to heavy bodies. During an eclipse he took photographs of a distant star to see if he could detect the influence of gravity on the light rays coming towards Earth. Eddington's experiment corroborated the theory.[4] But the key point is that it might not have. Relativity was vulnerable to experimental falsification. It remains so to this day.[5]

Compare this openness to failure with a pseudoscience like, say, astrology. Here, the predictions are hopelessly vague. On the day these words were written I looked at Horoscope.com to see its prediction for Libra. 'Big changes are brewing at home or work,' it said. This may seem like a testable assertion, but pretty much anything

---

* The precise relationship between failure and progress in science is a complex topic. There is much debate about when scientists can or should create new theories and paradigms in the light of challenging data. The philosopher Thomas Kuhn has written extensively on this subject. But the basic point that scientific theories should be testable, and therefore vulnerable, is almost universally agreed upon. Self-correction is a central aspect of how science progresses.

that happens in the life of anybody, Libra or otherwise, fits the prediction. We all have changes 'brewing' at home or work. This gives astrology a seductive strength: it is never 'wrong'. But the price it pays for immunity from failure is high indeed: it cannot learn. Astrology has not changed in any meaningful way for over two centuries.

Or take the theory, popular in the nineteenth century, that the world was created in 4004 BC. This seemed to have been disproved by the discovery of fossils, as well as by the later evidence of carbon dating. The new data pointed to the almost indisputable fact that the universe is substantially more than six thousand years old.

But in the nineteenth century a British naturalist called Philip Henry Gosse published a book called *Omphalos* in which he attempted to defend the creationist theory. His argument was nothing if not inventive. He asserted that the world had indeed been created in 4004 BC, but that God had created lots of apparent fossils at the same time so as to make the world look older than it actually is. He also argued that Adam had been given a navel by God in order to give him the appearance of human ancestry when he was really created out of mud (the title of his book *Omphalos* is 'navel' in Greek).[6]

In one way, Gosse had defended the theory of creationism in 4004 BC. His post hoc manoeuvre meant that the facts once again tallied with the theory. But he had done something else, too. He had made the theory invulnerable to failure. No amount of evidence, no amount of data, no amount of discovery could refute Gosse's position. Any new information suggesting that the world was older than 4004 BC would simply be held up as further evidence that God had played a trick on the world. The theory was confirmed, *come what may*. But this also meant that it could never adapt to meet the challenge of new evidence.

The same story can be told about the psychotherapeutic theories of Alfred Adler. These were very much in vogue in the 1920s and still have a lingering influence today. The central idea is that of the 'inferiority complex': the notion that behaviour emerges from a desire to prove oneself.

In 1919, Karl Popper met Adler personally to talk about a case that didn't seem to fit his theories at all. The specifics of the case are less important than Adler's response. Popper wrote:

> He [Adler] found no difficulty in analyzing in terms of his theory of inferiority feelings, although he had not even seen the child. Slightly shocked, I asked him how he could be so sure. 'Because of my thousand-fold experience,' he replied; whereupon I could not help saying: 'And with this new case, I suppose, your experience has become thousand-and-one-fold.'[7]

What Popper had in mind, here, is that Adler's theories were compatible with *anything*. If, say, a man saves a drowning child then, according to Adler, he is proving to himself that he has the courage to risk his life by jumping into a river. If the same man refuses to save the drowning child, he is proving to himself that he has the courage to risk social disapproval. In both cases, he has overcome his inferiority complex. The theory is confirmed, whatever happens. As Popper put it:

> I could not think of any human behaviour which could not be interpreted in terms of the theory. It was precisely this fact – that they always fitted, that they were always confirmed – which in the eyes of their admirers constituted the strongest argument in favour of the theory. It began to dawn on me that this apparent strength was in fact its weakness.

Most closed loops exist because people deny failure or try to spin it. With pseudosciences the problem is more structural. They have been designed, wittingly or otherwise, to make failure impossible. That is why, to their adherents, they are so mesmerising. They are compatible with everything that happens. But that also means they cannot learn from *anything*.

This hints, in turn, at a subtle difference between confirmation and falsification. Science has often been regarded as a quest for confirmation. Scientists observe nature, create theories, and then seek to prove them by amassing as much supporting evidence as possible. But we can now see that this is only a part of the truth. Science is not just about confirmation, it is also about falsification. Knowledge does not progress merely by gathering confirmatory data, but by looking for contradictory data.

Take the hypothesis that water boils at 100°C. This seems true enough. But, as we now know, the hypothesis breaks down when water is boiled at altitude. By finding the places where a theory fails, we set the stage for the creation of a new, more powerful theory: a theory that explains both why water boils at 100°C at ground level and a different temperature at altitude. This is the stuff of scientific progress.

This also reveals a subtle asymmetry between confirmation and falsification, between success and failure. If you are careful enough to limit your observations to low altitudes and open containers, you could find countless instances where water does indeed boil at 100°C. But none of this successful 'evidence' would have expanded our knowledge very much. Indeed, in one sense, it would not have even increased the probability of the assertion 'water always boils at 100°C.'[8]

This point was originally made by the Scottish philosopher David Hume in the eighteenth century, and popularised recently by Nassim Nicholas Taleb, the mathematician and author.[9] Taleb has pointed out that you could observe a million white swans, but this would not prove the proposition: all swans are white. The observation of a single black swan, on the other hand, would conclusively demonstrate its falsehood.

Failure, then, is hardwired into both the logic and spirit of scientific progress. Mankind's most successful discipline has grown by challenging orthodoxy and by subjecting ideas to testing. Individual scientists may sometimes be dogmatic but, as a community, scientists recognise that theories, particularly those at the frontiers of our knowledge, are often fallible or incomplete. It is by testing our ideas, subjecting them to failure, that we set the stage for growth.

Aviation is different from science but it is underpinned by a similar spirit. After all, an aeroplane journey represents a kind of hypothesis: namely, that this aircraft, with this design, these pilots, and this system of air traffic control, will reach its destination safely. Each flight represents a kind of test. A crash, in a certain sense, represents a falsification of the hypothesis. That is why accidents have a particular significance in improving system safety, rather as falsification drives science.

What is true at the level of the system also has echoes at the level of the individual. Indeed, this framework explains one of the deepest paradoxes in modern psychology. It is well known that experts with thousands of hours of practice can perform with almost miraculous accuracy. Chess grandmasters can instantly compute an optimal move; top tennis players can predict where the ball is going before their opponent has even hit it; experienced paediatric nurses can make almost instant diagnoses, which are invariably confirmed by later testing.

These individuals have not practised for weeks or months, but often for years. They have slowly but surely built up intuitions that enable them to perform with remarkable accuracy. These findings have led to the conclusion that expertise is, at least in part, about practice (the so-called 10,000-hour rule). Not everyone has the potential to become world champion, but most people can develop mastery with training and application.*

But further studies seemed to contradict this finding. It turns out that there are many professions where practice and experience do not have any effect. People train for months and sometimes years without improving *at all*. Research on psychotherapists, for instance, finds that trainees obtain results that are as good as those of licensed 'experts'. Similar results have been found with regard to college admissions officers, personnel selectors and clinical psychologists.† [10]

Why is this? How can experience be so valuable in some professions, but almost worthless in others?

---

* In my 2010 book *Bounce* I explore this area in some detail. In this section, I do not rely on the ideas in *Bounce*. The point here is merely that extended practice seems to be a prerequisite for expertise in predictable environments.

† The only thing that does change over time is not performance, but *confidence*. In one survey, 25 per cent of psychotherapists put themselves in the top 10 per cent of performers and none placed themselves below average.

To see why, suppose that you are playing golf. You are out on the driving range, hitting balls towards a target. You are concentrating and every time you fire the ball wide, you adjust your technique in order to get it closer to where you want it to go. This is how practice happens in sport. It is a process of trial and error.

But now suppose that instead of practising in daylight, you practise at night – in the pitch-black. In these circumstances, you could practise for ten years or ten thousand years without improving at all. How could you progress if you don't have a clue where the ball has landed? With each shot, it could have gone long, short, left or right. Every shot has been swallowed by the night. You wouldn't have any data to improve your accuracy.

This metaphor solves the apparent mystery of expertise. Think about being a chess player. When you make a poor move, you are instantly punished by your opponent. Think of being a clinical nurse. When you make a mistaken diagnosis, you are rapidly alerted by the condition of the patient (and by later testing). The intuitions of nurses and chess players are constantly checked and challenged by their errors. They are forced to adapt, to improve, to restructure their judgements. This is a hallmark of what is called deliberate practice.

For psychotherapists things are radically different. Their job is to improve the mental functioning of their patients. But how can they tell when their interventions are going wrong or, for that matter, right? Where is the feedback? Most psychotherapists gauge how their clients are responding to treatment not with objective data, but by observing them in clinic. But this data is highly unreliable. After all, patients might be inclined to exaggerate how well they are to please the therapist, a well-known issue in psychotherapy.

But there is a deeper problem. Psychotherapists rarely track their clients after therapy has finished. This means that they do not get any feedback on the lasting impact of their interventions. They have no idea if their methods are working or failing in terms of actually improving long-term mental functioning. And that is why the clinical judgements of many practitioners don't improve over time. They are effectively playing golf in the dark.[11]

Or take radiologists, who try to identify tumours by examining low-dose X-rays known as mammograms. When they diagnose a malignancy they obtain feedback on whether they are right or wrong only after exploratory surgery is undertaken sometime later. But by then they may have largely forgotten the reasons for the original diagnosis and become preoccupied by new cases. Feedback, when delayed, is considerably less effective in improving intuitive judgement.*

But more seriously, suppose that the doctor fails to diagnose a malignancy, and the patient goes home, relieved. If, some months or years later, this diagnosis turns out to be mistaken, and the cancer has developed, the radiologist may never find out about their original mistake. That means that they can't learn from the error. This explains, in part, why junior doctors learn so slowly, gradually approaching, but rarely exceeding, 70 per cent diagnostic accuracy.[12]

If we wish to improve the judgement of aspiring experts then, we shouldn't just focus on conventional issues like motivation and commitment. In many cases, the only way to drive improvement is to find a way of 'turning the lights on'. Without access to the 'error signal', one could spend years in training or in a profession without improving at all.

In the case of radiologists, imagine a training system where students have access to a library of digitised mammograms for which the correct diagnoses have already been confirmed. Students would be able to make diagnoses on an hour-by-hour basis and would receive instant feedback about their judgements. They would fail more, but this is precisely why they would learn more. The library of mammograms could also be indexed to encourage the student to examine a series of related cases to facilitate detection of some critical feature or type of tumour.[13]

And this takes us back to science, a discipline that has also learned from failure. Just look at the number of scientific theories that have

---

* Daniel Kahneman illustrates this point by inviting us to think about how rapidly we learn to steer a car. The feedback is instant and objective. It takes far longer to learn how to steer a ship, because there are long delays between actions and noticeable outcomes.

come and gone: the Emission Theory of Vision, Ptolemy's Law of Refraction, the Luminiferous Aether Theory, the Hollow Earth Theory, the Electron Cloud Model, the Caloric Doctrine, Phlogiston Theory, the Miasma Theory of Disease, the doctrine of Maternal Impression, and dozens more.

Some of these theories were, in practical terms, not much better than astrology. But the crucial difference is that they made predictions that could be tested. That is why they were superseded by better theories. They were, in effect, vital stepping stones to the successful theories we see today.

But notice one final thing: students don't study these 'failed' scientific theories any more. Why would they? There is a lot to learn in science without studying all the ideas that have been jettisoned over time. But this tendency creates a blind spot. By looking only at the theories that have survived, we don't notice the failures that made them possible.

This blind spot is not limited to science, it is a basic property of our world and it accounts, to a large extent, for our skewed attitude to failure. Success is always the tip of an iceberg. We learn vogue theories, we fly in astonishingly safe aircraft, we marvel at the virtuosity of true experts.

But beneath the surface of success – outside our view, often outside our awareness – is a mountain of necessary failure.

III

In 2002, Dr Gary S. Kaplan, the recently appointed chief executive of the Virginia Mason Health System in Seattle, visited Japan with fellow executives. He was keen to observe organisations outside healthcare in action: anything that might challenge his assumptions and those of his senior team.

It was while at the Toyota plant that he had a revelation. Toyota has a rather unusual production process. If anybody on the production line is having a problem, or observes an error, they pull a cord which halts production across the plant.

Senior executives rush over to see what has gone wrong and, if an employee is having difficulty performing their job, help them. The error is then assessed, lessons learned, and the system adapted. It is called the Toyota Production System, or TPS, and is one of the most successful techniques in industrial history.

'The system was about cars, which are very different from people,' Kaplan says when we meet for an interview. 'But the underlying principle is transferable. If a culture is open and honest about mistakes, the entire system can learn from them. That is the way you gain improvements.'

Kaplan has bright eyes and a restless curiosity. As he talks, his hands move animatedly. 'We introduced the same kind of system in Seattle when I returned from Japan,' he says. 'We knew that medical errors cost thousands of lives across America and we were determined to reduce them.'

One of his key reforms was to encourage staff to make a report whenever they spotted an error that could harm patients. It was almost identical to the reporting system in aviation and at Toyota. He instituted a twenty-four-hour hotline as well as an online reporting system. He called them Patient Safety Alerts.

The new system represented a huge cultural shift for staff. Mistakes were frowned on at Virginia Mason, just like elsewhere in healthcare. And because of the steep hierarchy, nurses and junior doctors were fearful of reporting senior colleagues. To Kaplan's surprise and disappointment, few reports were made. An enlightened innovation had bombed due to a conflict with the underlying culture.*

As Cathie Furman, who served as senior vice president for Quality, Safety and Compliance at Virginia Mason for fourteen years, put it: 'In healthcare around the world the culture has been one of blame and hierarchy. It [can prove] very difficult to overcome that.'[14]

---

* This may also help to explain why mortality and morbidity conferences – recurring meetings amongst clinicians designed to improve patient care – have not made a significant dent on avoidable mistakes. These are held regularly by medical centres and are supposed to give practitioners an opportunity to learn from mistakes. Clinicians are often nervous about speaking up, or reporting on their colleagues. Perhaps even more importantly, there is little attempt to probe systemic problems.

But in November 2004 everything changed at Virginia Mason. Mary McClinton, sixty-nine, a mother of four, died after she was inadvertently injected with a toxic antiseptic called chlorhexidine, instead of a harmless marker dye, during a brain aneurysm operation. The two substances had been placed side by side in identical stainless-steel containers and the syringe had drawn from the wrong one.[15] One of her legs was amputated and she died through multiple organ failure nineteen days later.

Gary Kaplan responded not by evading or spinning, but by publishing a full and frank apology – the opposite of what happened after the death of Elaine Bromiley. 'We just can't say how appalled we are at ourselves,' it read. 'You can't understand something you hide.' The apology was welcomed by relatives and helped them to understand what had happened to a beloved family member.

But the death provided something else, too: a wake-up call for the 5,500 staff at Virginia Mason. 'It was a tough time, but the death was like a rallying cry,' Kaplan says. 'It gave us the cultural push we needed to recognise how serious an issue this is.'

Suddenly, Patient Safety Alerts started to fly in. Those who reported mistakes were surprised to learn that, except in situations where they had been clearly reckless, they were praised, not punished. Dr Henry Otero, an oncologist, made a report after being told by a colleague that he had failed to spot the low magnesium level of a patient. 'I missed it,' he told a newspaper. 'I didn't know how I missed it. But I realised it's not about me, it's about the patient. The process needs to stop me making a mistake. I need to be able to say, "I might be the reason, fix me."'[16]

Today, there are around a thousand Patient Safety Alerts issued per month at Virginia Mason. A report by the US Department of Health found that these have uncovered latent errors in everything from prescription to care. 'After a pharmacist and nurse misinterpreted an illegible pharmacy order, leading to patient harm, the medical centre developed a step-by-step protocol that eliminates the likelihood of such incidents occurring,' the report said.

Another alert warned about wristbands: 'After a newly admitted patient received a colour-coded wristband signifying "Do Not

Resuscitate" instead of one indicating drug allergies (as a result of a nurse being colour blind), the medical centre added text to the wristbands.'

In 2002, when Kaplan became CEO, Virginia Mason was already a competent Washington hospital. In 2013, however, it was rated as one of the safest hospitals in the world. In the same year, it won the Distinguished Hospital Award for Clinical Excellence, the Outstanding Patient Experience Award and was named a Top Hospital by the influential Leapfrog group for the eighth successive year. Since the new approach was taken, the hospital has seen a *74 per cent reduction* in liability insurance premiums.[17]

This success is not a one-off or a fluke, it is a *method*. Properly instituted learning cultures have transformed the performance of hospitals around the world. Claims and lawsuits made against the University of Michigan Health System, for example, dropped from 262 in August 2001 to 83 in 2007 following the introduction of an open and disclose policy.[18] The number of malpractice claims against the University of Illinois Medical Center fell by half in two years after creating a system of open reporting.[19]

The example of the Virginia Mason System reveals a crucial truth: namely, that learning from mistakes has two components. The first is a system. Errors can be thought of as the gap between what we hoped would happen, and what actually did happen. Cutting-edge organisations are always seeking to close this gap, but in order to do so they have to have a system geared up to take advantage of these learning opportunities. This system may itself change over time: most experts are already trialling methods that they hope will surpass the Toyota Production System. But each system has a basic structure at its heart: mechanisms that guide learning and self-correction. Yet an enlightened system on its own is sometimes not enough. Even the most beautifully constructed system will not work if professionals do not share the information that enables it to flourish. In the beginning at Virginia Mason, staff did not file Patient Safety Alerts. They were so fearful of blame and reputational damage that they kept the information to themselves. Mechanisms designed to learn from mistakes are impotent in many contexts if people won't admit to them. It was only when the mindset of the organisation changed that the system started to deliver amazing results.

Think back to science. Science has a structure that is self-correcting. By making testable predictions, scientists are able to see when their theories are going wrong, which, in turn, hands them the impetus to create new theories. But if scientists as a community ignored inconvenient evidence, or spun it, or covered it up, they would achieve nothing.

Science is not just about a method, then, it is also about a mindset. At its best, it is driven forward by a restless sprit, an intellectual courage, a willingness to face up to failures and to be honest about key data, even when it undermines cherished beliefs. It is about method and mindset.

In healthcare, this scientific approach to learning from failure has long been applied to creating new drugs, through clinical trials and other techniques. But the lesson of Virginia Mason is that it is vital to apply this approach to the complex question of how treatments are delivered by real people working in large systems. This is what healthcare has lacked for so long, and explains, in large part, why preventable medical error kills more people than traffic accidents.

As Peter Pronovost, professor at the Johns Hopkins University School of Medicine and Medical Director for the Center for Innovation in Quality Patient Care, put it: 'The fundamental problem with the quality of American medicine is that we have failed to view the delivery of healthcare as a science. You find genes, you find therapies, but how you deliver them is up to you . . . That has been a disaster. It is why we have so many people being harmed.'[20]

Pronovost became interested in patient safety when his father died at the age of fifty due to medical error. He was wrongly diagnosed with leukaemia when he, in fact, had lymphoma. 'When I was a first-year medical student here at Johns Hopkins, I took him to one of our experts for a second opinion,' Pronovost said in an interview with the *New York Times*. 'The specialist said, "If you had come earlier, you would have been eligible for a bone marrow transplant, but the cancer is too advanced now." The word "error" was never spoken.

But it was crystal clear. I was devastated. I was angry at the clinicians and myself. I kept thinking, "Medicine has to do better than this."[21]

Over the following few years, Pronovost devoted his professional life to changing the culture. He wasn't going to shrug his shoulders at the huge number of deaths occurring every day in American hospitals. He wasn't prepared to regard these tragedies as unavoidable, or as a price worth paying for a system doing its best in difficult circumstances. Instead, he studied them. He compiled data. He looked for accident 'signatures'. He tested and trialled possible reforms.

One of his most seminal investigations was into the 30,000 to 60,000 deaths caused annually by central line infections (a central line is a catheter placed into a large vein to administer drugs, obtain blood tests and so on). Pronovost discovered a number of pathways to failure, largely caused by doctors and nurses failing to wear masks or put sterile dressings over the catheter site once the line was in.[22] Under the pressure of time professionals were missing key steps.

So, Pronovost instituted a five-point checklist to ensure that all the steps were properly taken, and, crucially, empowered nurses to speak up if surgeons failed to comply. Nurses would normally have been reluctant to do so, but they were provided with reassurance that they would be backed by the administration if they did. Almost instantly, the ten-day line-infection rate dropped from 11 per cent to 0. This one reform saved 1,500 lives and $100 million over the course of eighteen months in the state of Michigan alone. In 2008 *Time* magazine voted Pronovost as one of the most influential 100 individuals in the world due to the scale of suffering he had helped to avert.

In his remarkable book *Safe Patients, Smart Hospitals* Pronovost wrote:

> My dad had suffered and died needlessly at the premature age of fifty thanks to medical errors and poor quality of care. In addition, my family and I also needlessly suffered. As a young doctor I vowed that, for my father and my family, I would do all that I could to improve the quality and safety of care delivered to patients . . . [And that meant] turning the delivery of healthcare into a science.

Gary Kaplan, whose work at Virginia Mason has also saved thousands of lives, put the point rather more pithily: 'We learn from our mistakes. It is as simple and as difficult as that.'

The difference between aviation and healthcare is sometimes couched in the language of incentives. When pilots make mistakes, it results in their own deaths. When a doctor makes a mistake, it results in the death of someone else. That is why pilots are better motivated than doctors to reduce mistakes.

But this analysis misses the crucial point. Remember that pilots died in large numbers in the early days of aviation. This was not because they lacked the incentive to live, but because the system had so many flaws. Failure is inevitable in a complex world. This is precisely why learning from mistakes is so imperative.

But in healthcare, doctors are not supposed to make mistakes. The culture implies that senior clinicians are infallible. Is it any wonder that errors are stigmatised and that the system is set up to ignore and deny rather than investigate and learn?

To put it a different way, incentives to improve performance can only have an impact, in many circumstances, if there is a prior understanding of how improvement actually happens. Think back to medieval doctors who killed patients, including family members, with bloodletting. This happened not because they didn't care, but because they did care. They thought the treatment worked.

They trusted in the authority of Galen rather than trusting in the power of criticism and experimentation to reveal the inevitable flaws in his ideas, thus setting the stage for progress. Unless we alter the way we conceptualise failure, incentives for success can often be impotent.

IV

Virginia Mason and Michigan are two of the many bright spots that have emerged in healthcare in recent years. There are others too. In anaesthetics, for example, a study into adverse events in Massachusetts found that in half the anaesthetic machines, a clockwise turn of the dial increased the concentration of drugs, but in the other half the very same turn of the dial decreased it.

This was a defect of a similar kind to the one that had bedevilled the B-17 aircraft in the 1940s, which had identical switches with different functions side by side in the cockpit. But the flaw had not been spotted for a simple reason: accidents had never been analysed or addressed.

In the aftermath of the report, however, the machines were redesigned and the death rate dropped by 98 per cent.[23] This may sound miraculous, but we should not be altogether surprised. Think back to the redesign of the B-17 cockpit display, which pretty much eliminated runway crashes altogether.

But amid these bright spots, there remain huge challenges. The Mid Staffordshire NHS Foundation Trust in England, for example, did not address repeated failures for more than a decade, leading to potentially hundreds of avoidable deaths. Warning signs of neglect and sub-standard care were obvious for years, but were not only overlooked by staff at the hospital, but also by every organisation responsible for regulating the NHS, including the government's Department of Health.[24]

In many ways this reveals the depth of the cultural problem in healthcare. It wasn't just the professionals failing to be open about their errors (and, in some cases, neglect), the regulators were also failing to investigate those mistakes.

A different scandal at Furness General Hospital in the north of England revealed similar problems. Repeated errors and poor care in its maternity unit were not revealed for more than ten years. An influential 205-page report, published in 2015 found '20 instances of significant or major failures of care at FGH, associated with three maternal deaths and the deaths of 16 babies at or shortly after birth.'[25]

But these high profile tragedies are, in fact, the tip of the iceberg; the deeper problem is the 'routine' tragedies happening every day in hospitals around the world. It is about healthcare *in general*. Just weeks before this book went to print, a landmark report by the House of Commons Public Administration Select Committee revealed that the NHS is still struggling to learn from mistakes. 'There is no systematic and independent process for investigating incidents and learning from the most serious clinical failures. No single person or organisation is responsible and accountable for the quality of clinical investigations or for ensuring that lessons learned drive improvement in safety across the NHS.'

The Committee acknowledged that various reporting and incident structures are now in place, but made it clear that deeper cultural problems continue to prevent them from working. Scott Morrish, for example, a father who lost his son to medical error, found that the subsequent investigations were designed not to expose lessons, but to conceal them. 'Most of what we know now did not come to light through the analytical or investigative work of the NHS: it came to light despite the NHS,' he said in his evidence to the Committee. Looking at NHS England as a whole, the Committee concluded: 'the processes for investigating and learning from incidents are complicated, take far too long and are preoccupied with blame or avoiding financial liability.* The quality of most investigations therefore falls far short of what patients, their families and NHS staff are entitled to expect.'[26]

In the United States similar observations apply. In 2009 a report by the Hearst Foundation found that '20 states have no medical error reporting at all' and that 'of the 20 states that require medical error reporting, hospitals report only a tiny percentage of their mistakes, standards vary wildly and enforcement is often nonexistent'. It also found that 'only 17 states have systematic adverse-event reporting systems that are transparent enough to be useful to [patients]'.[27]

One particular problem in healthcare is not just the capacity to learn from mistakes, but also that even when mistakes *are* detected, the learning opportunities do not flow throughout the system. This is sometimes called the 'adoption rate'. Aviation, as we have seen, has protocols that enable every airline, pilot and regulator to access every

---

* In June 2015, it was reported that as many as 1,000 babies are dying before, during or after birth each year due to avoidable mistakes in the NHS. One simple error of failing to monitor babies' heart rates properly accounts for a quarter of negligence payouts.

new piece of information in almost real time. Data is universally accessible and rapidly absorbed around the world. The adoption rate is almost instantaneous.

However, in healthcare, the adoption rate has been sluggish for many years, as Michael Gillam, director of the Microsoft Medical Media Lab, has pointed out. In 1601, Captain James Lancaster, an English sailor, performed an experiment on the prevention of scurvy, one of the biggest killers at sea. On one of four ships bound for India, he prescribed three teaspoons of lemon juice a day for the crew. By the halfway point 110 men out of 278 had died on the other three ships. On the lemon-supplied ship, however, everyone survived.

This was a vital finding. It was a way of avoiding hundreds of needless deaths on future journeys. But it took another 194 years for the British Royal Navy to enact new dietary guidelines. And it wasn't until 1865 that the British Board of Trade created similar guidelines for the merchant fleet. That is a glacial adoption rate. 'The total time from Lancaster's definitive demonstration of how to prevent scurvy to adoption across the British Empire was 264 years,' Gillam says.[28]

Today, the adoption rate in medicine remains chronically slow. One study examined the aftermath of nine major discoveries, including one finding that the pneumococcal vaccine protects adults from respiratory infections, and not just children. The study showed that it took doctors an average of seventeen years to adopt the new treatments for half of American patients. A major review published in the *New England Journal of Medicine* found that only half of Americans receive the treatment recommended by US national standards.[29]

The problem is not that the information doesn't exist; rather, it is the way it is formatted. As Atul Gawande, a doctor and author, puts it:

> The reason . . . is not usually laziness or unwillingness. The reason is more often that the necessary knowledge has not been translated into a simple, usable and systematic form. If the only thing people did in aviation was issue dense, pages-long bulletins . . . it would be like subjecting pilots to the same deluge of almost 700,000 medical journal articles per year that clinicians must contend with. The

information would be unmanageable. Instead . . . crash investigators [distil] the information into its practical essence.[30]

Perhaps the most telling example of how far the culture of health-care still has to travel is in the attitude to autopsies. A doctor can use intuition, run tests, use scanners and much else besides to come up with a diagnosis while a patient is still alive. But an autopsy allows his colleagues to look inside a body and actually determine the precise cause of death. It is the medical equivalent of a black box.

This has rather obvious implications for progress. After all, if the doctor turns out to be wrong in his diagnosis of the cause of death, he may also have been wrong in his choice of treatment in the days, perhaps months, leading up to death. That might enable him to reassess his reasoning, providing learning opportunities for him and his colleagues. It could save the lives of future patients.

It is for this reason that autopsies have triggered many advances. They have been used to understand the causes of tuberculosis, how to combat Alzheimer's disease, and much else besides. In the armed forces, autopsies on American service men and women who died in Iraq and Afghanistan in the years since 2001 have yielded vital data about injuries from bullets, blasts and shrapnel.

This information revealed deficiencies in body armour and vehicle shielding and has led to major improvements in battlefield helmets, protective clothing and medical equipment[31] (just as the 'black box' analysis by Abraham Wald improved the armouring of bombers during the Second World War). Before 2001, however, military personnel were rarely autopsied, meaning that the lessons were not surfaced – leaving their comrades vulnerable to the same, potentially fatal, injuries.

In the civilian world around 80 per cent of families give permission for autopsies to be performed when asked, largely because it provides them with answers as to why a loved one died.[32] But despite this willingness, autopsies are hardly ever performed. Data in the United States indicates that less than 10 per cent of deaths are followed by an autopsy.[33] Many hospitals perform none at all. Since 1995, we don't know how many are conducted: the American National Center for Health Statistics doesn't collect the stats any longer.[*][34]

All of this precious information is effectively disappearing. A huge amount of potentially life-saving learning is being frittered away. And yet it is not difficult to identify why doctors are reluctant to access this precious data: it hinges on the prevailing attitude towards failure.

After all, why conduct an investigation if it might demonstrate you made a mistake?

This section is not intended as a criticism of doctors, nurses and other staff, who do heroic work every day. I have been looked after with diligence and compassion every time I have been in hospital. It is also worth pointing out that aviation is not perfect. There are many occasions when it doesn't live up to its noble ambition of learning from adverse events.

But the cultural difference between these two institutions is of deep importance if we are to understand the nature of closed loops, how they develop even when people are smart, motivated and caring – and how to break free of them.

It is also important to note that any direct comparison between aviation and healthcare should be handled with caution. For a start healthcare is more complex. It has a huge diversity of equipment: for example, there are 300 types of surgical pump but just two models of long-distance aircraft. It is also more hands-on, and rarely has the benefit of autopilot – all of which adds to the scope for error.

But this takes us to the deepest irony of all. When the probability of error is high, the importance of learning from mistakes is more essential, not less. As Professor James Reason, one of the world's leading experts on system safety, put it: 'This is the paradox in a nutshell: healthcare by its nature is highly error-provoking – yet health carers stigmatise fallibility and have had little or no training in error management or error detection.'[35]

---

* In England and Wales, autopsies are ordered whenever the cause of death is officially unknown, or when the death occurred in suspicious circumstances. In 2013, nearly 20 per cent of deaths required an autopsy.

There are, of course, limits to the extent to which you can transfer procedures from one safety-critical industry to another. Checklists have transferred successfully from aviation to some healthcare systems, but that is no guarantee other procedures will do so. The key issue however, is not about transferring procedures, but transferring an *attitude*.

As Gary Kaplan, CEO of Virginia Mason Health System, has said: 'You can have the best procedures in the world but they won't work unless you change attitudes towards error.'

The underlying problem is not psychological or motivational. It is largely conceptual. And until we change the way we *think* about failure, the ambition of high performance will often remain a mirage, not just in healthcare but elsewhere, too.

In May 2005 Martin Bromiley's persistence paid off. An investigation was commissioned by the general manager of the hospital where his wife died. It was headed by Michael Harmer, professor of Anaesthetics and Intensive Care Medicine at Cardiff University School of Medicine.

On 30 July Martin was called into the hospital to listen to its findings. The report listed a number of recommendations. Each of them could have been lifted directly from the National Transportation Safety Board's report into United Airlines 173 almost thirty years previously. It called for better communication in operating theatres so that 'any member of staff feels comfortable to make suggestions on treatment.'

It also articulated the concern over the limitations of human awareness. 'Given the problem with time passing unnoticed, should such an event occur again, a member of staff should be allocated to record timings of events and keep all involved aware of the elapsed time,' the report said.

The findings were, in one sense, obvious. In another sense they were revolutionary. Bromiley published the report (with the names of medical staff altered to protect anonymity). He gave it maximum exposure. He wanted all clinicians to read it and learn from it. He even managed to get a BBC television documentary commissioned that explored the case and its ramifications.

He then started a safety group to push forward reforms. The focus was not merely on the problem of blocked airways, but on the whole field of institutional learning. He heads the organisation – the Clinical Human Factors Group – in a voluntary capacity to this day.

Soon Martin started receiving emails from practising doctors. The messages were not just from clinicians in the UK, but from the United States, Asia and the rest of the world. One doctor wrote: '. . . for the first time in my career, I was recently faced with an unexpected "can't ventilate, can't intubate" situation. Despite the horror . . . we made the early decision to perform a surgical tracheostomy and the patient recovered with no neurological deficit of any kind.'

A doctor in Texas wrote:

After a 5 hour case today, my patient was turned supine . . . Because of the information I learned relating to your wife's case I pursued a surgical airway. An emergency tracheostomy was completed . . . The patient was transferred to ICU and when sedation was discontinued he woke up and responded appropriately. The good outcome in this case is directly related to the information you are sharing with medical professionals. I wanted to thank you.

Another wrote: 'Were it not for the work that you have tirelessly done to improve training in my profession, I do not think that this patient would have had such a successful outcome [the doctor had just performed an emergency tracheostomy]. I am greatly indebted to you.'

The final report into the death of Elaine Bromiley can be found via a simple search on Google.[36] It contains eighteen pages of detailed medical information. For all the technical language, however, the report can be seen, above all, as a heartfelt tribute to a beloved wife and mother.

At the bottom of the opening page, Martin, one of the most inspirational individuals I have ever interviewed, added a single, italicised sentence.

So that others may learn, and even more may live.

PART 2

Cognitive Dissonance

4

Wrongful Convictions

I

On 17 August 1992 Holly Staker, an eleven-year-old girl living in Waukegan, a small town in Illinois, took the short walk from her home to the apartment of Dawn Engelbrecht, a neighbour. She was babysitting Dawn's two young children, a daughter aged two and a son aged five.*

Dawn had met Holly's mother, Nancy, at the bar where she worked just a few blocks away. Little Holly often babysat when Dawn, who was recently divorced, was working at the bar in the evenings. The two families had become good friends.

Holly arrived at the two storey apartment building, on a tree-lined road called Hickory Street, as agreed, at 4 p.m. It was a fine day and Dawn greeted her warmly. A few minutes later, Dawn said goodbye to her children and Holly, and left for work. She had a long shift ahead.

By 8 p.m. Holly was dead. An unidentified intruder broke into the apartment, locked the door, and then violently raped Holly, stabbing her twenty-seven times in a frenzied assault. The corpse of the youngster was almost unrecognisable.

At just after 8 p.m. a neighbour went to the bar where Dawn worked to say that he had seen her son, who had been locked out of

---

* The case material is based on the work of the Innocence Project, interviews with Juan Rivera, Rivera's lawyers, and Barry Scheck, plus contemporaneous and archive newspaper and media reports, including email exchange with Andrew Martin, who wrote on the case for the *New York Times*.

the apartment and couldn't get back in. Dawn called the apartment, but there was no answer. She then called Holly's mother.

They met at the apartment, and Dawn unlocked the door. They saw that Dawn's two-year-old daughter seemed to be alone, and immediately called the police. Officers found Holly's bloodied corpse behind a bedroom door.

The local community descended into panic. The local police force pursued 600 leads and interviewed 200 people, but within a few weeks the trail had run cold. Parents were paranoid about letting their children out. Journalists described the community as 'traumatised'.

Then, through the testimony of a jailhouse informant, police happened upon a new suspect: Juan Rivera, a nineteen-year-old who lived a few miles south of the murder scene. Over four days, Rivera, who had a history of psychological problems, was subjected to a gruelling examination by the Lake County Major Crimes Task Force. At one point it seemed to get too much for him. He was seen by officers pulling out a clump of hair and banging his head on the wall.

On the third day, when the interview became accusatory, Rivera finally nodded his head when asked if he had committed the crime. By this time he was hog-tied (his hands were cuffed between his legs and his legs were shackled and linked to his handcuffs) and he was confined to a padded cell. Mental health staff at the jail determined that he had undergone a psychotic episode.

On the basis of his confession police prepared a statement for Rivera to sign. But the confession was so inconsistent with what was known about the crime that police had to go back the next day to obtain a new confession, with the inconsistencies removed. The final interrogation lasted almost twenty-four hours. Rivera signed the new confession as well.

At the trial, a few months later, the rewritten confession, which Rivera retracted hours after signing it, would form the central plank of the prosecution's case. There were no witnesses. Although Rivera had a history of psychological problems, there was nothing in his past suggesting that he was capable of violence. There was no physical evidence linking him to the attack, despite a crime scene rich with human tissue. There was blood, hair, skin fragments and many unidentified fingerprints, none of which matched Juan Rivera.

But there *was* a brutally murdered young girl, a community still in mourning, and that signed confession.

The jury didn't take long to make up its mind. Rivera was convicted of first-degree murder and sentenced to life in prison. The court declined a request to set the death penalty.

Many observers, including a number of local reporters, were uneasy at the verdict. They could see that the case hinged on the confession of a disturbed young man. But the police and prosecutors felt vindicated. It had been a troubling crime. A man had been convicted and sentenced. Holly's family could try to find closure. The panic had finally abated. The community could rest easy.

Or could it?

II

One of the key objectives of the criminal justice system is to ensure that people aren't punished for crimes they didn't commit. The idea of an innocent person serving time behind bars, deprived of his liberty by the state, offends deep sensibilities. As the English jurist William Blackstone put it: 'It is better that ten guilty persons escape than that one innocent suffer.'[1]

But miscarriages of justice have a quite different significance: they also represent precious learning opportunities. We saw in the last chapter that the aviation industry has made dramatic improvements by learning from failure. Investigators have examined data from accidents and reformed procedures. As a result the number of crashes has fallen. This is the anatomy of progress: adapting systems in the light of feedback.

There is a rather obvious trade-off between two of the key objectives of the justice system: convicting the guilty and acquitting the innocent. If you wanted to eliminate wrongful convictions altogether you could, say, increase the burden of proof required by the prosecution to 100 per cent. But this outcome would come at a hefty price. It would mean that many more criminals would walk free. How could a jury ever convict, even if it were virtually sure of guilt, with the requirement for 100 per cent certainty?

What we are interested in, then, is reducing the number of wrongful convictions *without compromising rightful convictions*, and vice versa. This would represent a win-win. It would please liberals worried about miscarriages of justice as well as conservatives worried about too many guilty people walking free. The question is: how to make it happen?

Think back to radiology, which we looked at in the last chapter. Here there are also two kinds of error. The first is when a doctor diagnoses a tumour which isn't actually there. This is sometimes called a Type One error: an error of commission. The second kind is when a doctor fails to diagnose a tumour that is there. This is called a Type Two error: an error of omission. It is possible to reduce one kind of error while simultaneously increasing the other kind by altering the 'evidence threshold', as in the criminal justice system. But this trade-off should not obscure the fact that it is possible to reduce both kinds of error at the same time. That is what progress is ultimately about.

Wrongful convictions are, in many ways, like plane crashes. If they can be established conclusively (a far from easy task, it has to be said), they hint at serious system failure. They offer an opportunity to probe what went wrong in everything from the police investigation, to the way the evidence was presented in court, to the deliberations of the jury, to the activities of the judge. By learning from failure we can design reforms that ensure similar mistakes don't happen again.

But, as we have seen, people don't like to admit to failure. How are the police going to feel when they are told that all their hard work to find a brutal killer has served only to put an innocent man in jail? How will prosecutors, who often make the decisive difference in court, feel when all those efforts have ruined the life of an innocent man? And how are judges and law officers going to react when they come face to face with evidence that the system they preside over has failed?

In Part 1, we interrogated the concept of failure through the contrast between aviation and healthcare. We found that in healthcare, professionals are so fearful of their mistakes that they cover them up in various ways, making it impossible to learn from them. We also noted that this tendency characterises the response to failure in many areas of our world.

In this section, we are going to ask, *why*? We are going to drill down into the precise psychological mechanisms that underpin error denial, investigate the contours of its subtle evasions, and see how closed loops are perpetrated by smart, honest people. The criminal justice system will provide the lens, but we will also look at some of the most breathtaking failures in politics, economics and business – and how progress has been thwarted again and again. We cannot learn if we close our eyes to inconvenient truths, but we will see that this is precisely what the human mind is wired up to do, often in astonishing ways.

It is not difficult to see why, in psychological terms, miscarriages of justice have been a sore topic for the legal system. The history is revealing. In 1932, Edwin Borchard, a law professor at Yale, compiled a list of wrongful convictions in his seminal book *Convicting the Innocent and State Indemnity for Errors of Criminal Justice*.[2] Many of the cases were unequivocal failures. Eight involved people convicted of murder when the 'victim' was missing, presumed dead, but who later turned out to be alive and well.

These examples offered an opportunity to identify error traps, to probe systemic weaknesses. But many prosecutors, police and judges (if not defence lawyers) drew very different conclusions. They were dismissive. Many regarded the very idea that the system was anything other than faultless as impertinent. As the district attorney of Worcester County put it: 'Innocent men are never convicted. Don't worry about it . . . It is a physical impossibility.'[3]

It is difficult to conceive of a more exquisite example of closed-loop thinking. After all, if miscarriages of justice are impossible, why spend any time learning from them?

'Historically, the legal system has been incredibly complacent,' Barry Scheck, a defence lawyer from New York, told me. 'When people were convicted, people took it as confirmation that the system was working just fine. There was very little serious work done on testing the system. In fact, the idea that wrongful conviction was common seemed outlandish.'

It is noteworthy that when a court of criminal appeal was first proposed in England and Wales in the early nineteenth century, the strongest opponents were judges. The court had a simple rationale: to provide an opportunity for redress. It was an institutional acknowledgement that mistakes were possible. The judges were against it, in large part, because they denied the premise. The creation of the court turned out to be 'one of the longest and hardest fought campaigns in the history of law reform' requiring 'thirty-one parliamentary bills over a sixty year period.'[4]

Over the next few decades, remarkably little changed. Well-attested miscarriages of justice were dismissed as 'one-offs' or as the price worth paying for a system that, on the whole, got decisions right. Scarcely anyone conducted systematic tests on police methods, court procedures, forensic techniques, or anything else. Why would they when the system is near to perfect?

As Edwin Meese, Attorney General of the United States under President Reagan, put it: 'The thing is, you don't have many suspects who are innocent of a crime. That's contradictory. If a person is innocent of a crime, then he is not a suspect.'

Then, on the morning of Monday 10 September 1984 everything changed.

It was at precisely 9.05 a.m. in a lab in Leicester, England that Alec Jeffreys, a research scientist, had a eureka moment while looking at an X-ray film of a DNA experiment. He realised that by examining variations in the genetic code it was possible to discover a genetic fingerprint, a unique marker that could provide almost definitive identification. Together with later work by Kary Mullis, a scientist who would go on to win the Nobel Prize, it set the stage for a revolution in criminology.[5]

Up until the work of Jeffreys, blood analysis represented pretty much the most sophisticated aspect of courtroom science. There are four blood groups, which meant that tissue found at a crime scene could narrow down the list of suspects, but not by much. In the UK, around 48 per cent of the population have blood group O.[6]

DNA evidence is quite different. In the absence of contamination, and provided the test is administered correctly, the odds of two unrelated people having matching DNA is roughly one in a billion. The ramifications were huge – and it didn't take long for the legal system to see them.

In a narrow group of cases it would be possible to identify conclusively the DNA of tissue at a crime scene. In a rape case, for example, if the police swabbed the sperm found in the victim, they could narrow down the number of potential suspects to just one. This is why DNA fingerprinting has helped to secure hundreds of convictions – it has a unique power in establishing guilt.

But DNA also has profound implications for cases that have already been tried: the power to exonerate. After all, if the DNA from the sperm in a rape victim has been stored, and if it does not match the DNA of the person serving time in prison, the conclusion is difficult to deny: it came from a different man, the real criminal.

'DNA testing is to justice what the telescope is for the stars: not a lesson in biochemistry, not a display of the wonders of magnifying optical glass, but a way to see things as they really are,' Scheck has said. 'It is a revelation machine.'[7]

DNA tests are not completely fail-safe, since they can be corrupted by human error, fraud, mislabelling or by flawed interpretations when there are only tiny fragments of human tissue.[8] But when they are undertaken honestly and systematically, they are pretty much definitive. By early 1989, the laboratory techniques pioneered by Jeffreys were ready to use in forensic labs. It set the stage for the most breathtaking experiment in legal history. And it didn't take long for the results to come rolling in.

On 14 August 1989, Gary Dotson, who had been convicted of rape in Chicago, was released from jail having consistently proclaimed his innocence. Underwear worn by the victim had been sent for DNA testing, which revealed that the semen belonged to a different man. Dotson had served more than ten years in jail.[9]

A few months later, Bruce Nelson, who had been convicted of rape and murder in Pennsylvania, had his sentence overturned after DNA testing eliminated him as the source of the saliva found on a cigarette and on the victim's breast, bra and hair. He had served nine years. Then Leonard Callace, convicted of the sexual assault of an eighteen-year-old in New York State, was released when DNA testing excluded him as the perpetrator. He had served almost six years.

The first DNA exoneration in the UK involved Michael Shirley, a young sailor who had been convicted of the rape and murder of Linda Cook, a barmaid working in Portsmouth, in 1986. A number of swabs had been taken from the victim and the original jury had been informed the blood group matched Shirley's (along with 23.3 per cent of the British adult male population).

Shirley mounted rooftop protests and engaged in hunger strikes. A journalist who campaigned for his release was sacked by his newspaper. The Home Secretary refused to refer his case to the Court of Appeal. The police claimed that the swabs containing the semen had been destroyed, but under pressure discovered the relevant material. A simple DNA test revealed that the semen found in the victim did not belong to Shirley. He had served sixteen years at the time of his release.[10]

By 2005 more than three hundred people had had their convictions overturned following DNA tests.[11] In situations where evidence had been stored, clients of the Innocence Project (a charity that helps prisoners protesting their innocence) were exonerated in *almost half the cases*.

These exonerations raised dozens of questions. Why were police pursuing the wrong suspects? Why were eyewitnesses misidentifying criminals? Why were interrogation techniques used by the police leading to false conclusions? Why were the courts failing? And what could be done about it?

There was a wider question, too: what about the system more generally? DNA is relevant in only a small number of cases (rapes, murders, etc. where human tissue had been found and stored). What about all the other cases, where convicted criminals had no recourse to DNA fingerprinting to establish their innocence? How many innocent people were behind bars in total?

Estimates are difficult to establish, but a study led by Samuel R.

Gross, a professor at the University of Michigan Law School, con-cluded: 'If we reviewed prison sentences with the same level of care that we devote to death sentences, there would have been over 28,500 non-death-row exonerations [in the United States] in the past 15 years rather than the 255 that have in fact occurred.'[12]

This should not surprise us. Systems that do not engage with fail-ure struggle to learn. 'The emerging picture is clear enough,' Barry Scheck, the lawyer, has written. 'The criminal justice system, from the police precinct to the Supreme Court, is a near shambles . . . A study by Colombia University reported that nationally two out of three death sentences imposed between 1973 and 1995 were consti-tutionally flawed and overturned by the courts.'[13]

In 2005 the lawyers representing Juan Rivera applied for a DNA test. At the time he had been in jail for almost thirteen years. Rivera was excited at the prospect of a method that could finally establish the truth about what had happened on that warm night in Waukegan, Illinois more than a decade earlier.

On 24 May the results came back. It showed that Rivera was not the source of the semen found inside the corpse of Holly Staker. He was, at first, overwhelmed. He couldn't quite take in the fact that people would finally see that he was innocent of such a horrendous crime. He told his lawyers that it felt like he was 'walking on air'. He celebrated that night in his cell.

But this wasn't the end of the story. In fact, it wasn't even the beginning of the end. Rivera would spend another six years in jail. Why? Think back to the police. Were they going to accept their mis-take? Were the prosecutors going to hold up their hands and admit they had got it wrong? Was the wider system going to accept what the DNA evidence was revealing about its defects?

Perhaps the most fascinating thing about the DNA exonerations is not how they opened the cell doors for wrongly convicted prisoners, but how excruciatingly difficult they were to push through; about how the system fought back, in ways both subtle and profound, against the very evidence that indicated that it was getting things wrong.

How did this happen? How does failure-denial become so deeply entrenched in human minds and systems? To find out we will take a detour into the work of Leon Festinger, arguably the most influential sociologist of the last half-century. It was his study into a small religious cult in Chicago that first revealed the remarkable truth about closed-loop behaviour.

III

In the autumn of 1954 Festinger, who at the time was a researcher at the University of Minnesota, came across an unusual headline in his local newspaper. 'Prophecy from Planet Clarion Call to City: Flee That Flood' it read. The story was about a housewife called Marian Keech* who claimed to be in psychic contact with a god-like figure from another planet, who had told her that the world would end before dawn on 21 December 1954.

Keech had warned her friends about the impending disaster and some left their jobs and homes, despite resistance from their families, to move in with the woman who had, by now, become their spiritual leader. They were told that true believers would be saved from the apocalypse by a spaceship that would swoop down from the heavens and pick them up from the garden of Keech's small house in suburban Michigan, at midnight.

Festinger, an ambitious scientist, glimpsed a rare opportunity. If he could get close to the cult, perhaps even infiltrate it by claiming to be a believer, he would be able to observe how the group behaved as the apocalyptic deadline approached. In particular, he was fascinated by how they would react *after the prophecy had failed*.

Now, this may seem like a rather obvious question. Surely the group would go back to their former lives. They would conclude that Keech was a fraud who hadn't been in touch with any god-like figure at all. What other conclusion could they possibly reach if the prophecy wasn't fulfilled? It is difficult to think of a more graphic failure, both for Keech and those who had put their trust in her.

---

* Her real name was Dorothy Martin but, in order to protect her anonymity, Festinger changed the name in his seminal book *When Prophecy Fails*.

But Festinger predicted a different response. He suspected that far from disavowing Keech, their belief in her would be unaffected. Indeed, he believed they would become *more committed* to the cult than ever before.

In early November, Festinger and his colleagues contacted Keech by phone and went about trying to gain her confidence. One of them invented a story about having had a supernatural experience while travelling in Mexico; another pretended to be a businessman who had become intrigued by the newspaper story. By late November they had been granted access to Keech's cult, and were ensconced in her house, observing a small coterie of people who believed that the end of the world was imminent.

Sure enough, as the deadline for the apocalypse passed without any sign of a spaceship (still less a flood), Festinger and his colleagues watched the group in the living room (Keech's husband, who was a non-believer, had gone to his bedroom and slept through the whole thing). At first the cult members kept checking outside to see if the spaceship had landed. Then, as the clock ticked past midnight, they became sullen and bemused.

Ultimately, however, they became defiant. Just as Festinger had predicted, the faith of hardcore members was unaffected by what should have been a crushing disappointment. In fact, for some of them, their faith seemed to strengthen.

How is this possible? After all, this was an unambiguous failure. Keech had said the world would end, and that a spaceship would save true believers. Neither had happened. The cult members could have responded by altering their beliefs about the supernatural insights of Keech. Instead, they altered the 'evidence'.

As Festinger recounts in his classic book *When Prophecy Fails*,[14] they simply redefined the failure. 'The godlike figure is so impressed with our faith that he has decided to give the planet a second chance' they proclaimed (I am paraphrasing only a little). 'We saved the world!' Far from abandoning the cult, core members went out on a recruitment drive. As Festinger put it: 'The little group, sitting all night long, had spread so much light that God had saved the world from destruction.' They were 'jubilant'.

Now, this is important not because of what it tells us about cults, but because of what it reveals about all of us. Festinger showed that this behaviour, while extreme, provides an insight into psychological mechanisms that are universal. When we are confronted with evidence that challenges our deeply held beliefs we are more likely to *reframe* the evidence than we are to alter our beliefs. We simply invent new reasons, new justifications, new explanations. Sometimes we ignore the evidence altogether.

Let us move away from religious cults, for a moment, and take a look at something as everyday as politics. Specifically, let's take the Iraq War. In the build-up to the conflict, much of the justification centred on Iraq's alleged possession of weapons of mass destruction (WMD). The idea that WMD had been stockpiled by Saddam Hussein was used by leaders on both sides of the Atlantic as a core part of the case for action. The problem was that, as early as 2003, it was clear that there were no WMD in Iraq.

This was not an easy thing for those who had endorsed the policy to accept. It implied a failure of judgement. Many had spent months arguing for the intervention, and backing the leaders who had pushed it through. They strongly believed that military action was the right course. The lack of WMD didn't show that the intervention was necessarily a mistake, but it did, at the very least, weaken its legitimacy, given that it had been a central plank of the original justification.

What is important for our purposes, however, is not whether the Iraq intervention was right or wrong, but how different people responded to the new evidence. The results were startling. According to a Knowledge Networks poll published in October 2003,[15] more than half of Republicans, who had voted for George W. Bush, simply ignored it. They said that they believed that weapons *had been found*.

As the survey's director put it: 'For some Americans, their desire to support the war may be leading them to screen out information that weapons of mass destruction have not been found. Given the intensive news coverage and high levels of public attention to the topic, this level of misinformation [is remarkable].'

Think about that for a moment. The evidence of the lack of WMD had vanished. These people had watched the news, seen the stories about the absence of WMD, but then managed to forget all about it. Democrats, on the other hand, were perfectly aware of the lack of WMD. Many of those who opposed the war had it seared on their memories. But more than half of Republicans? Nope, they couldn't remember it at all.

'Cognitive dissonance' is the term Festinger coined to describe the inner tension we feel when, among other things, our beliefs are challenged by evidence. Most of us like to think of ourselves as rational and smart. We reckon we are pretty good at reaching sound judgements. We don't like to think of ourselves as dupes. That is why when we mess up, particularly on big issues, our self-esteem is threatened. We feel uncomfortable, twitchy.

In these circumstances we have two choices. The first is to accept that our original judgements may have been at fault. We question whether it was quite such a good idea to put our faith in a cult leader whose prophecies didn't even materialise. We pause to reflect on whether the Iraq War was quite such a good idea given that Saddam didn't pose the threat we imagined.

The difficulty with this option is simple: it is threatening. It requires us to accept that we are not as smart as we like to think. It forces us to acknowledge that we can sometimes be wrong, even on issues on which we have staked a great deal.

So, here's the second option: denial. We reframe the evidence. We filter it, we spin it, or ignore it altogether. That way, we can carry on under the comforting assumption that we were right all along. We are bang on the money! We didn't get duped! What evidence that we messed up?

The cult members had a lot riding on Keech. They had left their jobs and risked the anger of their families. They had been ridiculed by their neighbours, too. To admit they were wrong was not like admitting they had taken the wrong turning on the way to the supermarket. Their credibility was on the line. They were highly motivated to believe Keech was the guru she claimed to be.

Think how shaming it would have been to walk out of that house. Think of how excruciating to admit they had put their trust in a crank. Doesn't it make sense that they were desperate to reinterpret the failure as a success in disguise (a very good disguise!), just as it was easier for many Republicans to edit out the lack of WMD than confront the facts full-on? Both mechanisms helped to smooth out the feelings of dissonance and retain the reassuring sense that they are smart, rational people.

In one experiment by the leading psychologist Elliot Aronson and his colleague Judson Mills, students were invited to join a group that would be discussing the psychology of sex.[16] Before joining the group the students were asked to undergo an initiation procedure. For some students this was highly embarrassing (reciting explicit sexual passages from racy novels) while for others it was only mildly embarrassing (reading sexual words from a dictionary). The students were then played a tape of a discussion taking place between members of the group they had just joined.

Aronson had staged the discussion so that it was totally boring. So boring, in fact, that any unbiased person would have been forced to conclude that it was a mistake to join up. The members discussed the secondary sexual characteristics of birds: their plumage, colouring, etc. They droned on and on. Many didn't even know their material, kept hesitating, and failed to reach the end of their sentences. It was utterly tedious.

At the end of the tape the students were asked to rate how interesting they found the discussion. Those who had undergone the mild initiation found it boring. Of course they did. They could see the discussion for what it was. They were irritated by a member who admitted that he hadn't done the reading on the mating rituals of a breed of rare bird. 'What an irresponsible idiot!' they said. 'He didn't even do the basic reading! He let the group down! Who'd want to be in a group with him!'[17]

But what about those who had undergone the highly embarrassing initiation? For them, everything changed. As Aronson put in his fascinating book (co-authored with Carol Tavris) *Mistakes Were Made (but Not by Me)*: '. . . they rated the discussion as interesting and exciting and the group members as attractive and sharp. They forgave the irresponsible idiot. His candour was refreshing! Who wouldn't want to be in a group with such an honest guy? It was hard to believe they were listening to the same recording.'

What was going on? Think about it in terms of cognitive dissonance. If I have put up with a lot to become a member of a group, if I have voluntarily subjected myself to acute embarrassment, I would have to be pretty stupid if the group turned out to be anything less than wonderful. To protect my self-esteem I will want to convince myself that the group is pretty damn good. Hence the necessity to talk it up, to reframe my perceptions in a positive direction.

None of this applies, of course, if the initiation is simple. If the group turns out to be a waste of time, one can say to oneself, honestly, and without any threat to one's self-esteem 'this place is not worth bothering with'. It is only when we have staked our ego that our mistakes of judgement become threatening. That is when we build defensive walls and deploy cognitive filters.

In a similar experiment led by the psychologist Charles Lord, volunteers were recruited who were either adamantly in favour of capital punishment or adamantly against.[18] Those in favour of capital punishment were the kind of people who shout at the TV when liberals argue for clemency; who regale their friends about the deterrent effects of capital punishment. Those against it were the kind of people who are horrified by 'state-sanctioned murder', and who worry about how it brutalises society.

Lord gave these two groups two research projects to read. He made sure that both research projects were impressive. Both seemed to marshal well-researched evidence about the issue. The reports were robust and weighty. But here's the thing: one report collated all evidence that called into question the legitimacy of capital punishment while the other articulated evidence that supported it.

Now, at the very least, you might have expected this contradictory evidence to have shown that capital punishment has arguments on both sides. You might have expected people on either side of the divide, reading all this, to have shifted a little closer together in their views. In fact, the opposite happened. The two groups became more polarised. Those in favour were more convinced of the logic of their position; ditto those against.

When asked about their attitudes afterwards, those in favour of capital punishment said that they were deeply impressed with the dossier citing evidence in line with their views. The data, they said, was rigorous. It was extensive. It was robust. But the other dossier? Well, it was full of holes, shoddy, weak points everywhere. How could any self-respected academic publish such rubbish?

Precisely the opposite conclusions were drawn by those who were against capital punishment. It was not just that they disagreed with the conclusions. They also found the (neutral) statistics and methodology unimpressive. From reading exactly the same material, the two groups moved even further apart in their views. They had each reframed the evidence to fit in with their pre-existing beliefs.

Festinger's great achievement was to show that cognitive dissonance is a deeply ingrained human trait. The more we have riding on our judgements, the more we are likely to manipulate any new evidence that calls them into question.

Now let us take these insights back to the subject with which we started this chapter. For it turns out that cognitive dissonance has had huge and often astonishing effects on the workings of the criminal justice system.

IV

On 20 March 1987 a young girl was attacked in her home in Billings, Montana. The Innocence Project, the non-profit organisation set up by two New York lawyers, Barry Scheck and Peter Neufeld, to help prisoners obtain DNA tests, describes the crime as follows:

> The young girl was attacked by an intruder who had broken in through a window. She was raped ... The perpetrator fled after stealing a purse and jacket. The victim was examined the same day. Police collected her underwear and the bed sheets upon which the crime was committed. Semen was identified on the underwear and several hairs were collected from the bed sheets.[19]

The police produced a composite sketch of the intruder based upon the description given by the victim and this led an officer to interview Jimmy Ray Bromgard, an eighteen-year-old who lived in the area, and who resembled the sketch. Bromgard eventually agreed to participate in a line-up. He was picked out by the victim, but not with any real confidence. She said she was '60, 65 per cent sure'.

When the case came to trial, most of the prosecution case was based on forensic evidence related to hair found at the crime scene. This evidence (it was later established) was largely concocted by the 'expert' called by the prosecution. There were no fingerprints, and no physical evidence beyond the flawed hair testimony. Bromgard, who said he was at home asleep at the time of the crime, was found guilty and sentenced to forty years in prison.

The Innocence Project took up the case in 2000. A DNA test excluded Bromgard as the source of the semen found on the victim's underwear. This represented powerful evidence that he was not the perpetrator. 'The original case was flimsy and the new evidence invalidated the conviction,' Barry Scheck told me. 'The prosecutors could have dropped the case. They could have put their hands up and admitted they got the wrong man. But they didn't.'

Or perhaps they just couldn't.

Michael McGrath, the state prosecutor, responded to the new evidence by coming up with an interpretation that, in many ways, is even more novel than the explanation given by the cult for the failure of the Keech prophecy. As Kathryn Schulz explains in her excellent book *Being Wrong*, McGrath claimed that Bromgard might be a 'chimera'.[20] This is where a single person has two different blood types due to the death of a twin in the womb. It has only been reported around thirty times in history. It represented a reframing of the evidence of a quite breathtaking kind.

Sadly, for McGrath at least, further testing proved that Bromgard was not a chimera, but the prosecutor wasn't finished yet. When Bromgard sued the state of Montana for wrongful conviction, Peter Neufeld from the Innocence Project came face to face with McGrath during the deposition. McGrath was still adamant that Bromgard was the prime suspect. Nothing seemed to prise him from that belief:

no amount of persuasion, no amount of testimony, no amount of evidence.

Neufeld questioned him on what had become, by this stage, an unshakable belief. If Bromgard is guilty, Neufeld asked, how could McGrath explain the presence of semen from a different man in the victim?

Kathryn Schulz quotes from the transcript of the exchange:

McGrath: The semen could have come from multiple different sources.

Neufeld: Why don't you tell me what those multiple sources are?

McGrath: It's potentially possible that [the victim] was sexually active with somebody else

(The victim was 8 years old)

McGrath: It's possible that her sister was sexually active with somebody else

(Her sister was 11 at the time)

McGrath: It's possible that a third person could have been in the room. It's possible. It's possible that the father could have left that stain in a myriad of different ways.

Neufeld: What other different ways?

McGrath: He could have masturbated in that room in those underwear . . . The father and mother could have had sex in that room in that bed, or somehow transferred a stain to those underwear . . . [The father] could have had a wet dream; could have been sleeping in that bed; he could have had an incestual relationship with one of the daughters.

The transcript runs on for another 249 pages of similar outlandish claims.

'So we have four possibilities,' Schulz writes. 'The eight-year-old was sexually active; her eleven-year-old sister was sexually active while wearing her sister's underpants; a third party was in the room (even though the victim had testified to a single intruder); or the father had deposited the semen in one perverse way or another.'

There was, of course, a fifth possibility, but it required McGrath to accept the evidence for what it was, rather than what he wanted it to be. Bromgard was innocent. The state of Montana eventually paid Bromgard $3.5 million in damages. And McGrath failed in his attempt to ban publication of the exchange with Neufeld.

What was going on? The only way to make sense of this exchange is through the prism of cognitive dissonance. Many prosecutors see their work as more than a job; it is more like a vocation. They have spent years training to reach high standards of performance. It is a *tough* initiation. Their self-esteem is bound up with their competence. They are highly motivated to believe in the probity of the system they have joined.

In the course of their investigations, they get to know the bereaved families well and quite naturally come to empathise with their trauma. And they want to believe that in all those long hours spent away from their own families pursuing justice, they have helped to make the world a safer place.

Imagine what it must be like to be confronted with evidence that they have assisted in putting the wrong person in jail; that they have ruined the life of an innocent person; that the wounds of the victim's family are going to be reopened. It must be stomach churning. In terms of cognitive dissonance, it is difficult to think of anything more threatening.

As Richard Ofshe, a social psychologist, has put it: '[convicting the wrong person is] one of the worst professional mistakes you can make – like a physician amputating the wrong arm.'[21]

Just think of how desperate they would be to reframe the fatality. The theory of cognitive dissonance is the only way to get a handle on the otherwise bewildering reaction of prosecutors and police (and, indeed, the wider system) to exonerating DNA evidence. 'It is almost like a state of denial,' Scheck says. 'They just couldn't see the new evidence for what it was.'

In an adversarial system you would expect any new evidence secured by the defence to be looked at with healthy scepticism by prosecutors. You would expect them to give it scrutiny and to look at the wider context to be sure it stacks up. But in case after case contested by the Innocence Project, the sense of denial from many prosecutors and police went a lot further.

Nothing seemed to budge them from their conviction that the man who had been sent to prison was guilty. Even after the test had been performed. Even after the conviction had been overturned. Even after the prisoner had been released from jail. The problem was not the strength of the evidence, which was often overwhelming, it was the psychological difficulty in accepting it.

The reframing exercise often took a distinctive path. First the prosecutors would try to deny access to DNA evidence in the first place. When that strategy was batted away by judges, and the test had excluded the convict as the source of the DNA, they would claim that it had not been carried out correctly.

This didn't last long, either, because when the test was redone it would invariably come back with the same result. The next stage was for the prosecutor to argue that the semen belonged to a different man *who was not the murderer*. In other words, the victim had had consensual sex with another man, but had subsequently been raped by the prisoner, who had used a condom.[22]

This is the domino effect of cognitive dissonance: the reframing process takes on a life of its own.

The presence of an entirely new man, not mentioned at the initial trial, for whom there were no eyewitnesses, and who the victim often couldn't remember having sex with, may seem like a desperate ploy to evade the evidence. But it has been used so often that it has been given a name by defence lawyers: 'the unindicted coejaculator'.

It is a term that usefully captures the power of cognitive dissonance.

Schulz quotes from a fascinating interview with Peter Neufeld of the Innocence Project:

> We'll be leaving the courtroom after an exoneration and the prose-cutor will say 'We still think your client is guilty and we are going to retry him.' Months go by and then finally the prosecutor comes back and says 'We're agreeing to dismiss the charges, not because your client is innocent but because with the passage of time it's too

difficult to get the witnesses' . . . There's a whole category of prosecutors and detectives who still say 'I can't tell you how, I can't give
you a logical explanation, but there's no doubt in my mind that your
guy is guilty.'

Some of these contortions would be almost comical if the subject
matter were not so serious. In an investigation by Andrew Martin of
the *New York Times* dozens of surreal explanations were uncovered:

> In Nassau County on Long Island, after DNA evidence showed that
> the sperm in a 16-year-old murder victim did not come from the
> man convicted of the crime, prosecutors argued that it must have
> come from a consensual lover, even though her mother and best
> friend insisted she was a virgin. In Florida, after DNA showed that
> the pubic hairs at the scene of a rape did not belong to the convicted
> rapist, prosecutors argued that the hairs found on the victim's bed
> could have come from movers who brought furniture to the bed-
> room a week or so earlier.[23]

Of course, the prosecution has a duty to test the claims of the
defence. After all, it is *possible* that the semen in a rape victim was
deposited by someone else who was not the murderer. Exploring the
context is reasonable and, in many circumstances, necessary. They
are only doing their job.

But notice the contrast here. When prosecutors are assessing evidence at the beginning of a case, DNA is held up as the most powerful
evidence there is. That is why it has helped to secure so many convictions. But once prosecutors have secured a conviction, exonerating
DNA evidence suddenly becomes highly suspect. Why is this?
Festinger would have found it pretty easy to explain: DNA evidence
is indeed strong, but not as strong as the desire to protect one's
self-esteem.

There may also be external incentives at work in the behaviour of
prosecutors as Brandon Garret, a law professor at the University of
Virginia, has pointed out. 'Legal scholars looking at the issue suggest
that prosecutors' concerns about their political future and a culture

that values winning over justice also come into play,' he said in an interview with the *New York Times*. 'They are attached to their convictions, and they don't want to see their work called into question.'[24]

But often the scale of denial went way beyond any of this. As Scheck told me: 'I am not a psychologist, but it seems pretty obvious that some prosecutors just couldn't bring themselves to accept that they had got it wrong. It was just too raw.'

And this brings us back to Juan Rivera. You'll remember that, as a nineteen-year-old, he was convicted of the rape and murder of an eleven-year-old girl on the basis of a confession signed in the middle of a psychotic episode during a four-day interrogation. You will also remember that the DNA test excluded him as the source of the semen found inside the victim.

'When the DNA results came back showing that Juan Rivera was absolutely not the person responsible for the rape of Holly Staker everyone assumed that that was the end of the case,' Larry Marshall, professor of law at Stanford University, has said. 'It was the classic exoneration.'[25]

But that is not how it seemed to state prosecutors. They came up with a new story to account for the DNA evidence, a story very different from the one they had presented at the original trial. Holly, an eleven-year-old child, had had consensual sex with a lover a few hours before the attack, prosecutors claimed. This accounted for the semen. And Rivera? He had happened upon Holly *after* intercourse had taken place. Rivera may not have deposited the semen, they claimed, but he did murder her.

'It was a grotesque way of squaring the new evidence with their unshakable belief that Rivera was guilty,' Steven Art, one of Rivera's lawyers, told me. 'But it was also totally inconsistent with the overwhelming evidence that Holly had been raped, quite brutally. There were signs of vaginal and anal trauma and stab wounds in her genitals.'

The prosecutor's new story may have seemed outlandish and improbable, but the consequences were very real. Rivera did not escape prison for another six years. In a retrial in 2009 the jury discounted the DNA evidence. The power of a signed confession, and the graphic nature of the murder, were simply too strong to ignore.

I asked Rivera, who was eventually released in 2012 after a fourth trial, what it was like to sit in his cell while the system resisted the exonerating evidence. He was understandably emotional. He said:

> When the DNA result came back, I was so happy. It showed that I had been telling the truth all along. It showed to the community that I was not a rapist or a murderer. It was an incredible relief.
>
> But when my attorneys came into my cell to tell me the result there was always a fear at the back of my mind that it wasn't over. I knew the prosecutors would resist the new evidence. I had this sense of dread that they would find a way of keeping me in prison. But even I was shocked at the new story they came up with. There didn't seem to be *anything* that could convince them that I hadn't done it.

The nineteen years in prison took an extraordinary toll. 'I got stabbed twice and endured three attempted rapes,' he said. 'People wanted to hurt me; they thought that I was a child rapist. But perhaps the toughest thing of all, was knowing that I was innocent. No matter how often they twisted the story to fit in with the new evidence, I could at least hold onto that truth.'

V

The criminal justice system takes evidence seriously. You could almost say that the entire system is founded on the notion that evidence is sacrosanct and that the best way of arriving at the right answer is to examine it without prejudice. Verdicts are likely to be flawed otherwise. But if trained prosecutors lose their bearings because of a fear of failure, what hope is there for the rest of us?

Not all trials followed the pattern of Rivera or Bromgard, however. Many prosecutors accepted the strength of the DNA tests, and after suitable scrutiny accepted that wrongful convictions had taken place.

Indeed, many support the work of the Innocence Project and recognise that these failures provide an opportunity to adapt the system. But the wider sense of denial has been unmistakable. Sometimes, the system itself seems designed not to learn from mistakes, but to bury them. Until recently, for example, many US states denied access to DNA tests through so-called 'finality doctrines'. These put a time limit on reopening old cases and, by implication, thwarted access to the very evidence that could prove a wrongful conviction had taken place.[26]

'The Innocence Project and other advocates have spent hundreds of hours just arguing against finality doctrines that are used to block inquiries that no fair person would resist,' Scheck has written.[27]

Until 1999 New York and Illinois were the only two states that permitted DNA tests after conviction: they also, unsurprisingly, had the most exonerations. Today, all fifty states have statutes allowing post-conviction DNA testing, but many retain time limits. Others do not allow access to DNA evidence if the suspect originally confessed (like Rivera), even if the test could exonerate them.[28]

And then there is the attitude of those at the top. It is remarkable that many of the highest courts around the world, including the Supreme Court in the United States, have effectively stated that they would only retry cases if it could be shown that there was a mistake in procedure rather than in fact. As William Renquist, the former Chief Justice, put it: 'A claim of actual innocence is not in itself a constitutional claim.'*

Think about that for a moment, because it has darkly comic overtones. Defective systems create errors *even when procedures are followed*. Think of United Airlines 173, where the pilots followed procedure but the plane crashed. It was precisely because of the evidence provided by the crash that procedures were altered (the introduction of Crew Resource Management, for example). That is one of the key ways in which progress happens.

---

* Justice Antonin Scalia has gone even further. In a case in 2009, he said: 'This Court has never held that the Constitution forbids the execution of a convicted defendant who has had a full and fair trial but is later able to convince a . . . court that he is "actually" innocent.'

But the highest courts were refusing to listen to claims of factual innocence unless the original trials contained procedural errors. It meant that factual errors, created by procedural flaws, would not be investigated, still less addressed. For innocent people behind bars, it was a catch-22 of monumental proportions. And it revealed the breathtaking scale of closed-loop behaviour within the legal system.

In Chapter 6 we will look at reform of the criminal justice system (and catch up with what happened to Juan Rivera). We will see that when wrongful convictions were investigated by the Innocence Project, systematic defects were revealed in everything from police procedures to forensic science. If these investigations had taken place earlier, and the problems been addressed, hundreds of innocent people could have been spared wrongful conviction. As Scheck has written:

> In the United States there are grave consequences when an airplane falls from the sky . . . Serious inquiries are made: what went wrong? Was it a systemic breakdown? An individual's mistake? Was there official misconduct? Can anything be done to prevent it from happening again? . . . [But] America keeps virtually no records when a conviction is vacated based on new evidence of innocence. Judges typically write one-line orders, not official opinions, meaning that they don't analyse what went wrong. Neither does anyone else.[29]

5
Intellectual Contortions

I

The phenomenon of cognitive dissonance is often held up as a testament to the quirkiness of human psychology. It is easy to laugh when we see just how far we are prepared to go to justify our judgements, sometimes to the point of filtering out evidence that contradicts them. It is all part of the elusive trickery of the human brain, it is said, a charming if occasionally troubling aspect of our eccentricity as a species.

But we can now see that it is so much more than that. So far in this book, it has been argued that progress in most human activities depends, in large part, on our willingness to learn from failure. If we edit out failure, if we reframe our mistakes, we are effectively destroying one of the most precious learning opportunities that exists.

And the scariest thing of all is that we scarcely realise we are doing it. When, in the initiation experiment discussed in the previous chapter, the students who had been subject to the embarrassing initiation were told the real reasons they had found such a tedious discussion so fascinating, they wouldn't accept it. 'After each participant had finished, I explained the study in detail and went over the theory [of cognitive dissonance] carefully,' Aronson has said.

> Although everyone who went through the severe initiation said they found the hypothesis intriguing and that they could see how most people would be affected in the way I predicted, they all took pains to assure me that their preference for the group had nothing to do with the severity of the initiation. They each claimed that they liked

the group because that is how they really felt. Yet almost all of them liked the group more than any of the people in the mild initiation condition did.[1]

This reveals a subtle difference between external and internal deception. A deliberate deception (misleading one's colleagues, or a patient, or a boss) has at least one clear benefit. The person doing the deceiving will, by definition, recognise the deceit and will inwardly acknowledge the failure. Perhaps he will amend the way he does his job to avoid such a failure in the future.

Self-justification is more insidious. Lying to oneself destroys the very possibility of learning. How can one learn from failure if one has convinced oneself – through the endlessly subtle means of self-justification, narrative manipulation, and the wider psychological arsenal of dissonance-reduction – that a failure didn't actually occur?

It is worth noting here, too, the relationship between the ambiguity of our failures and cognitive dissonance. When a plane has crashed, it's difficult to pretend the system worked just fine. The failure is too stark, too dramatic. This is what engineers call a red flag: a feature of the physical world that says 'you are going wrong'. It is like driving to a friend's house, taking a wrong turn, and hitting a dead end. You have to turn around.

Most failure is not like that. Most failure can be given a makeover. You can latch on to any number of justifications: 'it was a one-off', 'it was a unique case', 'we did everything we could'. You can selectively cite statistics that justify your case, while ignoring the statistics that don't. You can find new justifications that did not even occur to you at the time, and which you would probably have dismissed until they – thankfully, conveniently – came to your rescue.

Psychologists often point out that self-justification is not entirely without benefits. It stops us agonising over every decision, questioning every judgement, staying awake at night wondering if getting married/taking that job/going on that course was the right thing to do. The problem, however, is when this morphs into mindless self-justification: when we spin automatically; when we reframe wantonly; when failure is so threatening we can no longer learn from it.

And this takes us back to a question that has been lingering since the opening section of this book when we examined the scale of deaths from preventable medical error. How could doctors and nurses preside over such suffering? How could these honourable people cover up their mistakes in such a brazen way? How could they live with themselves?

Our exploration of cognitive dissonance finally provides us with the answer. It is precisely in order to live with themselves, and the fact that they have harmed patients, that doctors and nurses reframe their errors in the first place. This protects their sense of professional self-worth and morally justifies the practice of non-disclosure. After all, why disclose an error if there wasn't really an error, after all?

And this pierces to the very heart of the distinction between internal and external deception. If nurses and doctors were fully aware of the fatal errors they were making, non-disclosure would *add* to their emotional anguish. They would know that they had harmed a patient, know that they had deliberately deceived patients, and know that they had made mistakes more likely in the future.

It is hardly likely that health professionals would engage in this kind of deceit on such a large scale. The vast majority of doctors and nurses are committed and decent people. Indeed, many are heroic in their care for their patients. And therein lies the tragedy of cognitive dissonance. It allows good, motivated people to harm those they are working to protect, not just once, but again and again.

To put it a slightly different way, the most effective cover-ups are perpetrated not by those who are covering their backs, but by those who don't even realise that they have anything to hide.

In his book *Medical Errors and Medical Narcissism*, John Banja, professor of medical ethics at Emory University, looked in detail at the reframing techniques used by clinicians.[2] The words may be different, but the underlying semantics are uncannily similar to those used by prosecuting lawyers when faced with DNA exonerations. They are a way of taking the sting out of mistakes and of justifying non-disclosure:

'Well, we did our best. These things happen.'

'Why disclose the error? The patient was going to die anyway.'

'Telling the family about the error will only make them feel worse.'

'It was the patient's fault. If he wasn't so (obese, sick etc.), this error wouldn't have caused so much harm.'

'If we're not totally and absolutely certain the error caused the harm, we don't have to tell.'

Banja writes: 'Health professionals are known to be immensely clever at covering up or drawing attention away from an error by the language they use. There is good reason to believe that their facility with linguistic subterfuge is cultivated during their residency years or on special training.'[3]

A landmark three-year investigation published in the *The Social Science and Medical Journal* revealed similar findings, namely that physicians cope with their errors through a process of denial. They 'block mistakes from entering conscious thought' and 'narrow the definition of a mistake so that they effectively disappear, or are seen as inconsequential'.*

The same conclusion is also revealed in direct surveys of health professionals. A study in 2004, for example, polled medical

---

* This narrowing of the definition of a mistake has an echo in the 'wrong' approach to science. In Chapter 3 we looked at the example of a hypothesis: namely that water boils at 100°C. We now know that this breaks down when water is boiled at altitude. But we could salvage the initial hypothesis by simply narrowing its content, as the philosopher Bryan Magee has pointed out. We could reformulate the hypothesis as: 'water boils at 100°C at sea-level atmospheric pressure'. And when we discover that water does not boil at 100°C in sealed containers, we could narrow the hypothesis still further: 'Water boils at 100°C at sea-level atmospheric pressure in open containers'. But to go down this route, placing ever more caveats upon the hypothesis, thereby progressively narrowing its empirical application, would be to destroy its usefulness. It would also obscure the most important feature of the situation, namely that the failure of the initial hypothesis was an opportunity not to salvage it, but to reform it. It was a chance to come up with a theory that explains *both* why water boils at 100°C at sea level and why it does not boil at altitude and in sealed containers. Science is not just about detecting errors but about responding in a progressive way.

practitioners at conferences in Dallas, Kansas City, Richmond and Columbus. They were asked whether 'rationalisations that excuse medical errors (and excuse the need to disclose and report those errors) are common in hospitals'. As astonishing 86 per cent of respondents, who actually work within the healthcare system, either agreed or strongly agreed.[4]

Consider again the doctors who operated on Elaine Bromiley, the case explored at the start of the book. At the time their behaviour may have seemed like a blatant attempt to avoid the external repercussions of their mistake, like a reprimand from management or legal action from the patient's family. But we can now see that it also bears the classic hallmarks of dissonance-reduction. The doctors didn't want to admit their mistake *to themselves*.

They had spent years training to reach high standards of performance. It was a tough initiation. As with most good doctors, healthcare was more than a job, it was a vocation. Their self-esteem was bound up with their clinical competence. They came into medicine to reduce suffering, not to increase it. And now they were confronted with having killed a healthy thirty-seven-year-old woman.

Just think of how desperate they would have been to reframe the fatality as a mere 'complication'. Think, too, of the investigation into the way doctors report errors by the researcher, Nancy Berlinger. She wrote of 'the depths of physicians' resistance to disclosure and the lengths to which some will go to justify the habit of nondisclosure – it was only a technical error, things just happen . . .'

This research may have looked like an indictment of healthcare culture, but we can now see that this is a painfully accurate description of the effects of cognitive dissonance. Self-justification, the desire to protect one's self-image, has the potential to afflict us all. The healthcare and criminal justice systems are but two strands in a wider story that represents a clear and present danger to our future progress.

II

Let us return briefly to the Iraq War, for it will allow us to drill deeper into the psychological mechanisms associated with cognitive dissonance. To avoid controversy, we will not take a stand on whether the invasion was right or wrong.* Instead, we will look at the intellectual contortions of the leaders who took us to war. This will provide a glimpse at how the reframing exercise can take on a life of its own.

Remember that for a man like Tony Blair, this was the biggest decision of his political life. He was not just a voter who supported the war, he was a prime minister who had gambled his career on the conflict, committing troops on the ground, of whom 179 would lose their lives. His political reputation, to a large extent, hinged on the decision. If anyone would be motivated to defend it, he would.

So, let us explore the contortions.

On 24 September 2002, before the conflict, Blair made a speech to the House of Commons about Saddam Hussein's weapons of mass destruction: 'His WMD programme is active, detailed and growing,' he said. 'Saddam has continued to produce them, . . . he has existing and active military plans for the use of chemical and biological weapons, which could be activated within 45 minutes . . .'

Of course, within months of the invasion the problem with these claims became clear. First of all Saddam's troops did not use these supposedly devastating weapons to repel the advancing Western forces. Further, the search for WMD in the immediate aftermath of Saddam's fall drew a rather conspicuous blank.

But as social psychologists Jeff Stone and Nicholas Fernandez of the University of Arizona detail in a powerful essay on the Iraq conflict,[5] Blair parried. In a speech to the House of Commons, he said: 'There are literally thousands of sites . . . but it is only now that the Iraq Survey Group has been put together that a dedicated team of people, which includes former UN inspectors, scientists and experts, will be able to go in and do the job properly . . . I have no doubt that

---

* Was it right or wrong? With some decisions, it is very difficult to reach definitive answers. The situation is complex, and you can't rewind the clock to see if an alternative approach would have worked better. This is sometimes called the 'counterfactual problem'. In the next section, we will look at how to learn in situations such as these.

they will find the clearest possible evidence of Saddam's weapons of mass destruction.'

So, to Blair, the lack of WMD did not show that these weapons were not actually there, but rather provided evidence that inspectors hadn't been looking hard enough. Note another thing, too. The absence of WMD had *strengthened* his conviction that they would be found.

This is a classic response predicted by cognitive dissonance: we tend to become more entrenched in our beliefs (like those in the capital punishment experiment, whose views became more extreme after reading evidence that challenged their views and the members of the cult who became more convinced of the truth of their beliefs after the apocalyptic prophecy failed). 'I have *no doubt* that they will find the *clearest possible evidence* of Saddam's weapons of mass destruction [my italics],' Blair said.

Twelve months later, when the Iraq survey group, Blair's inspectors of choice, couldn't find the weapons either, he changed tack again. Speaking to the House of Commons Liaison Committee, he said: 'I have to accept we haven't found them and we may never find them, we don't know what has happened to them . . . They could have been removed, they could have been hidden, they could have been destroyed.'

The evidential dance was now at full tilt. The lack of evidence for WMD in Iraq, according to Blair, was no longer because troops had not had enough time to find them, or because of the inadequacy of the inspectors: rather, it was because the Iraqi troops had spirited them out of existence.

But this stance, within a few months, became untenable too. As the search continued in a state of near desperation, it became crystal clear that not only were there no WMD, but there were no remnants of them, either. Iraqi troops could not have spirited them away. So Blair parried again. In a set-piece speech at the Labour Party Conference, he finally accepted that Saddam did not have chemical or biological weapons, but argued that the decision to go to war was right anyway.

'The problem is that I can apologise for the information that turned out to be wrong, but I can't, sincerely at least, apologise for removing Saddam,' he said. 'The world is a better place with Saddam in prison . . .'

These contortions continued for the next ten years. At times Blair struggled to remember their precise chronology, and appeared strained when trying to keep track of them under questioning. When so-called Islamic State began a major offensive in Iraq in 2014, and the country was on the brink of a Civil War – which some commentators linked to the 2003 conflict – Blair found another avenue of justification.

He pointed to the policy of non-intervention in Syria, which had descended into its own bloody civil war. In an article written for his personal website, he said: 'In Syria we called for the regime to change, took no action and it is in the worst state of all.'[6] In other words, 'if things look bad in Iraq now, they would have been even more awful if we had not invaded in 2003'.

The most important thing, for our purposes, is not whether Blair was right or wrong on this point. The vital thing to realise is that had non-intervention in Syria achieved the most heavenly outcome (peace, happiness, doves circling above), Blair would likely still have found a way to interpret that evidence through the lens of the rightness of his decision to invade Iraq. In fact, he would probably have become *more convinced* of its rightness, not less so. That is the domino effect of cognitive dissonance. A similar domino effect can be seen in the behaviour of George W. Bush. Almost all of Bush's claims in the build-up to war and its aftermath turned out to be mistaken. He was wrong that Saddam had WMD and wrong that the Iraqi leader had links with Al Qaeda. When he stood under a banner proclaiming 'Mission Accomplished' six weeks after the invasion began and stated that 'major combat operations in Iraq have ended', he was wrong about that, too.

But he seemed able to effortlessly reframe any inconvenient evidence. As Aronson and Tarvis put it in their book *Mistakes were Made (but Not by Me)*:

Bush [responded by finding] new justifications for the war: getting rid of a 'very bad guy', fighting terrorists, promoting peace in the

Middle East . . . increasing American security, and finishing the task [our troops] gave their lives for . . . In 2006, with Iraq sliding into civil war . . . Bush said to a delegation of conservative columnists: 'I've never been more convinced that the decisions I made are the right decisions.'

If it is intolerable to change your mind, if no conceivable evidence will permit you to admit your mistake, if the threat to ego is so severe that the reframing process has taken on a life of its own, you are effectively in a closed loop. If there are lessons to be learned, it has become impossible to acknowledge them, let alone engage with them.

This is not intended as an argument against Blair or Bush or their followers. Issues of war and peace are complex and there are always arguments on both sides (we will look at how to learn in situations of complexity in Part 3). No political party has a monopoly on making mistakes, either. But what this does show is that intelligent people are not immune from the effects of cognitive dissonance.

This is important because we often suppose that bright people are the most likely to reach the soundest judgements. We associate intelligence, however defined, as the best way of reaching truth. In reality, however, intelligence is often deployed in the service of dissonance-reduction. Indeed, sometimes the most prestigious thinkers are the most adept at deploying the techniques of reframing, often in such subtle ways that it is difficult for us, them, or anyone else, to notice them.

In December 2012 I briefly interviewed Tony Blair. Our paths had crossed a few times before and, for the first few minutes we chatted about what he had been doing since leaving Downing Street in 2007. He was talkative and, as always, courteous. He was also somewhat strained: public disapproval for the Iraq War had been steadily growing.

After a minute or two I asked the question I was most keen to ask. Given what he now knew, with the thousands of deaths that had occurred, the absence of WMD, the huge upheaval, did he still think that his decision over Iraq was the right one. 'Decisions of war and peace are controversial, and I would be lying if I said the decision was easy,' he said. 'But do I think I made the right decision? Yes, I am more sure than I have ever been.'

A few months later, I met with Alastair Campbell, Blair's former head of communications and one of his most trusted lieutenants. We talked at length about the phenomenon of cognitive dissonance. Campbell was characteristically thoughtful, talking about the build-up to war and the pressure cooker atmosphere in Downing Street.

I asked him if he still backed the decision to go to war. 'There are times when I wonder about it, particularly when news comes through of more deaths,' he said. 'But on balance, I think we were right to get rid of Saddam.' Do you think it is possible that you could ever change your mind, I asked? 'It would be difficult, given what we have been through, but it's not impossible,' he said.

And what about Tony, I asked. 'Think about what it would mean if he admitted he was wrong,' Campbell replied. 'It would overshadow everything he had ever worked for. It would taint his achievements. Tony is a rational and strong-minded guy, but I don't think he would be able to admit that Iraq was a mistake. It would be too devastating, even for him.'

III

In November 2010, a group of renowned economists, high-profile intellectuals and business leaders wrote an open letter to Ben Bernanke, then chairman of the Federal Reserve.[7] The bank had just announced its second tranche of so-called quantitative easing. They proposed to purchase bonds with newly printed money, introducing, over time, an additional $600 billion into the US economy.

The signatories were worried about this policy. In fact, they thought it might prove disastrous. In the letter, which was published in the *Wall Street Journal*, they argued that the plan was not 'necessary or advisable under current circumstances' and that it would not 'achieve the Fed's objective of promoting employment'. They concluded that it should be 'reconsidered and discontinued'.

The signatories included some of the most celebrated individuals in their fields, including Michael J. Boskin, the former chairman of the president's Council of Economic Advisers, Seth Klarman, the billionaire founder of the Baupost Group, an investment company, John Taylor, professor of economics at Stanford University, Paul Singer, the billionaire founder of Elliott Management Corporation, and Niall Ferguson, the renowned professor of history at Harvard University.

Perhaps their greatest concern was over inflation, the fear that printing money would lead to run-away price increases. This is a worry often associated with economists within the 'monetarist' school of policymaking. The signatories warned that quantitative easing would risk 'currency debasement and inflation' and 'distort financial markets'.

The letter, which was also published as a full-page advert in the *New York Times*, made headlines around the world. The fears were well expressed, well argued, and the prediction of trouble ahead for the US economy caused a minor tremor in financial markets.

But what actually happened? Did the prediction turn out to be accurate? Did inflation soar out of control?

At the time the letter was published the inflation rate was 1.5 per cent. Four years later, in December 2014, inflation had not merely remained at historically low levels, it had actually fallen. According to the Consumer Prices Index published monthly by the Bureau of Labour Statistics, inflation was at 0.8 per cent. By January 2015, just before these words were written, it had fallen into negative territory. Inflation had become deflation. The headline rate in the United States was minus 0.1 per cent.

It is probably fair to say, then, that the predictions did not materialise quite as expected. In fact, the US economy seemed to go in a different direction altogether. It is not just inflation that failed to balloon out of control. Jobs were also growing, despite the warning by the signatories that they didn't think the policy would 'promote employment'. By autumn 2014 the US economy was creating jobs at the fastest pace since 2005 and unemployment had dropped from 9.8 per cent to 6.1 per cent. American companies were also faring well, reporting low debts, high levels of cash, and record profits.[8]

There is nothing wrong with making mistakes in forecasting, of course. The world is complex and there are many uncertainties, particularly in the economic arena. Indeed, there was something intellectually courageous about the group choosing to make their predictions so public in the first place. Certainly, the violation of their expectations handed them a gilt-edged opportunity to revise or enrich their theoretical assumptions. After all, that is what failure means.

But how did the signatories actually react? In October 2014, Bloomberg, the media company, invited them to reflect on the content of their letter in the light of subsequent events.[9] What is striking about the responses (nine of the signatories accepted the request for interview*) was not that these thinkers attempted to explain why the predictions had failed, or what they had learned; rather, it is that they didn't think the prediction had failed *at all*.

Indeed, many of them thought they had got their analysis bang on.

David Malpass, former deputy assistant Treasury secretary, said: 'The letter was correct as stated.'

John Taylor, professor of economics at Stanford University, said: 'The letter mentioned several things – the risk of inflation, employment, it would destroy financial markets, complicate the Fed's effort to normalize monetary policy – and all have happened.'

Jim Grant, publisher of *Grant's Interest Rate Observer*, said: 'People say, you guys are all wrong because you predicted inflation and it hasn't happened. I think there's plenty of inflation – not at the check out counter, necessarily, but on Wall Street.'

It was almost as if they were looking at a different economy.

Others argued that the prediction may not have materialised yet, but it soon would. Douglas Holtz-Eakin, former director of the Congressional Budget Office, said: 'They are going to generate an uptick in core inflation. They are going to go above 2 percent. I don't know when, but they will.'

This last response is certainly true in the sense that inflation will

---

* Some refused the interview request, others did not respond. One of the signatories had died during the intervening period.

rise, perhaps sharply, above its recent historic lows. But it is also reminiscent of the fan of Brentford Football Club who predicted at the beginning of the 2012 to 2013 season that his team would win the FA Cup. When they were knocked out by Chelsea, he was asked what had gone wrong with his prediction. He said: 'I said they would win the FA Cup, but I didn't say when.'

This example is yet another illustration of the reach of cognitive dissonance. Dissonance is not just about Tony Blair, or doctors, or lawyers, or members of religious cults, it is also about world-famous business leaders, historians and economists. Ultimately, it concerns how our culture's stigmatising attitude towards error undermines our capacity to see evidence in a clear-eyed way. It is about big decisions and small judgements: indeed, anything that threatens one's self-esteem.

A quick personal example. When I was in the process of writing this chapter, I joined a gym a few miles from where I live. It was an expensive membership and my wife warned that I wouldn't use it because of the long journey. She pointed out that a less-expensive gym next door to our house would be a much better bet. She worried that the travel time would eat into the day. I disagreed.

Day after day at the end of work I would drive over to the gym. The journey was increasingly time-consuming. Sometimes it took more than thirty minutes. I found myself rushing there and back while my wife enjoyed the proximity of the gym next door. The tougher the journey, the more I kept travelling over. It took me a year to realise that all these constant trips were attempts at justifying my original decision. I didn't want to admit that it was a mistake to join in the first place.

My wife, who read an early draft of this chapter, smiled after one such trip. 'Cognitive dissonance,' she suggested. And she was right. Twelve months after paying an expensive membership fee, I finally joined the gym next door. Had I admitted my mistake sooner, I would have saved twelve months of frustration. But my ego just wouldn't let me. It was too difficult to admit that I had been wrong all along – and that I had wasted a lot of money.

This may sound like a trivial example, but it reveals the scope of cognitive dissonance. Think back to the various examples touched upon so far in the book, which involved decisions of far greater magnitude – and thus a bigger threat to self-esteem. An accident in an operating theatre became 'one of those things'; an exonerating DNA test pointed to an 'unindicted co-ejaculator'; the failure of an apocalyptic prophecy proved that 'God has been appeased by our actions.'

For the signatories to the open letter to Bernanke, the same analysis applies. The failure of an economic prediction showed not that they were mistaken, but that they were right all along. If inflation had soared, they would doubtless have taken this as a vindication. And yet they also felt entitled to claim success when inflation stayed low, just as Blair claimed vindication for his strategy in Iraq when events flatly contradicted his initial expectations. Heads I win; tails I don't lose.

It is probably fair to say that economics, as a subject, has a particular problem with its attitude to failure. It is not just the signatories to the letter, but the wider culture. As an economics student in the early 1990s I observed how many of us split into rival schools, such as Keynesians or Monetarists, at an early stage of the course. The decision to join one group or another was often based on the flimsiest of pretexts, but it had remarkably long term consequences. Very few economists alter their ideological stance. They stick to it for life.

A poll (albeit a straw one) of economists revealed that fewer than 10 per cent change 'schools' during their careers, or 'significantly adapt' their theoretical assumptions.* Professor Sir Terry Burns, a former economic adviser to Margaret Thatcher (who later became chairman of Santander UK), told me: 'It is roughly as common as Muslims converting to Christianity or vice versa.'

This is surely a warning sign that instead of learning from data, some economists are spinning it. It hints at the suspicion that the intellectual energy of some of the world's most formidable thinkers is directed, not at creating new, richer, more explanatory theories, but

---

* Interviews by the author with twelve economists, three academic and nine working for financial institutions.

at coming up with ever-more tortuous rationalisations as to why they were right all along.

And this takes us back to perhaps the most paradoxical aspect of cognitive dissonance. It is precisely those thinkers who are most renowned, who are famous for their brilliant minds, who have the most to lose from mistakes. And that is why it is often the most influential people, those who ought to be in the best position to help the world learn from new evidence, who have the greatest incentive to reframe it. And these are also the kinds of people (or institutions) who often have the capacity to employ expensive PR firms to bolster their post hoc justifications. They have the financial means, in addition to a powerful subconscious urge, to bridge the gap between beliefs and evidence, not by learning, but by spinning. It is the equivalent of a golfer hitting the ball out of bounds and then hiring a slick PR company to convince the world that it had nothing to do with him, it was a sudden gust of wind!

Perhaps this phenomenon was most vividly revealed in a celebrated study by Philip Tetlock, a psychologist from the University of Pennsylvania. In 1985 Tetlock invited 284 experts to assign probabilities that particular, well-defined events would occur in the not too distant future.[10] All were acknowledged leaders in their fields, with more than half holding PhDs. Hypothetical events included things like 'would Gorbachev be ousted in a coup?' and 'would there be a nonviolent end to apartheid in South Africa?' All told, he gathered thousands of predictions.

A few years later Tetlock compared the predictions with what actually happened. He found that the predictions of experts were somewhat better than those of a group of undergraduates, but not by much. This is not surprising. The world is complex. Even for well-informed experts, it is not easy to say what will happen when there are lots of variables interacting in dynamic ways. As Tetlock put it: 'We reach the point of diminishing marginal predictive returns for knowledge disconcertingly quickly.'

But perhaps the most striking finding of all was that the celebrated experts, the kinds of people who tour television studios and go on book tours, were the worst of all. As Tetlock put it: 'Ironically, the more famous the expert, the less accurate his or her predictions tended to be.'

Why is this? Cognitive dissonance gives us the answer. It is those who are the most publicly associated with their predictions, whose livelihoods and egos are bound up with their expertise, who are most likely to reframe their mistakes – and who are thus the least likely to learn from them.

These findings have huge implications not just for economics, healthcare and the law, but for business, too. After all, you might suppose that the higher up you go in a company, the less you will see the effects of cognitive dissonance. Aren't the people who get to the top of big companies supposed to be rational, forensic and clear-sighted? Isn't that supposed to be their defining characteristic?

In fact, the opposite is the case. In his seminal book, *Why Smart Executives Fail: And What You Can Learn from Their Mistakes*, Sydney Finkelstein, a management professor at Dartmouth College, investigated major failures at over fifty corporate institutions.[11] He found that error denial *increases* as you go up the pecking order.

Ironically enough, the higher people are in the management hierarchy, the more they tend to supplement their perfectionism with blanket excuses, with CEOs usually being the worst of all. For example, in one organization we studied, the CEO spent the entire forty-five-minute interview explaining all the reasons why others were to blame for the calamity that hit his company. Regulators, customers, the government, and even other executives within the firm – all were responsible. No mention was made, however, of personal culpability.

The reason should by now be obvious. It is those at the top of business who are responsible for strategy and therefore have the most to lose if things go wrong. They are far more likely to cling on to the idea that the strategy is wise, even as it is falling apart, and to reframe any evidence that says otherwise. Blinded by dissonance, they are also the least likely to learn the lessons.

IV

A common misperception of the theory of cognitive dissonance is that it is about external incentives. People have a lot to lose if they get their judgements wrong; doesn't it therefore make sense that they would want to reframe them? The idea here is that the learning advantage of adapting to a mistake is outweighed by the reputational disadvantage of admitting to it.

But this perspective does not encompass the full influence of cognitive dissonance. The problem is not just the external incentive structure, it is the internal one. It is the sheer difficulty that we have in admitting our mistakes even when we are incentivised to do so.

To see this most clearly, consider the so-called disposition effect, a well-studied phenomenon in the field of behavioural finance. Say you have a portfolio of shares, some of which have lost money, and some of which have gained. Which are you likely to sell? And which are you likely to keep?

A rational person should keep those shares most likely to appreciate in the future while selling those likely to depreciate. Indeed, this is what you *must* do if you are attempting to maximise your financial return. The stock market rewards those who buy low and sell high.

But we are actually more likely to keep the shares that have lost money, regardless of their future prospects. Why? Because we hate to crystallise a loss. The moment a losing stock is sold, a paper loss becomes a real loss. It is unambiguous evidence that the decision to buy that stock in the first place was a mistake. This is why people hold on to losing stocks far too long, desperately hoping they will rebound.

But when it comes to winning stocks, everything changes. Suddenly there is a subconscious desire to lock in the gain. After all, when you sell a winning stock you have bona fide proof that your initial judgement was right. It is a vindication. This is why there is a bias in selling winning stocks, even when they might rise in the future, thus robbing you of all that additional gain.

A study by Terrance Odean, professor of finance at UCL Berkeley, found that the winning stocks investors sold outperformed the losing stocks they didn't sell by 3.4 per cent. In other words, people were holding on to losing stocks too long, because they couldn't bring themselves to admit they had made a mistake. Even professional stock pickers – supposedly ultra-rational people who operate according to cold, hard logic – are susceptible: they tend to hold losing stocks around 25% longer than winning stocks.[12]

But avoiding failure in the short term has an inevitable outcome: we lose bigger in the longer term. This is, in many ways, a perfect metaphor for error-denial in the world today: the external incentives – even when they reward a clear-eyed analysis of failure – are often overwhelmed by the internal urge to protect self-esteem. We spin the evidence even when it costs us.

Confirmation bias is another of the psychological quirks associated with cognitive dissonance. The best way to see its effects is to consider the following sequence of numbers: 2, 4, 6. Suppose that you have to discover the underlying pattern in this sequence. Suppose, further, that you are given an opportunity to propose alternative sets of three numbers to explore the possibilities.

Most people playing this game come up with a hypothesis pretty quickly. They guess, for example, that the underlying pattern is 'even numbers ascending sequentially'. There are other possibilities, of course. The pattern might just be: 'even numbers'. Or 'the third number is the sum of the first two'. And so on.

The key question is: how do you establish whether your initial hunch is right? Most people simply try to *confirm* their hypothesis. So, if they think the pattern is 'even numbers ascending sequentially', they will propose '10, 12, 14' and when this is confirmed, they will propose '100, 102, 104'. After three such tests most people are pretty certain that they have found the answer.

And yet they may be wrong. If the pattern is actually 'any ascending numbers', their guesses will not help them. Had they used a different strategy, on the other hand, attempting to *falsify* their hypothesis rather than confirm it, they would have discovered this far quicker. If they had, say, proposed 4, 6, 11 (fits the pattern), they would have found that their initial hunch was wrong. If they had followed up with, say, 5, 2, 1, (which doesn't fit), they would now be getting pretty warm.

As Paul Schoemaker, research director of the Mack Institute for Innovation Management at the Wharton School of the University of Pennsylvania, puts it:

> The pattern is rarely uncovered unless subjects are willing to make mistakes – that is, to test numbers that violate their belief. Instead most people get stuck in a narrow and wrong hypothesis, as often happens in real life, such that their only way out is to make a mistake that turns out not to be a mistake after all. Sometimes, committing errors is not just the fastest way to the correct answer; it's the only way. College students presented with this experiment were allowed to test as many sets of three numbers as they wished. Fewer than 10 per cent discovered the pattern.[13]

This is confirmation bias in action, and is eerily reminiscent of early medicine (where doctors interpreted any outcome in their patients as an affirmation of bloodletting). It provides another reason why the scientific mindset, with a healthy emphasis on falsification, is so vital. It acts as a corrective to our tendency to spend our time confirming what we think we already know, rather than seeking to discover what we don't know.

As the philosopher Karl Popper wrote: 'For if we are uncritical we shall always find what we want: we shall look for, and find, confirmations, and we shall look away from, and not see, whatever might be dangerous to our pet theories. In this way it is only too easy to obtain ... overwhelming evidence in favour of a theory which, if approached critically, would have been refuted.[14]'

V

For one final example, let us examine an incident that neatly draws together the various insights so far. It involved Peter Pronovost, the doctor we met in Chapter 3 who cut central line infections from 11 per cent to 0 at Johns Hopkins University Hospital by introducing an intensive care checklist.

Early in his career, Pronovost, an anaesthetist by training, was in the operating theatre assisting with surgery on a patient suffering with a recurrent hernia.[15] Ninety minutes into the operation the patient started wheezing, her face reddened, and her blood pressure plummeted. Pronovost strongly suspected that she had a latex allergy and that the surgical gloves of the surgeon could be at fault.

He provided a dose of epinephrine, the recommended drug, and her symptoms dissipated. He then advised the surgeon to change to an alternative pair of gloves, which were stored nearby. But the surgeon disagreed. 'You're wrong,' he said. 'This can't be a latex allergy. We have been operating for an hour and a half and the patient didn't experience a reaction to latex during any of her previous procedures.'

The stakes were now set. The surgeon had expressed his judgement. He was the boss, the captain in charge, the man at the pinnacle of the hierarchy. Any new evidence or argument from this point on was likely to be interpreted not as an opportunity to do what was right for the patient, but as a challenge to his competence and authority. In short, cognitive dissonance was now in play.

Pronovost, however, didn't drop his concern. He had a deep knowledge of allergies and tried to explain his reasoning. 'Latex allergies often develop after a patient, like this one, has had multiple surgeries and they can start anytime during the case,' he said. 'You just got into her abdomen and the latex only recently came in contact with her blood, which is why we didn't see the reaction before.'

But he wasn't getting through. The surgeon continued with the operation, the patient's symptoms returned, and Pronovost had to deliver another dose of epinephrine. Again he explained to the surgeon that the latex was endangering the patient, but once again the surgeon disagreed. This was a medical issue, not a surgical one. Pronovost was more qualified to express an opinion. But the surgeon was in charge – and he wasn't budging.

By this time, with the argument escalating, the junior doctor in the room and the nurses were pale-faced. Pronovost was now certain that this was a latex allergy, given the second adverse reaction, and that if the surgeon didn't change gloves the patient would die, possibly within minutes. So he changed tack, trying to nudge the argument away from the threat to the status of the surgeon and on to the basic calculation that would surely resolve the argument once and for all.

'Let's think through this situation,' he said gently. 'If I'm wrong you will waste five minutes changing gloves. If you are wrong the patient dies. Do you really think this risk-benefit ratio warrants you not changing your gloves?'

At this point, you might imagine that the surgeon would be forced to accept the logic of the situation. Surely he could not persist. But the theory of cognitive dissonance offers a different possibility. The risk-benefit ratio was not about weighing the life of a patient against the few moments it would have taken to change gloves. Rather, the risk-benefit ratio was about weighing the life of a patient against the prestige of a surgeon whose entire self-esteem was constructed upon the cultural insinuation of his own infallibility.

The weighing exercise wasn't even close. The surgeon became more entrenched; more utterly certain of his own judgement; he scarcely even considered the calculation that Pronovost had suggested. 'You're wrong,' the surgeon said. 'This is clearly not an allergic reaction, so I'm not changing my gloves.'

This could have been the end of it, and normally it would have been. After all, the surgeon is in charge. You are not supposed to challenge his judgement. But Pronovost, who had lost his own father to medical error and had chosen to devote his life to patient safety, stuck to his guns. He instructed the nurse to telephone the dean and the president of Johns Hopkins Hospital so that they could overrule the surgeon.

The atmosphere in the theatre was now one of stunned silence. The nurse picked up the phone, but hesitated, looking at the two men. She was unsure what to do. Even now the life of the patient hung by a thread. Further contact with the latex gloves could prove fatal. 'Page them now,' Pronovost said firmly. 'This patient is having a latex allergy. I cannot allow her die because we did not change gloves.'

Only as the phone was being dialled did the surgeon finally budge.

He swore, dropped his gloves, and strode out to change them. The tension finally began to abate.

Once the operation was over, tests confirmed what Pronovost had suspected all along: the patient had a latex allergy. If the surgeon had got his own way, as he would have done 99.9 per cent of the time, she would almost certainly have died.

And this reveals the inextricable link between the lack of progress in key areas of our world and the absence of learning from failure. The context is healthcare, but the lessons extend far wider.

Think of it this way: doctors are sometimes oblivious to their mistakes because they have already reframed them. They are not dishonest people; they are often unaware of the reframing exercise because it is largely subconscious. If there were independent investigations into adverse events, these mistakes would be picked up during the 'black box' analysis and doctors would be challenged on them, and learn from them. But proper independent investigation is almost non-existent. Moreover, such investigations generally rely on the information provided by professionals, which is often withheld in a culture that stigmatises error.

This means that doctors make the same mistakes again and again, while growing in the mistaken conviction that they are infallible. This, in turn, increases the cognitive dissonance associated with mistakes, tightening the noose still further. Admitting to error becomes so threatening that in some cases surgeons (decent, honourable people) would rather risk killing a patient than admit they might be wrong. The renowned physician David Hilfiker put it this way:

> Doctors hide their mistakes from patients, from other doctors, even from themselves . . . The drastic consequences of our mistakes, the repeated opportunities to make them, the uncertainty about our culpability, and the professional denial that mistakes happen all work together to create an intolerable dilemma for the physician. We see the horror of our mistakes, yet we cannot deal with their enormous emotional impact.[16]

Now consider one final study into the scale of evasion in health-care. What we haven't yet done is try to break the numbers down into their component parts. Who is involved in the most cover-ups? Is it nurses, the junior members of staff? Or is it the doctors, the senior members, the ones with the prestigious educations and the remit to lead the industry forward?

It will not surprise you to hear that it is the latter. Intelligence and seniority when allied to cognitive dissonance and ego is one of the most formidable barriers to progress in the world today. In one study in twenty-six acute care hospitals in the United States, nearly half of the errors reported were made by registered nurses. Physicians contributed less than 2 per cent.[17]

If Peter Pronovost hadn't been in the operating theatre on the day when the patient was reacting adversely to the latex surgical gloves, it isn't just one patient who would have died. The deeper tragedy is that nobody would have learned from it. The failure would have been reframed: the blame would have been pinned on the patient's unusual symptoms, rather than on the surgeon's failure to remove his gloves. It would have left the surgeon free to make the same mistake again.

Today, Pronovost is arguably the most influential doctor in American healthcare. His crusading work into medical error has saved thousands of lives. He has been awarded a MacArthur Fellowship, otherwise known as a genius grant. In 2008 he was named as one of the most influential 100 people in the world. But back in that operating theatre, he was still a junior clinician. Even now he acknowledges that saving the life of the patient was a close-run thing. He has said:

> The patient was fortunate because I was already gaining a reputation as a safety leader. That gave me the courage to speak up . . . What if I was just starting out in my career? Would I have taken such a risk? Perhaps not. If the patient had died, it would have been blamed primarily on her allergy, not the surgeon. Similar dramas play out day after day in hospitals across the country. How many patients have been harmed or died as a result? Will we ever really know?[18]

6

Reforming Criminal Justice

I

Trofim Lysenko was a dark-haired, bright-eyed biologist. He came from peasant stock in the west of what would become the Soviet Union and was spotted by the political leaders of the Communist revolution in the 1920s when he claimed to have found a way to enhance crop yields.[1]

The technique was not as successful as Lysenko claimed, but the young scientist was ambitious and politically savvy. Over a period of ten years he gradually moved up the academic ranks. In 1934, he was appointed to the Lenin All-Union Academy of Agricultural Sciences.

It was then that he took a major gamble. In the early twentieth century, the science of genetics, based on the work of Gregor Mendel, a German friar and scientist, was just beginning to take off. It proposed that heredity was encoded in small units called genes and could be described using statistical rules. Lysenko became an outspoken critic of this new theory, positioning himself against a rising tide of scientific opinion.

Lysenko was not stupid. He calculated that this stance would endear him further to the political elite. Marxism was based on the idea that human nature is malleable. Genetics, which held that certain traits are passed down from generation to generation, seemed like a threat to this doctrine. Lysenko started to defend a different idea: the notion that traits acquired during one's lifetime could be passed on. It is sometimes called Lamarckism, after the original proponent of the theory.

Scientific ideas should succeed or fail according to rational argument and evidence. It is about data rather than dogma. But Lysenko realised that he couldn't silence the geneticists through argument alone. Thousands of scientists up and down the country were excited by the new genetic approach. They sincerely believed that it had intellectual merit and that it should, therefore, be pursued. And they had data to back up their beliefs.

So Lysenko tried a different approach: instead of engaging in debate, he tried to shut it down. He called upon Stalin to outlaw the new theory of genetics. Stalin agreed, not because genetics had been proved wanting scientifically, but because it didn't tally with Communist ideology. Together they declared genetics 'a bourgeois perversion'. The ideas of Lamarck, on the other hand, were given the Communist seal of approval.

Those who dissented from the Party line were ruthlessly persecuted. Many geneticists were executed, including Israel Agol, Solomon Levit, Grigorii Levitskii, Georgii Karpechenko and Georgii Nadson, or sent to labour camps. Nikolai Vavilov, one of the most eminent Soviet scientists, was arrested in 1940 and died in prison in 1943. All genetic research was forbidden and at scientific meetings around the country geneticists were condemned and dismissed.

Lysenko had silenced his critics and pretty much guaranteed that his own ideas would triumph. But this 'success' had a familiar sting in its tail. By protecting his ideas from dissent, he had deprived them of a valuable thing: the possibility of failure. He proposed all sorts of techniques to improve crop yields, but nobody tested them out of fear of persecution. Science had effectively been detached, by political decree, from the feedback mechanism of falsification.

The results were devastating. Before the rise of Lysenko, Russian biology had been flourishing. Dmitry Ivanovsky discovered plant viruses in 1892. Ivan Pavlov won the Nobel Prize for Medicine in 1904 for his work on digestion. Ilya Mechnikov won the Nobel Prize in 1908 for his theories on the cellular response to infection. In 1927, Nikolai Koltsov proposed that inherited characteristics are double-stranded giant molecules, anticipating the double helix structure of DNA.

By the end of the purges, however, Russian science had been decimated. As Valery Soyfor, a Russian scientist persecuted during the

Lysenko era, put it: 'The progress of science was slowed or stopped, and millions of university and high school students received a distorted education.'[2] This had knock-on effects on the quality of life for millions of Russians, not least because the agricultural techniques proposed by Lysenko were often ineffective. This is what happens when ideas are not allowed to fail.

For Communist China, which had also embraced Lysenko's ideas, the results were, in many ways, even more catastrophic. Lysenko had publicly come out in favour of a technique of close planting of crop seeds in order to increase output. The theory was that plants of the same species would not compete with each other for nutrients.

This fitted in with Marxist and Maoist ideas about organisms from the same class living in harmony rather than in competition. 'With company, they grow easy,' Mao told colleagues. 'When they grow together, they will be comfortable.' The Chinese leader drew up an eight-point Lysenko-inspired blueprint for the Great Leap Forward, and persecuted Western-trained scientists and geneticists with the same kind of ferocity as in the Soviet Union.[3]

The theory of close-planting should have been put to the test. It should have been subject to possible failure. Instead it was adopted on ideological grounds. 'In Southern China, a density of 1.5 million seedlings per 2.5 acres was usually the norm,' Jasper Becker writes in *Hungry Ghosts, Mao's Secret Famine*. 'But in 1958, peasants were ordered to plant 6.5 million per 2.5 acres.'

Too late, it was discovered that the seeds did indeed compete with each other, stunting growth and damaging yields. It contributed to one of the worst disasters in Chinese history, a tragedy that even now has not been fully revealed. Historians estimate that between 20 and 43 million people died during one of the most devastating famines in human history.

The Lysenko incident is rightly regarded as one of the most scandalous episodes in the history of science. It has been the subject of dozens of books (including the magisterial *Lysenko and the Tragedy of Soviet Science*), hundreds of journal articles and it is familiar to almost all researchers. It serves as a stark warning about the dangers of protecting ideas from the possibility of failure.

Yet a different and more subtle form of the Lysenko tendency exists in the world today. Ideas and beliefs of all kinds are protected from failure, but not by a totalitarian state. Instead they are protected from failure *by us*.

Cognitive dissonance doesn't leave a paper trail. There are no documents that can be pointed to when we reframe inconvenient truths. There is no violence perpetrated by the state or anyone else. It is a process of *self*-deception. And this can have devastating effects, not least on those who were the subject of Chapter 4: the wrongly convicted.

And this brings us back to the DNA exoneration era. We have seen that these cases were difficult for the police and prosecutors to accept. But to close this section, let us explore these graphic failures in the criminal justice system and see what they tell us about how the system should be reformed to prevent them ever happening again.

The answer, it turns out, starts with creating a system that is sensitive to the inherent flaws in human memory*.

II

Neil deGrasse Tyson is an eminent astrophysicist, popular science writer and media personality. He has eighteen honorary doctorates and was once voted the sexiest astrophysicist in the world. He is also a prolific public speaker. Many of his performances are on YouTube.

For many years after 9/11, Tyson told a particular story about George W. Bush. The former president had made a speech in the

---

* An element of Lamarckism has resurfaced in recent years due to advances in epigenetics, which refers to changes in organisms caused by modification of gene expression rather than alteration of the genetic code itself. But this should not be held up as evidence that Lysenko was, in some curious way, right. After all, the phenomenon is being debated via testing and data rather than threats and intimidation. And it certainly doesn't imply that it is legitimate to base science on ideology rather than evidence.

days after the attack on the twin towers. Tyson quoted Bush as saying in this speech: 'Our God is the God who named the stars.'[4]

To Tyson this was a destructive thing for the president to say. He felt that Bush was seeking to divide Christians and Muslims in the aftermath of an attack by Islamic extremists. It was an insinuation that Christians believed in the true God, given that He had named the stars.

As Tyson put it: 'George Bush, within a week of [the attacks] gave us a speech attempting to distinguish "we" from "they". And who are "they"? These were the Muslim fundamentalists . . . And how does he do it? He says . . . "Our God is the God who named the stars."'

But Tyson wasn't finished. Bush was not just being bigoted, he said, but also inaccurate. In the next sentence Tyson revealed that two thirds of identified stars actually have Arabic names, having been discovered by Muslim scholars. 'I don't think Bush knew this,' Tyson said. 'That would confound the point he was making.'

The speech was highly effective. It mesmerised audiences and made an acute political point. It also positioned Bush as an irresponsible president, using a tragedy to divide Americans at a moment of great sensitivity. But there was a small problem. When a journalist from the Federalist website went looking for the Bush quote, he couldn't find it. He searched the TV and newspaper archives for the statements of the president after 9/11, but the 'stars quote' didn't seem to be there.[5]

When Tyson was contacted, he was adamant that he could remember Bush making the statement. 'I have explicit memory of those words being spoken by the President,' he said. 'I reacted on the spot, making a note for possible later reference in my public discourse. Odd that nobody seems to be able to find the quote anywhere.'

But no matter how hard journalists looked for it, they couldn't find it. The only speech that Bush had made in the aftermath of the attacks had been very different from the one highlighted by Tyson. 'The enemy of America is not our many Muslim friends,' Bush said. 'It is not our many Arab friends. Our enemy is a radical network of

terrorists and every government that supports them.' This was rec-
onciliatory and, as for stars, he didn't mention them at all.

Only later did researchers uncover a quote where Bush *did* mention stars, but it wasn't made after 9/11; it was spoken in the aftermath
of the Space Shuttle Columbia disaster. 'The same creator who names
the stars also knows the names of the seven souls we mourn today,'
Bush said.

Needless to say this put an entirely different gloss on the quote,
and made something of a mockery of Tyson's interpretation. This
was a president offering words of comfort and hope for the families
of those who had died in the Columbia tragedy – and he was making
no contrast with Islam.

But Tyson was nothing if not insistent. He said that he had a clear
memory of Bush saying the words after 9/11. For a while, he wouldn't
budge. Only after weeks of being asked to find a scrap of evidence for
the original quote did he finally issue a retraction. 'I here publicly
apologize to the President for casting his quote in the context of con-
trasting religions rather than as a poetic reference to the lost souls of
Columbia,'[6] he said.

The post 9/11 'stars' speech by George W. Bush never happened.

This episode is revealing because it shows that even practising scientists are suckers for the seemingly inviolable power of memory.
When we remember seeing something, it feels as if we are accessing
a videotape of a real, tangible, rock-solid event. It feels like it *must*
have happened. When people question one's memory it is natural to
get irate.

But Tyson is not the first to have created a fictitious memory. In a
study in Scotland, members of the public were adamant that they
could remember a nurse removing a skin sample from their little
finger. But this never happened. A week earlier these volunteers had
been asked by researchers to *imagine* a nurse removing the sample.
But somehow, on recollection, it had morphed into a real event. They
were four times as likely to recall it as real compared with those who
had not been asked to imagine it.[7]

In a different study, volunteers were asked to look at films of car
bumpers in which no windows or headlights were broken. Later, they

were asked how fast the cars were going when they 'smashed' into each other. Suddenly they started reporting memories of glass shattering when no glass had smashed at all. They had re-engineered the memory to encompass the new information provided by the word 'smashed'.[8]

Memory, it turns out, is not as reliable as we think. We do not encode high-definition movies of our experiences and then access them at will. Rather, memory is a system dispersed throughout the brain, and is subject to all sorts of biases. Memories are suggestible. We often assemble fragments of entirely different experiences and weave them together into what seems like a coherent whole. With each recollection, we engage in editing.*

By retrieving, editing and integrating disparate memories, we have imagined an entirely new event. People with amnesia, however, are unable to do this. They struggle to remember the past, but they also cannot imagine the future.

In short, the very fact that memory is so malleable may lead us astray when it comes to recollection. But it could also play a crucial role in imagining and anticipating future events.

We try to make the memory fit with what we now know rather than what we once saw. In the case of Jean Charles de Menezes, for example, who was shot by police in an Underground station in the aftermath of the London terrorist atrocities in 2005, eyewitnesses said that he had been wearing a bulky jacket, had run away from police, and had vaulted a ticket barrier.

But it turned out that all of this was untrue. Menezes, an innocent passenger, was actually 'wearing a light denim shirt or jacket, walked through the barriers having picked up a free newspaper, and only ran when he saw his train arriving'.[9] The witnesses had transposed what they had seen with what they had read about the event subsequently in the newspapers.

---

* Recent research suggests that this feature of memory may have benefits in terms of our imagination. For example, we can all imagine going to a cafe with David Beckham and drinking cappuccino. We simply retrieve a memory of the last time we went to a cafe and splice it together with an image of David Beckham, and a time when we drank coffee.

With this in mind it will not seem surprising that when the Innocence Project started to investigate the signatures of wrongful convictions, they discovered that mistaken eyewitness identification was a contributing factor in an astonishing 75 per cent of cases.[10] People were testifying in open court that they had seen people at the scene of a crime who in fact were elsewhere at the time.

These witnesses were not necessarily lying. They were not making it up. But then neither was Neil Tyson when he talked about Bush's stars speech. When the witnesses said they remembered seeing the suspect at the scene of the crime, they were telling the truth. They did *remember* seeing him there, but they didn't actually see him there. These are two quite different things.

This is not to say that eyewitness testimony is worthless; quite the reverse. In certain circumstances it is invaluable in order to secure convictions. Rather, it is to say that memories should be coaxed out of witnesses with sensitivity to the biases that might otherwise contaminate the evidence. The tragedy is that the techniques used by police, until recently, had little of this sophistication.

The practice of 'drive-bys', for example, has been used and abused for decades: this is where an eyewitness is taken by police to see a suspect on the street, or at their place of work. Given that the witness knows that the police have suspicions about the person – why else would they be going there? – the technique is dangerously suggestive.

And one obvious problem is that once a person has viewed the suspect they are liable to transpose his face onto that of the real criminal. Each time they recall the crime scene, they will become more certain that the suspect was really there. A tentative identification is rapidly transformed into cast-iron certainty. As Donald Thomson, a psychologist in Melbourne, put it: 'Two months down the track, they go into the witness box and say they are absolutely sure.'

Line-ups – where a suspect and a number of fillers are placed side by side in a room – are more reliable than drive-bys, but these, too, have been open to abuse. Often they are conducted by an officer who already knows the identity of the suspect, opening up the possibility that he might inadvertently influence the selection with verbal and non-verbal cues. In other cases line-ups have been conducted where only one person, the suspect, matches the description.*

And so it goes on. There were so many error traps in the methods used by police that entire book chapters have been written about them. If miscarriages of justice had been investigated, these latent problems would have been discovered, and could have been addressed. Instead, these procedures were used, with only minor variations, for decades.

This was not just bad for suspects, but also for the police, prosecutors and the public. After all, mistaken identifications cause police to ignore other leads. This often allows the real criminal to roam the streets, perpetrating more crimes.

The Innocence Project has campaigned for a number of reforms. It argues that line-ups should always be administered by an officer who doesn't know the identity of the suspect. It also calls for sequential line-ups, where suspects and fillers are shown one at a time rather than simultaneously.

When these procedures have been tested, they have significantly reduced mistaken identifications *without compromising accurate identifications*. A field study in 2011, for example, found that 'double-blind sequential line-ups as administered by police departments across the country resulted in the same number of suspect identifications but fewer known-innocent filler identifications than double blind simultaneous line-ups'.[11]

Some have disputed these findings and have proposed more tests. But this, in itself, represents progress. Systems are being trialled. People are using experiments. As of 2014, three US states are using double-blind sequential administration, and six others have recommended them. This is what an open loop looks like.

A second error trap identified by the Innocence Project is false confessions, which contributed to 30 per cent of wrongful convictions.[12] These are often secured from vulnerable people, who are

---

* There is a famous newspaper cartoon with a line-up consisting of a refrigerator, a hen and a man with an Afro.

tricked or intimidated into confessing to crimes they didn't commit. Juan Rivera, you will remember, was a vulnerable young man with a history of psychological problems who confessed after days of interrogation. Police experts said he had experienced a psychotic episode.

One reform that could help to eliminate false confessions would be to make the videotaping of interrogations compulsory. This would undermine any incentive to bully or mislead suspects into confessions.

Some police forces worry that such a change might impede their ability to secure confessions from people who are actually guilty. If true, this would count against reform. But a comprehensive review by the Department of Justice found that police departments that had voluntarily taped interviews had not compromised their capacity to secure genuine confessions. As a district attorney in Minnesota put it: 'During the past eight years it has become clear that videotaped interrogations have strengthened the ability of police and prosecutors to secure convictions against the guilty.'[13]

Another area requiring major reform is forensic science. Some of these techniques, such as hair microscopy, have limited scientific legitimacy. In one murder case, experts 'matched' seventeen hairs found at a crime scene with the hair taken from a suspect. He was subsequently convicted. But later testing using hard DNA evidence demonstrated that all seventeen hairs had been misidentified. A pubic hair matched to a male suspect actually belonged to the female victim.[14]

It turns out that hair matching is highly subjective. In 2013 the FBI admitted that in more than two thousand cases between 1985 and 2000, analysts may have exaggerated the significance of hair analysis or reported them inaccurately.[15] The National Academy of Science has said that hair matching is 'unreliable'.[16] It was this error trap that condemned Jimmy Ray Bromgard, mentioned in Chapter 4, to fifteen years in prison for a crime he didn't commit.

And so it goes on. In case after case the Innocence Project discovered predictable pathways to failure; weaknesses that should have been identified and addressed. Other signatures of wrongful conviction include government misconduct, bad advice by lawyers, the use of prison informants (often offered undisclosed incentives to testify against the suspect) and scientific fraud.

Scheck has suggested reform in each of these areas. But perhaps the most significant reform he has called for is the establishment of Criminal Justice Reform Commissions. These are independent bodies mandated to investigate wrongful convictions and to recommend reforms, along the lines of air-accident investigation teams. As of publication, only eleven US states had such commissions.

In the UK a Reform Commission of sorts was set up in 1995 following a series of spectacular miscarriages of justice, including the Birmingham Six and the Guildford Four. The Criminal Cases Review Commission, an independent body, has the authority to refer questionable verdicts to the Court of Appeal. Between 1997 and the end of October 2013 the commission referred a total of 538 cases.

Of these, 70 per cent succeeded at appeal.

There is an intriguing coda to the Tyson/Bush episode, as Christopher Chabris and Daniel Simons, two psychologists, point out in an essay for the *New York Times*.[17] For it turns out that George W. Bush was wrong about his memories of 9/11 too.

The former president has often claimed that he saw the first plane crashing into the north tower before going into a classroom in Florida. But he didn't. There was no live footage of a plane hitting the tower so he couldn't have seen it before going into the classroom. As Chabris puts it: 'Mr. Bush must have combined information he acquired later with the traces left by his actual experience to produce a new version of events, just as Dr. Tyson did.'

This faulty recollection from Bush also had another effect. People assumed that if he saw footage of the crash before going into the classroom, he must have known about the attacks in advance. Had he also been involved in planning them? people asked. This is the stuff of a now familiar conspiracy theory. But, in fact, there was no conspiracy. It is just that presidents misremember as well.

III

In our discussion of the criminal justice system, we have largely focused on wrongful convictions. But this shouldn't obscure equally pressing issues. Methods of detection need to be improved to bring unsolved crimes to trial. There is also vital work that needs to be undertaken to reduce the rate at which guilty people walk free. These are tragedies, too, because victims are denied justice and the deterrent effect of the system is undermined.

There is also the problem of the large number of trials where innocent defendants are put in the dock. The data suggests that the acquittal rate is high. That is often hailed as evidence that the justice system is rigorously acquitting the innocent, but it could also mean that millions of pounds are being wasted on unnecessary trials, with the real culprit still at large.

The key issue in all of this, however, is not to allow the perceived trade-offs between these objectives to obscure the deeper fact that progress can be made on each of them *at the same time*. That was the point about wrongful convictions: reforms wouldn't blunt the teeth of the justice system; on the contrary, they would, in many cases, make them sharper.

There are also other deep-lying problems, features so integral to the fabric of the system that they tend to go unquestioned. Trial by jury, for example, is often held up as sacrosanct, and it may be the most effective form of deliberation in criminal cases. But shouldn't it be tested? If juries are coming to the wrong conclusions in predictable ways, doesn't it make sense that procedures should be reformed so that these latent problems are addressed?

To see how, consider an experiment not on juries, but on judges. Over a ten-month period, Shai Danziger, a neuroscientist at Tel Aviv University, and colleagues analysed the parole decisions of eight Israeli judges.[18] Every day each judge considered between fourteen and thirty-five real-life cases, spending around six minutes on each decision. The verdicts represented 40 per cent of the parole decisions made in Israel over the ten-month period. Each judge had an average of twenty-two years of experience.

Now, judges are supposed to be rational and deliberative. They are supposed to make decisions on hard evidence. But Danziger found something quite different: if the case was assessed by a judge just after he had eaten breakfast, the prisoner had a 65 per cent chance of getting parole. But as time passed through the morning, and the judges got hungry, the chances of parole *gradually diminished to zero*. Only after the judges had taken a break to eat did the odds shoot back up to 65 per cent, only to decrease back to 0 over the course of the afternoon.

The judges were oblivious to this astonishing bias in their deliberations. Criminologists and social workers were also unaware of it. Why? Because it had never been analysed. As one of the co-authors of the study put it: 'There are no checks about the judges' decisions because no one has ever documented this tendency before. Needless to say, I would expect there to be something put into place after this.'[19]

With regard to juries, things are even worse. It is illegal in the UK to even conduct a study on how juries go about their deliberations. The unstated rationale for this prohibition is that if the public find out how juries operate, they might lose confidence in the system. It is an 'ignorance is bliss' approach. But this is as intellectually fraudulent as removing the black box from an aeroplane to ensure that people won't ever find out about pilot error. The result is inevitable: the same mistakes will be made, over and over.

None of this is to argue that the jury system should be abolished. Many juries do brilliant work under stressful circumstances. It is merely to highlight the almost total lack of evidence as to whether juries are working effectively compared with possible alternatives.* We cannot sustain this approach indefinitely because miscarriages of justice and other high profile mistakes are corroding trust in the system. Criminal justice, like so many other areas of public life, needs

---

* Some people argue that juries are important independently of how well they reach accurate verdicts; that having a lay component in the justice system is an important aspect of democracy and has a legitimising function. But, even so, this should not prevent us from trying to improve the way that juries operate. After all, this is what justice means.

to undergo a high performance revolution based on something that has historically proved almost impossible: learning from mistakes.

More than twenty years after Juan Rivera was sentenced to life imprisonment for the murder of eleven-year-old Holly Staker, a DNA test was conducted on a blood-stained piece of timber that had been used in a different murder. A man called Delwin Foxworth, who also lived in Lake County, had been savagely beaten with the timber, doused with gasoline and set on fire. He later died of his injuries having suffered burns over 80 per cent of his body.[20]

The murderer was never found, but the DNA test was conclusive. The DNA of the blood found on the four-by-two matched that of the semen found in Holly Staker. Police are now almost certain that the man who got away with the rape and murder of an innocent eleven-year-old back in 1992 went on to commit another murder eight years later. Therefore Foxworth may be yet another victim of the wrongful conviction of Juan Rivera – it allowed the real culprit to get away with it, and kill again.

'When we think about miscarriages of justice, we often focus on the person who has been jailed for a crime he didn't commit,' Steve Art, a New York lawyer, said.[21] 'But there are other consequences, too. When you convict the wrong person, the real criminal is left to roam the streets, committing crimes with sometimes with devastating effects. It is yet another reason why we need to learn the lessons.'

As for Rivera, he was finally released on 6 January 2012. 'I can't explain it. It's life all over again,' he said as he walked free. 'I just want to experience life. Watch a football game. Just walk on the sidewalk and know that I'm free.' Somebody in the crowd handed him a slice of pizza, which he carried with some embarrassment to a car that had been arranged by supporters.

His friends have rallied around, but he will never get back the nineteen years he spent in prison. 'I would be lying if I said that I have come to terms with what I went through,' he told me. 'Even now, I am uneasy and nervous. I can't sleep at night. I can't go into crowded supermarkets. When I am walking down the road, I keep looking around. Nineteen years in prison for a crime you didn't commit leaves a mark.'

But what about those who were responsible for sending him to jail? How do they feel about it today? Perhaps it should come as no surprise that even now many remain convinced of Rivera's guilt. In October 2014, Charles Fagan, an investigator who helped obtain Rivera's confessions, was asked by the *Chicago Tribune* if he still believed that Rivera committed the murder. 'I think so,' he said.[22]

And what of the prosecutors? Even after Rivera was released, some Lake County lawyers wanted to put him back on trial. Only with a further conviction would they be able to say that they had been right all along. Only with a conviction could they quell their dissonance. Rivera walking around free was like an accusation against their competence.

It was left to the Illinois Appellate Court to take what might otherwise seem to be an astonishing step: it barred Lake County from ever prosecuting Juan Rivera for the murder of Holly Staker again.

PART 3

Confronting Complexity

7

The Nozzle Paradox

I

Unilever had a problem. They were manufacturing washing powder at their factory near Liverpool, in the north-west of England, in the usual way – indeed, the way washing powder is still made today. Boiling hot chemicals are forced through a nozzle at super-high levels of pressure and speed out of the other side; as the pressure drops they disperse into vapour and powder.

The vapour is siphoned away while the powder is collected in a vat, where collagen and various other ingredients are added. Then it is packed into boxes, branded with names like Daz and Bold, and sold at a hefty mark up. It is a neat business concept, and has become a huge industry. Annual sales of washing powders are over $3 billion in the United States alone.

But the problem for Unilever was that the nozzles didn't work smoothly. To quote Steve Jones, who briefly worked at the Liverpool soap factory in the 1970s before going on to become one of the world's most influential evolutionary biologists, they kept clogging up.[1] 'The nozzles were a damn nuisance,' he has said. 'They were inefficient, kept blocking and made detergent grains of different sizes.'

This was a major problem for the company, not just because of maintenance and lost time, but also in terms of the quality of the product. They needed to come up with a superior nozzle. Fast.

And so they turned to their crack team of mathematicians. Unilever, even back then, was a rich company so it could afford the brightest and best. These were not just ordinary mathematicians, but experts in high-pressure systems, fluid dynamics and other aspects of chemical analysis. They had special grounding in the physics of 'phase transition': the processes governing the transformation of matter from one state (liquid) to another (gas or solid).

These mathematicians were what we today might call 'intelligent designers'. These are the kind of people we generally turn to when we need to solve problems, whether business, technical or political: get the right people, with the right training, to come up with the optimal plan.

They delved ever deeper into the problems of phase transition, and derived sophisticated equations. They held meetings and seminars. And, after a long period of study, they came up with a new design.

You have probably guessed what is coming: it didn't work. It kept blocking. The powder granularity remained inconsistent. It was inefficient.

Almost in desperation, Unilever turned to its team of biologists. These people had little understanding of fluid dynamics. They would not have known a phase transition if it had jumped up and bitten them. But they had something more valuable: a profound understanding of the relationship between failure and success.

They took ten copies of the nozzle and applied small changes to each one, and then subjected them to failure by testing them. 'Some nozzles were longer, some shorter, some had a bigger or smaller hole, maybe a few grooves on the inside,' Jones says. 'But one of them improved a very small amount on the original, perhaps by just one or two per cent.'

They then took the 'winning' nozzle and created ten slightly different copies, and repeated the process. They then repeated it again, and again. After 45 generations and 449 "failures", they had a nozzle that was outstanding. It worked 'many times better than the original'.

Progress had been delivered not through a beautifully constructed masterplan (*there was no plan*), but by rapid interaction with the world. A single, outstanding nozzle was discovered as a consequence of testing, and discarding, 449 failures.

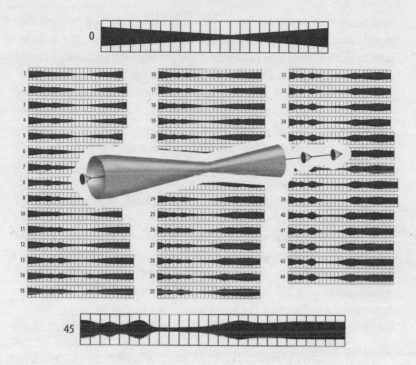

(*The original nozzle is at the top. The final nozzle, after 45 generations and 449 rejected designs, is at the bottom. It has a shape no mathematician could possibly have anticipated.*)

II

So far in the book, we have seen that learning from mistakes relies on two components: first, you need to have the right kind of system – one that harnesses errors as a means of driving progress; and second, you need a mindset that enables such a system to flourish.

In the previous section we concerned ourselves with the mindset aspect of this equation. Cognitive dissonance occurs when mistakes are too threatening to admit to, so they are reframed or ignored. This can be thought of as the internal fear of failure: how we struggle to admit mistakes to ourselves.

In sections 5 and 6, we will return to this crucial issue. We will look at how to create a culture where mistakes are not reframed or suppressed, but wielded as a means of driving progress. We will also look at the external fear of failure – the fear of being unfairly blamed or punished – which also undermines learning from mistakes.

Ultimately, we will see that strong, resilient, growth-orientated cultures are built from specific psychological foundations, and we will look at practical examples of cutting-edge companies, sports teams and even schools that are leading the way.

But now we are going to delve into the system side of the equation. We have already touched upon this in our examination of institutions that successfully learn from mistakes, such as aviation and the Virginia Mason Health System. But now we are going to look at the rich theoretical framework that underpins these examples. We will see that *all* systems that learn from failure have a distinctive structure, one that can be found in many places, including the natural world, artificial intelligence and science. This will then give us an opportunity to examine the ways in which some of the most innovative organisations in the world are harnessing this structure – with often startling results.

It is this structure that is so marvellously evoked by the Unilever example. What the development of the nozzle reveals, above all, is the power of testing. Even though the biologists knew nothing about the physics of phase transition, they were able to develop an efficient nozzle by trialling lots of different ones, rejecting those that didn't work and then varying the best nozzle in each generation.

It is not coincidental that the biologists chose this strategy: it mirrors how change happens in nature. Evolution is a process that relies on a 'failure test' called natural selection. Organisms with greater 'fitness' survive and reproduce, with their offspring inheriting their genes subject to a random process known as mutation. It is a system, like the one that created the Unilever nozzle, of trial and error.

In one way, these failures are different from those we examined in aviation, healthcare and the criminal justice system. The biologists realised they would create many failures: in fact they did so deliberately to find out which designs worked and which didn't. In aviation nobody sets out to fail deliberately. The whole idea is to minimise accidents.

But despite this difference there is a vital similarity. Failures in aviation set the stage for reform. The errors are part and parcel of the dynamic process of change: not just real accidents and failures, but also those that occur in simulators and near-miss events. Likewise, the rejected nozzles helped to drive the progression of the design. They all share an essential pattern: an adaptive process driven by the detection and response to failure.

Evolution as a process is powerful because of its *cumulative* nature. Richard Dawkins offers a neat way to think about cumulative selection in his wonderful book *The Blind Watchmaker*. He invites us to consider a monkey trying to type a single line from *Hamlet*: 'Methinks it is like a weasel.' The odds are pretty low for the monkey to get it right.

If the monkey is typing at random and there are 27 letters (counting the space bar as a letter), it has a 1 in 27 chance to get the first letter right, a 1 in 27 for the next letter, and so on. So just to get the first three in a row correct are 1/27 multiplied by 1/27 multiplied by 1/27. That is one chance in 19,683. To get all 28 in the sequence, the odds are around 1 in 10,000 million, million, million, million, million, million.

But now suppose that we provide a selection mechanism (i.e. a failure test) that is cumulative. Dawkins set up a computer programme to do just this. It's first few attempts at getting the phrase is random, just like a monkey. But then the computer scans the various nonsense phrases to see which is closest, however slightly, to the target phrase. It rejects all the others. It then randomly varies the winning phrase, and then scans the new generation. And so on.

The winning phrase after the first generation of running the experiment on the computer was: WDLTMNLT DTJBSWIRZREZLMQCO P. After ten generations, by honing in on the phrase closest to the target phrase, and rejecting the others, it was: MDLDMNLS ITJISWHRZREZ MECS P. After twenty generations, it looked like this: MELDINLS IT ISWPRKE Z WECSEL. After thirty generations, the resemblance is visible to the naked eye: METHINGS IT ISWLIKE B WECSEL. By the forty-third generation, the computer got the right phrase. It took only a few moments to get there.

Cumulative selection works, then, if there is some form of 'memory': i.e. if the results of one selection test are fed into the next, and into the next, and so on. This process is so powerful that, in the natural world, it confers what has been called 'the illusion of design': animals that look as if they were designed by a vast intelligence when they were, in fact, created by a blind process.

An echo of this illusion can be seen in the nozzle example. The final shape is so uniquely suited to creating fine-grained detergent that it invites the thought that a master designer must have been at work. In fact, as we have seen, the biologists used no 'design' capability at all. They simply harnessed the power of the evolutionary process.

There are many systems in the world that are essentially evolutionary in nature. Indeed, many of the greatest thinkers of the last two centuries favoured free market systems because they mimic the process of biological change,[2] as the author Tim Harford notes in his excellent book *Adapt*.[3] Different companies competing with each other, with some failing and some surviving, facilitate the adaptation of the system. This is why markets – provided they are well regulated – are such efficient solvers of problems: they create an ongoing process of trial and error.

The equivalent of natural selection in a market system is bankruptcy. When a company goes bust it is a bit like the failure of a particular nozzle design. It reveals that something (product, price, strategy, advertising, management, process, etc.) wasn't working compared with the competition. Weaker ideas and products are jettisoned. Successful ideas are replicated by other companies. The evolution of the system is driven, just like the design of the Unilever nozzle, by cumulative adaptation.

The failure of companies in a free market, then, is not a defect of the system, or an unfortunate by-product of competition; rather, it is an indispensable aspect of *any* evolutionary process. According to one economist, 10 per cent of American companies go bankrupt every year.[4] The economist Joseph Schumpeter called this 'creative destruction'.

Now, compare this with centrally planned economies, where there are almost no failures at all. Companies are protected from failure by subsidy. The state is protected from failure by the printing press, which can inflate its way out of trouble. At first, this may look like an enlightened way to go about solving the problems of economic production, distribution and exchange. Nothing ever fails and, by implication, everything looks successful.

But this is precisely why planned economies didn't work. They were manned by intelligent planners who decided how much grain to produce, how much iron to mine, and who used complicated calculations to determine the optimal solutions. But they faced the same problem as the Unilever mathematicians: their ideas, however enlightened, were not tested rapidly enough – and so had little opportunity to be reformed in the light of failure.

Even if the planners were ten times smarter than the businessmen operating in a market economy, they would still fall way behind. Without the benefit of a valid test, the system is plagued by rigidity. In markets, on the other hand, it is the thousands of little failures that lubricate and, in a sense, guide the system. When companies go under, other entrepreneurs learn from these mistakes, the system creates new ideas, and consumers ultimately benefit.

In a roughly similar way, accidents in aviation, while tragic for the passengers on the fatal flights, bolster the safety of future flights. The failure sets the stage for meaningful change.

That is not to say that markets are perfect. There are problems of monopoly, collusion, inequality, price-fixing and companies that are too big to fail, and are therefore protected by a taxpayer guarantee. All these things militate against the adaptive process. But the underlying point remains: markets work not in spite of the many business failures that occur, but because of them.

It is not just systems that can benefit from a process of testing and learning; so, too, can organisations. Indeed, many of the most innovative companies in the world are bringing some of the basic lessons of evolutionary theory into the way they think about strategy. Few companies tinker randomly like the Unilever biologists, because with complex problems it can take a long time to home in on a solution.

Rather, they make judicious use of tests, challenge their own assumptions, and wield the lessons to guide strategy. It is a mix of top-down reasoning (as per the mathematicians) and bottom-up iteration (as per the biologists); the fusing of the knowledge they already have with the knowledge that can be gained by revealing its inevitable flaws. It is about having the courage of one's convictions, but also the humility to test early, and to adapt rapidly.

An echo of these ideas can be seen in the process of technological change. The conventional way we think about technology is that it is essentially top-down in character. Academics conduct high-level research, which creates scientific theories, which are then used by practical people to create machines, gadgets and other technologies.

This is sometimes called the linear model and it can be represented with a simple flowchart: Research and theory → Technology → Practical applications. In the case of the Industrial Revolution, for example, the conventional picture is that it was largely inspired by the earlier scientific revolution; the ideas of Boyle, Hooke and Locke gave rise to the machinery that changed the world.

But there is a problem with the linear model: in most areas of human development, it severely underestimates the role of bottom-up testing and learning of the kind adopted by the Unilever biologists. In his book *The Economic Laws of Scientific Research*, Terence Kealey, a practising scientist, debunks the conventional narrative surrounding the Industrial Revolution:

> In 1733, John Kay invented the flying shuttle, which mechanised weaving, and in 1770 James Hargreaves invented the spinning jenny, which as its name implies, mechanised spinning. These major developments in textile technology, as well as those of Wyatt and Paul (spinning frame, 1758), Arkwright (water frame, 1769), presaged the Industrial Revolution, yet they owed nothing to science; they were empirical developments based on the trial, error and experimentation of skilled craftsmen who were trying to improve the productivity, and so the profits, of their factories.[5]

Note the final sentence: these world-changing machines were developed, like Unilever's nozzle, through trial and error. Amateurs and artisans, men of practical wisdom, motivated by practical problems, worked out how to build these machines, by trying, failing and learning. They didn't fully understand the theory underpinning their inventions. They couldn't have talked through the science. But – like the Unilever biologists – they didn't really need to.*

And this is where the direction of causality can flip. Take the first steam engine for pumping water. This was built by Thomas Newcomen, a barely literate, provincial ironmonger and Baptist lay preacher, and developed further by James Watt. The understanding of both men was intuitive and practical. But the success of the engine raised a deep question: *why* does this incredible device actually work (it broke the then laws of physics)? This question inspired Nicolas Léonard Sadi Carnot, a French physicist, to develop the laws of thermodynamics. Trial and error inspired the technology, which in turn inspired the theory. This is the linear model in reverse.

In his seminal book *Antifragile*, Nassim Nicholas Taleb shows how the linear model is wrong (or, at best, misleading) in everything from cybernetics, to derivatives, to medicine, to the jet engine. In each case history reveals that these innovations emerged as a consequence of a similar process utilised by the biologists at Unilever, and became encoded in heuristics (rules of thumb) and practical know-how. The problems were often too complex to solve theoretically, or via a blueprint, or in the seminar room. They were solved by failing, learning and failing again.

Architecture is a particularly interesting case, because it is widely believed that ancient buildings and cathedrals, with their wonderful

---

* There is something of an analogy with sport. A top footballer can take a free kick from thirty yards and bend it into the top corner of the goal. In order to do this he must solve differential equations and various problems of aerodynamics. But he does not solve these equations mathematically. His knowledge is practical: he solves these problems implicitly. Where does this practical understanding come from? Again it comes through trial and error (i.e. practice). Over thousands of hours he kicks balls at a target and gradually reduces the gap between where the ball lands and the target by varying and improving his technique.

shapes and curves, were inspired by the formal geometry of Euclid. How else could the ancients have built these intricate structures? In fact, geometry played almost no role. As Taleb shows, it is almost certain that the practical wisdom of architects inspired Euclid to write his Book of Elements, so as to formalise what the builders already knew.

'Take a look at Vitruvius' manual, *De architectura*, the bible of architects, written about three hundred years after Euclid's Elements,' Taleb writes. 'There is little formal geometry in it, and, of course, no mention of Euclid, mostly heuristics, the kind of knowledge that comes out of a master guiding his apprentices ... Builders could figure out the resistance of materials without the equations we have today – building that are, for the most part, still standing.'[6]

These examples do not show that theoretical knowledge is worthless. Quite the reverse. A conceptual framework is vital even for the most practical men going about their business. In many circumstances, new theories have led to direct technological breakthroughs (such as the atom bomb emerging from the Theory of Relativity).

The real issue here is speed. Theoretical change is itself driven by a feedback mechanism, as we noted in Chapter 3: science learns from failure. But when a theory fails, like say when the Unilever mathematicians failed in their attempt to create an efficient nozzle design, it takes time to come up with a new, all-encompassing theory. To gain practical knowledge, however, you just need to try a different-sized aperture. Tinkering, tweaking, learning from practical mistakes: all have speed on their side. Theoretical leaps, while prodigious, are far less frequent.

Ultimately, technological progress is a complex interplay between theoretical and practical knowledge, each informing the other in an upward spiral*. But we often neglect the messy, iterative, bottom-up aspect of this change because it is easy to regard the world, so to

---

* Francis Bacon, the philosopher, identified this dynamic interplay as early as the seventeenth century. In his book *Novum Organum* he writes: 'Let no man look for much progress in the sciences – especially in the practical part of them – unless natural philosophy be carried on and applied to particular sciences, and particular sciences be carried back again to natural philosophy.'

speak, in a top-down way. We try to comprehend it from above rather than discovering it from below.

You can even see the basic contours of this perspective in the modern history of artificial intelligence. When the chess grand-master Garry Kasparov was defeated by Deep Blue in the famous 'victory of the machine' match in 1997, it created a storm. The popular interpretation was 'computers are better than humans!'

In fact, the real surprise was that Kasparov came so close. Humans can only search three or so moves per second. Deep Blue could search 200-million moves per second. It was designed to look deep into the various possibilities. But, crucially, it could not search every possibility due to the vast number of permutations (chess is charac-terised by a certain kind of complexity). Moreover, although it had been pre-progammed with a great deal of chess knowledge, it couldn't learn from its own mistakes as it played the games.

This gave Kasparov a fighting chance, because he had something the computer largely lacked: practical knowledge developed through trial and error. He could look at the configuration of pieces on a board, recognise its meaning based upon long experience, and then instantly select moves. It was this practical knowledge which almost propelled him to victory despite a formidable computational deficit. Deep Blue won the series three and a half to two and a half.

But artificial intelligence has moved on since then.[7] One of the vogue ideas is called *temporal difference learning*. When designers created TD-Gammon, a program to play backgammon, they did not provide it with any pre-programmed chess knowledge or capacity to conduct deep searches. Instead, it made moves, predicted what would happen next, and then looked at how far its expectations were wide of the mark. That enabled it to update its expectations, which it took into the next game.

In effect, TD-Gammon was a trial and error program. It was left to play day and night against itself, developing practical knowledge. When it was let loose on human opponents, it defeated the best in the world. The software that enabled it to learn from error was sophisticated, but its main strength was that it didn't need to sleep, so could practise all the time.

In other words it had the opportunity to fail more often.

III

Before we go on to look at what all this means in practice, and how we might harness the evolutionary process in organisations and in our lives, let us deal with a question that immediately arises: isn't it just *obvious* that we should test our assumptions if there is a cost-effective way of doing so? Why would any business leader, politician or, indeed, sports team do otherwise?

It turns out, however, that there is a profound obstacle to testing, a barrier that prevents many of us from harnessing the upsides of the evolutionary process. It can be summarised simply, although the ramifications are surprisingly deep: we are hardwired to think that the world is simpler than it really is. And if the world is simple, why bother to conduct tests? If we already have the answers, why would we feel inclined to challenge them?

This tendency to underestimate the complexity around us is now a well-studied aspect of human psychology and it is underpinned, in part, by the so-called narrative fallacy. This term was coined by the philosopher Nassim Nicholas Taleb and has been studied by the Nobel Prize-winner Daniel Kahneman: it refers to our propensity to create stories about what we see *after the event*.

You see the narrative fallacy in operation when an economist pops up on the early evening news and explains why the markets moved in a particular direction during the day. His arguments are often immaculately presented. They are intuitive and easy-to-follow. But they raise a question: why, if the market movements are so easy to understand, was he unable to predict the market movement in advance? Why is he generally playing catch-up?

Another example of the narrative fallacy comes from sports pun-ditry. In December 2007, Fabio Capello, an Italian, became head coach of the England football team. He was a disciplinarian. He ordered players to arrive at meetings five minutes early, clamped down on mobile phones and even banned tomato ketchup in the canteen. These actions were highly visible and well reported. This is what psychologists call 'salience'. And the results on the pitch were, at the outset, very good.

Rather like the economists on the early evening news, football journalists began to tell a simple and convincing story as to why the team was doing well: it was about Capello's authoritarian manner. His methods were eulogised. Finally, a coach who was willing to give the players a kick up the rear! At last, a coach who has provided discipline to those slackers! One flattering headline read: 'The Boss!'

But at the FIFA World Cup, the biggest competition in the sport, England bombed. They limped through the qualifying stage before being decisively eliminated with a 4–1 defeat by Germany. Almost instantly the narrative flipped. Capello is too tough! He is taking the fun out of the game! The Italian is treating our players like children! Many football journalists didn't even notice that they had attempted to explain contradictory effects with the same underlying cause.

That is the power of the narrative fallacy. We are so eager to impose patterns upon what we see, so hardwired to provide explanations, that we are capable of 'explaining' opposite outcomes with the same cause without noticing the inconsistency.

In truth, England's football results were not caused not by the salient features of Capello's actions, but by myriad factors that were not, in advance, predictable. That is why football journalists who are brilliant at explaining why teams won or lost after the event are not much better than amateurs at predicting who is going to win or lose beforehand. Daniel Kahneman has said:

> Narrative fallacies arise inevitably from our continuous attempt to make sense of the world. The explanatory stories that people find compelling are simple; are concrete rather than abstract; assign a larger role to talent, stupidity, and intentions than to luck; and focus on a few striking events that happened rather than on the countless events that failed to happen. Any recent salient event is a candidate to become the kernel of a causal narrative.[8]

But think about what this means in practice. If we view the world as simple, we are going to expect to understand it without the need for testing and learning. The narrative fallacy, in effect, biases us towards top-down rather than bottom-up. We are going to trust our hunches, our existing knowledge, and the stories that we tell our-selves about the problems we face, rather than testing our assumptions, seeing their flaws, and learning.

But this tendency, in turn, changes the psychological dynamic of organisations and systems. The greatest difficulty that many people face, as we have seen, is in admitting to their personal failures, and thus learning from them. We have looked at cognitive dissonance, which becomes so severe that we often reframe, spin and sometimes even edit out our mistakes.

Now think of the Unilever biologists. They didn't regard the rejected nozzles as failures because they were part and parcel of how they learned. All those rejected designs were regarded as central to their strategy of cumulative selection, not as an indictment of their judgement. They knew they would have dozens of failures and were therefore not fazed by them.

But when we are misled into regarding the world as simpler than it really is, we not only resist testing our top-down strategies and assumptions, we also become more defensive when they are chal-lenged by our peers or by the data. After all, if the world is simple, you would have to be pretty stupid not to understand it.

Think back to the divide between aviation and healthcare. In avi-ation there is a profound respect for complexity. Pilots and system experts are deeply aware that they are dealing with a world they do not fully understand, and never will. They regard failures as an inev-itable consequence of the mismatch between the complexity of the system and their capacity to understand it.

This reduces the dissonance of mistakes, increases the motivation to test assumptions in simulators and elsewhere, and makes it 'safe' for people to speak up when they spot issues of concern. The entire system is about preventing failure, about doing everything possible to stop mistakes happening, but this runs alongside the sense that failures are, in a sense, 'normal'.

In healthcare, the assumptions are very different. Failures are seen not as an inevitable consequence of complexity, but as indictments of those who make them, particularly among senior doctors whose self-esteem is bound up with the notion of their infallibility. It is difficult to speak up about concerns, because powerful egos come into play. The consequence is simple: the system doesn't evolve.

Now, let us take these insights into the real world and, in particular, the rapidly-growing industry of high technology.

IV

Drew Houston was getting frustrated. A young computer programmer from Massachusetts, he had a creative idea for a high-tech start-up. It was an online file sharing and storage service, which seamlessly uploads files and replicates them across all computers and devices.

Houston thought of the idea while travelling on a bus from Boston to New York. He opened his laptop but realised he had forgotten his flash drive, which meant that he couldn't do the work he wanted to. 'I had a big list of things I wanted to get done. I fished around in my pockets only to find out I'd forgotten my thumb drive,' he said. 'I was like: "I never want to have this problem again."'[9]

He was so annoyed with himself that he started to write some code that would remove the need for a flash drive. Then he realised that this was something everyone could benefit from. 'This wasn't a problem unique to me; it was a problem that everyone faced. As a product, it might really sell,' he said.

Houston toured venture capital companies but they kept raising the same issue. The market for storage and file sharing was already pretty crowded. Houston explained that these alternative products were rarely used because they were clunky and time-consuming. A more streamlined product would be different, he said. But he couldn't get through.

'It was a challenge to raise our first money because these investors would say: "There are a hundred of these storage companies. Why does the world need another one of them?" I would respond with: "Yes, there are a lot of these companies out there, but do you use any of them?" And invariably, they would say: "Well, no".'

Houston was clever enough to know that his product wasn't a guaranteed winner. Predicting whether consumers will actually buy a product is often treacherous. But he was quietly confident and wanted to give it a go. However, after a year he wondered if he would ever get a shot. He was close to desperate.

Let us leave Houston for a moment or two and look at two other tech entrepreneurs – Andre Vanier and Mike Slemmer, grappling with a different problem. They had an idea for a free online information service called 1-800-411-SAVE. Unlike Houston they had the money to develop the software. But they had very different ideas about how to write the code, as the author Peter Sims reveals in his book *Little Bets*.[10]

Vanier, a former consultant with McKinsey, thought they should spend plenty of time in the office getting the software absolutely right, so that it was capable of supporting all the millions of users they hoped to attract. He believed that the people at the company had great ability and, given time, would come up with bug-free and efficient software. This is the old perspective on development, with its emphasis on rigorous top-down planning.

Slemmer had a different view. He had already started two tech companies and realised something profound: it is pretty much impossible to come up with perfect code first time around. It is only when people are using the software, putting it under strain, that you see the bugs and deficiencies you could never have anticipated. By putting the code out there and subjecting it to trial and error you learn the insights that create progress. Why, he asked Vanier, would you try to answer every question before you have a single user?

The debate between Slemmer and Vanier echoes the contrast between the biologists and mathematicians at Unilever (and at a higher level of abstraction between Kealey's idea of progress and those who think progress always emerges from theoretical advance): it is pitting top-down against bottom-up. Vanier wanted to get everything right via a blueprint while Slemmer wanted to test early, and then iterate rapidly while receiving feedback from consumers, thus developing new insights. He wanted to test his assumptions.

Slemmer's arguments won out. The company got the software out at an early stage of development, and rapidly learned the inevitable flaws in their pre-market reasoning. They had to rewrite large sections, learning new insights that increased in direct proportion to the growing user base. Ultimately they developed arguably the most sophisticated software in the industry.

'Although they competed against substantially larger, better-resourced companies . . . they were consistently first to identify new features and services such as driving directions and integrated web-phone promotional offers', Peter Sims, the tech author who followed the company's progress, has written. 'As Vanier explains, if he can launch ten features in the same time it takes a competitor to launch one, he'll have ten times the amount of experience to draw from in figuring out what has failed the test of customer acceptance and what has succeeded.'[11]

This story hints at the dangers of 'perfectionism': of trying to get things right first time. The story of Rick, a brilliant computer scientist living in Silicon Valley, will highlight the problem even more starkly.

Rick had the idea of creating a web service that would allow people to post simple text articles online. He had this idea well before the blogging revolution. He could sense the potential and worked on it fifteen hours a day. Soon he had a working prototype. But instead of giving consumers a chance to use it, perceive its weaknesses, and then make changes, he decided the software would run more efficiently if he could design a more sophisticated programming language. He spent the next four years designing this new language. It proved disastrous. Two psychologists, Ryan Babineaux and John Krumboltz, have written:

> Over the next four years, he got more and more mired in technical details and lost sight of his original idea. Meanwhile, other entrepreneurs began to build blogging platforms that were neither perfect nor technologically advanced. The difference was that they quickly put their flawed efforts out into the world for others to try. In doing so, they received crucial feedback, evolved their software, and made millions of dollars.[12]

The desire for perfection rests upon two fallacies. The first resides in the miscalculation that you can create the optimal solution sitting in a bedroom or ivory tower and thinking things through rather than getting out into the real world and testing assumptions, thus finding their flaws. It is the problem of valuing top-down over bottom-up.

The second fallacy is the fear of failure. Earlier on we looked at situations where people fail and then proceed to either ignore or conceal those failures. Perfectionism is, in many ways, more extreme. You spend so much time designing and strategising that you don't get a chance to fail at all, at least until it is too late. It is *pre-closed loop* behaviour. You are so worried about messing up that you never even get on the field of play.

In their book *Art and Fear* David Bayles and Ted Orland tell the story of a ceramics teacher who announced on the opening day of class that he was dividing the students into two groups. Half were told that they would be graded on quantity. On the final day of term, the teacher said he would come to class with some scales and weigh the pots they had made. They would get an 'A' for 50 lbs of pots, a 'B' for 40 lbs, and so on. The other half would be graded on quality. They just had to bring along their one, perfect pot.

The results were emphatic: the works of highest quality were all produced by the group graded for *quantity*. As Bayles and Orland put it: 'It seems that while the "quantity" group was busily churning out piles of work – and learning from their mistakes – the "quality" group had sat theorizing about perfection, and in the end had little more to show for their efforts than grandiose theories and a pile of dead clay.'[13]

You see this in politics, too. Politicians come up with theories (bordering on ideologies) about whether, say, wearing school uniform improves discipline. They talk to psychologists and debate the issue in high-level meetings. It is an elaborate, top-down waste of time. They end up with dead clay. They should conduct a test, see what works, and what doesn't. They will fail more, but that is precisely why they will learn more.

Babineaux and Krumboltz, the two psychologists, have some advice for those who are prone to the curse of perfectionism. It involves stating the following mantras: 'If I want to be a great musician, I must first play a lot of bad music.' 'If I want to become a great tennis player, I must first lose lots of tennis games.' 'If I want to become a top commercial architect known for energy-efficient, min-imalist designs, I must first design inefficient, clunky buildings.'

The notion of getting into the trial and error process early informs one of the most elegant ideas to have emerged from the high-tech revolution: *the lean start-up*. This approach contains a great deal of jargon, but is based upon a simple insight: the value of testing and adapting. High-tech entrepreneurs are often brilliant theorists. They can perform complex mathematics in their sleep. But the lean start-up approach forces them to fuse these skills with what they can discover from failure.

How does it work? Instead of designing a product from scratch, techies attempt to create a 'minimum viable product' or MVP. This is a prototype with sufficient features in common with the proposed final product that it can be tested on early adopters (the kind of con-sumers who buy products early in the life cycle and who influence other people in the market).

These tests answer two vital questions. The first is the fundamen-tal one of: will people buy our product? If the MVP sufficiently resembles the proposed final product, but none of the early adopters have any interest in it, then you can be pretty sure that the entire business plan is worth ripping up. You have saved a huge amount of time and money by failing early.

But if the MVP looks like a possible winner, you can now find out how it can be improved further. This is the second question answered by the lean start-up approach. You can see what features the con-sumers like, what they don't like; you can see flaws in the concept, vary its assumptions, as you develop towards the final product. In other words, you have hardwired the evolutionary process into the design of the business.

And this brings us back to Drew Houston. His problem, you'll remember, was that he couldn't raise the funds to get his file sharing idea off the ground. Investors were not confident his idea would get anywhere.

What's worse, it was almost impossible to create a working proto-type. After all, Houston's basic pitch was that the file sharing product would only prove its value if it could seamlessly integrate multiple platforms and operating systems. To do that in even minimal form required a huge amount of work, based on deep knowledge of the various systems.

But Houston had an insight. He realised that the MVP doesn't need to be a working prototype at all. All it has to do is mimic the essential features of the final product. Provided it is sufficiently rep-resentative it can demonstrate whether consumers really want to buy it and thus kick-start the process of trial and error.

So Houston created a video that showed how the product would work in practice. There was no software, no code, but he didn't need these for his MVP. After all, how do you decide if you want a piece of software? You often look over the shoulder of someone who has got it, and is raving about it, and watch what it does. That is precisely what Houston did with his video.[14]

Eric Ries, the technology entrepreneur and author, picks up the story:

> The video is banal, a simple three-minute demonstration of the technology as it is meant to work, but it was targeted at a commu-nity of early adopters. Drew narrates the video personally, and as he's narrating, the viewer is watching his screen. As he describes the kinds of files he'd like to synchronise, the viewer can watch his mouse manipulate his computer. Of course, if you're paying atten-tion, you start to notice that the files he's moving around are full of in-jokes and humorous references that were appreciated by this community of early adopters.[15]

The effects were breathtaking. 'It drove hundreds of thousands of people to the website,' Houston has said. 'Our beta waiting list went from 5,000 people to 75,000 people literally overnight. It totally blew us away.'[16]

Houston had demonstrated that people wanted the product. It ena-bled him to raise more capital and continue product development with confidence. But it also enabled him to interact with the early adopters, develop practical knowledge and refine the product. That is the value of the lean start-up.

Nick Swinmurn, another technology entrepreneur, created a rather different MVP. He reckoned the world needed a website in order to purchase a stylish collection of shoes. He could have gone about this in the usual way: raising millions in capital, creating a vast inventory, and developing relationships with all the various manufacturers: i.e. designing the entire company from scratch from a blueprint. In other words, top-down.

Instead, he toured various shops and asked if he could take photos of their shoes. In return for allowing him to take the pictures and posting them online, he said he would come back and purchase the shoes at full price if customers registered their interest. By this process, Swinmurn was able to test the so-called value hypothesis: do customers actually want to buy shoes online? It turned out that they did.

But he discovered a host of other things, too. By interacting with real customers he learned things he could never have imagined in advance. He had to deal with returns, complaints, and taking online payment. 'This is decidedly different from market research,' Ries writes. 'If Swinmurn had relied on existing market research or conducted a survey, it could have asked what customers thought they wanted. By building a product instead, albeit a simple one, the company learned much more.'[17]

In 2009 Swinmurn sold his company, Zappos, to Amazon for $1.2 billion.

Steve Jobs is a man who is often held up for his vision. He wasn't interested in feedback and iteration, he wanted to change the world. We will explore how big, creative leaps happen in Chapter 10. But in the meantime it is worth noting that when it came to many of his strategic decisions, Jobs harnessed feedback in often powerful ways.

When he took Apple into retail in the early 2000s, for example, he didn't buy a string of stores and try to make the whole thing fly instantly. Rather, he bought a warehouse and started to test his hunches and convictions, and those of his retail experts. The first approach bombed, as Jim Collins reveals in his book *Great by Choice*. 'We were like, "Oh God, we're screwed!"' Jobs said.

So along with Ron Johnson, his retail leader, he kept redesigning and testing. Eventually they opened two stores in Virginia and Los Angeles, enabling them to test some more. Only when they had learned from direct feedback and early failures did they roll out big, across the nation, with disciplined consistency.[18]

The lean start-up approach has many parallels in the modus operandi of innovative companies. In its early days, 3M, the technology conglomerate, relied on a team of product developers for new ideas. They would brainstorm, think deeply, and then, when they had developed completed products, they would show them to end users to see how they reacted. It seemed like a rational process – but it was too slow.

In the mid-1990s they transformed their approach by bringing early adopters into the design process itself. They asked them to try early prototypes, observed them as they used the products, noticed what they liked and what they didn't. This enabled them to test their assumptions again and again.

3M then compared the two approaches. The results weren't even close. As the author Peter Sims puts it: 'A study published in 2002 found that using [the] active user strategy to identify and develop ideas generated an average of $146 million after five years, more than eight times higher than the average project developed using traditional, in-house 3M idea-generation methods.'[19]

Many other 'failure-based' notions are finding their way into business. Agile scrum development and the fail-fast approach are just two of these. Some are doubtless more effective than others. All would benefit from further testing (systems devoted to trial and error themselves benefit from trial and error). None should be used in the wrong context.

But the key significance of this family of ideas, which have helped to develop many of the world's most innovative products, is that they present a riposte to the historic presumption of top-down over bottom-up.

Drew Houston, the entrepreneur we started with in this section, has learned an important psychological lesson too. To leverage the power of failure, you have to be resilient and open. In other words, you have to have the right mindset as well as the right system. If you run away from mistakes, you won't get anywhere. 'It is a very gruelling experience,' he said. 'One day you are on top of the world . . . the next day there is a huge bug and the site is down and you are tearing your hair out . . . And guess what: that is still true today.'[20]

In 2014 Houston's company was valued at just over $10 billion. It is called Dropbox.

V

There is a metaphor that neatly summarises these insights. It comes from David Lane, professor at Henley Business School and a leading thinker on complexity.[21] The problem today, he says, is that we operate with a *ballistic model* of success. The idea is that once you've identified a target (creating a new website, designing a new product, improving a political outcome) you come up with a really clever strategy designed to hit the bullseye.

You construct the perfect rifle. You create a model of how the bullet will be affected by wind and gravity. You do your sums to get the strategy just right. Then you calibrate the elevation of the rifle, pull the trigger, and watch as the bullet sails towards the target.

This approach is flawed for two reasons: firstly the real world contains greater complexity than just wind and gravity: there are endless variables and interdependencies. Take a policy as simple as reducing the dangers of smoking by cutting tar and nicotine in cigarettes. It sounds great in theory, particularly when used in conjunction with a clever marketing campaign. It looks like a ballistic strategy perfectly designed to hit an important public health target.

But when this idea was implemented in practice, it failed. Smokers compensated for the lack of nicotine by smoking more cigarettes and taking longer and deeper drags. The net result was an *increase* in carcinogens and carbon monoxide.[22] That is what happens in systems populated by human beings: there are unintended consequences.

And this is why it is difficult to formulate an effective strategy from on high, via a blueprint. The second problem is even more elemental. By the time you have designed the rifle, let alone pulled the trigger, the target will have moved. This is the problem of a rapidly changing world. Just look at how IT products are becoming obsolete even before they roll off the production line. This kind of rapid change is only likely to accelerate.

What to do? Professor Lane recommends an entirely different concept of success: the *guided-missile* approach. Sure, you want to design a great rifle, you want to point it at the target, and you want to come up with a decent model of how it will be affected by the known variables, such as the wind and gravity. But it is also vital to react to what happens *after you pull the trigger*.

As soon as the bullet leaves the muzzle, as soon as it comes into contact with the real world – this is when you start to discover the flaws in the blueprint. You find out that the wind is stronger than you anticipated, that it is raining, and that there are unknown variables, interacting with each other as well as with the bullet, which you couldn't possibly have anticipated in advance.

The key is to adjust the flight of the bullet, to integrate this new information into the ongoing trajectory. Success is not just dependent on *before-the-event reasoning*, it is also about *after-the-trigger adaptation*. The more you can detect failure (i.e. deviation from the target), the more you can finesse the path of the bullet onto the right track. And this, of course, is the story of aviation, of biological evolution and well-functioning markets.

This reasoning illustrates the balance between top-down and bottom-up. If the original ballistic plan is hopeless, if the bullet just dribbles out of the muzzle, precision guidance is not going to help very much. But likewise, if you just rely on a ballistic plan, however sophisticated, you are going to hit thin air. It is by getting the balance right between top-down strategy and a rigorous adaptation process that you hit the target. It is fusing what we already know, and what we can still learn.

In the coming decades, Professor Lane argues, success will not just be about intelligence and talent. These things are important; but they should never overshadow the significance of identifying where one's strategy is going wrong, and evolving.

Systems and organisations that foster the growth of knowledge of all kinds will dominate. This is the insight that the high-tech world has been gravitating towards and which much of the rest of the world, with only a few heroic exceptions, is studiously resisting.

Think about the ratio of Unilever again: 449 failures to create a single success. Has your company failed that often, and been honest enough to admit it? Has your school? Has your government depart ment? If they haven't, you are likely to be off target.

It is pointless getting upset about this. Clinging on to cherished ideas because you are personally associated with them is tantamount to ossification. As the great British economist John Maynard Keynes put it: 'When my information changes, I alter my conclusions. What do you do, sir?'

VI

To conclude this chapter, let us take one final example that reveals the dangers of trusting narrative above testing and learning. It is from the field of international development and a powerful case study because it reveals that the consequences of relying on top-down intuition can sometimes be measured in lost lives.

Specifically, let us take the scourge of AIDS and HIV in Africa. There are a number of alternative approaches to preventing and treating this disease that, on the face of it, seem highly plausible. All of them look like positive ways to alleviate a pressing (and often lethal) problem. But which is the most effective? What does top-down judgement tell you?

OPTION 1: surgical treatment for Kaposi's sarcoma, an AIDS defining illness

OPTION 2: antiretroviral therapy to combat the virus in infected people

OPTION 3: prevention of transmission from mother to baby during pregnancy

Option 4: condom distribution to prevent general transmission
Option 5: education for high-risk groups like sex workers

They all sound pretty good, don't they? You can imagine that each approach has its own charity with its own website, glossy material, testimonies from people who have personally benefited from the programme, and promotional video. This is how most charities operate. And, on this basis, you would probably invest your money with the organisation with the most convincing narrative. In the absence of data, narrative is the best we have.

But this is why we need to conduct tests, to challenge our hunches, and the narrative fallacies upon which they are often based. And when proper trials have been conducted, it turns out that these different programmes, which all look so impressive, have vastly different outcomes. It is not just that some of the approaches are a couple of times better; or five times better; or even ten times. The best of the options listed above is *1,400 times as cost-effective* as the worst option.[23]

On the graph below, the treatment for Kaposi's sarcoma doesn't even register.

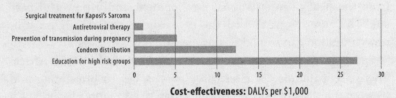

Cost-effectiveness: DALYs per $1,000

It is for this reason that many of the most influential development campaigners argue that the most important issue when it comes to charitable giving is not just raising more money, but conducting tests, understanding what is working and what isn't, and learning. Instead of trusting in narrative, we should be wielding the power of the evolutionary mechanism.

'Ignoring effectiveness does not mean losing 10% or 20% of the potential value that a health budget could have achieved, but can easily mean losing 99% or more,' Toby Ord, a philosopher at Oxford

University, has said. 'In practical terms, this can mean hundreds or thousands or millions of additional deaths due to a failure to prioritise. In non-life-saving contexts, it means thousands or millions of people with untreated disabling conditions.'[24]

The problem is not just that the donors don't know the effectiveness of rival approaches; neither do many of the charities. The power of the narrative fallacy, the stories of the lives being saved, the testimonies told by people who have benefited, are as convincing to people running charities as to those donating to them. Indeed, why would you wish to collect data when you can meet and talk to those whose lives have been saved?

But given that there may be an alternative treatment that can save more lives, benefit more people – sometimes hundreds or even thousands more – our faith in the evidence of our own eyes is often insufficient. It is by testing that we gain access to the feedback that drives progress, and, in the case of charities, saves lives.

One of the ironies of charitable spending is that the one statistic many donors *do* tend to look at can actually undermine the pursuit of evidence. The so-called overhead ratio measures the amount of money spent on administration compared with the front line. Most donors are keen for charities to keep this ratio low: they want money to go to those who really need it rather than office staff.

But given that evidence-gathering counts as an administrative cost rather than treatment, this makes it even more difficult for charities to conduct tests. As Ord puts it: 'You might think that organizations would know the most effective treatment. But often they don't and one of the reasons for that is because they don't do as much program evaluation as we would like because they're trying to keep the overhead ratio low. Also, they just generally aren't aware of these figures.'[25]

Ord has set up an organisation that encourages people to give 10 per cent of their lifetime income to charity, but only to those projects with a proven track record of success.[26] 'Our intuitions about what works are often wrong,' he says. 'We have to test and learn if we are serious about saving lives and alleviating suffering.'

8
Scared Straight?

I

On a cool morning in the spring of 1978, seventeen teenagers from New Jersey and New York were driven across town to Rahway State Prison, one of the most notorious detention centres in North America. As they walked up the gravel path to the forbidding set of buildings the youngsters joked and giggled. They were cocky, had lots of swagger.

The kids – fourteen boys, three girls, of different ethnic groups, aged between fifteen and seventeen – had one thing in common: all had been in trouble with the law. Terence, a seventeen-year-old African American, had stolen cars. Lori, a pretty white sixteen-year-old with a wide smile and large earrings, was a thief and a drug dealer. Angelo, a teenager with unkempt hair and a wispy moustache, had robbed shops in his neighbourhood.[1]

Nearly half of all serious crime in America was, at the time, committed by children between ten and seventeen. Arrests for burglary were reportedly 54 per cent juvenile; those for car theft were 53 per cent juvenile.[2] Rape had been on the rise. These seventeen kids, still joking as they reached the gates of the prison, were not just an isolated group of delinquents, they were symbolic of a wider social problem facing the United States.

Their visit to Rahway was part of a crime-reduction programme called 'Scared Straight'. The idea was that by giving these youngsters a glimpse of prison life – what it is really like inside a maximum security installation – they would be shocked, or at least nudged, into a change of behaviour. The programme, which had been conceived by the inmates, had been running for two years.

The kids didn't buy the premise, of course. Nobody was going to frighten them out of stealing and mugging. They were too tough to be intimidated by anyone, least of all the jailbirds at Rahway. 'They don't scare me,' one of the youngsters said with a shrug of the shoulders. 'I think it's going to be great going in and seeing all them burnouts,' Lori said, laughing.

As they walked through the metal detector at the entrance of the prison, however, the youngsters experienced a first tremor of apprehension. 'Line up against the wall!' a sergeant shouted. 'You may think this is a sightseeing trip. It isn't. When you went through the door, the man who brought you lost jurisdiction over you. You're in our hands. You'll do as we say. The first thing is to stop smoking! And don't chew gum! And take off those hats!'

This was not what they were expecting. They were ordered to walk in single file into the main prison area as an iron door slammed behind them. They were now in the bowels of a maximum security prison. Up on the balcony convicted prisoners looked down on them. 'There's a sweet mother****** right there, with the yellow shirt on!' a muscular black convict yelled. 'When you are here, you'll be my bitch,' another said menacingly. The kids looked at the guards for a reaction, but there was no response. Their fear heightened.

They were then walked through a cell block called 'the hole', populated by prisoners in solitary confinement. The sexual jibes at this stage are too shocking to report. The kids became ever more uncertain. The swagger had vanished. You could see the confusion and fear on their faces. But they were not even thirty minutes into their initiation.

For the next two hours, they were locked in a small room with twenty lifers: prisoners who have been given minimum sentences of twenty-five years. Together, their terms added up to nearly a thousand years. This is where the intervention really began. One at a time, the lifers stood up and offered an insight into what the youngsters could expect if they ever came to Rahway.

'Two of you guys I don't like,' a convict with a life sentence for murder screamed at the kids. 'I don't like you and I don't like you. You got one time to smile at me and I am going to turn your teeth upside down. You understand? I have just got out of the hole today and I am going to turn your teeth upside down.'

The kids had arrived at Rahway with the vague idea that prison was an easy ride. They thought they could just breeze through. They thought they were tough. As they listened, they were systematically disabused of their naivety. Another inmate asked:

When we got sexual desires, who do you think we get? Take a wild guess . . . We get young, dumb mother*******, just like you. I am in here ten years and I am going to die in this stinking joint. And if they want to give me these three bitches right here I would leap over them like a kangaroo just to get to one young, pretty . . .

One day you are lying on your blanket, and your mind is drifting over those thirty foot walls and you are thinking about who's with your girl when three guys will slide into your cell, wrap you up in that blanket, and I don't care how tough you think you are or how strong you might be, but they are going to kick you onto the side of that bed, and they are going to [rape you].

None of the kids were talking now. One or two were crying. The lifers were not acting out of spite. They were, in effect, issuing warnings, admonishing the kids to change before it was too late. This was an attempt to deter the next generation of criminals. The lifers didn't want the youngsters to make the same mistakes they had.

'We don't get paid for doing this,' the kids were told. 'We don't get no extra reward, no extra benefits, no nothing. We do it because we *want* to do it. Because we might help you.' Another convict said: 'I have been here seven years. I regret every day I have been here . . . You have the best opportunity in the world [to avoid prison] . . . You would have to be a fucking fool not to take it.'

The kids were inside Rahway for three hours, but it seemed like three days. They had seen the reality of prison and were adamant they would never go back. Crime no longer seemed cool, but a game that led to hopelessness and desperation. On the way home they were silent. At one point the driver had to stop the car so that one of the boys could vomit.

'I was just so scared, I don't want to go to one of them things,' Lori, the girl with the big earrings, said. 'It scared the shit out of me, I didn't like it at all.'

'I think it will change my life,' another said, wide-eyed. 'I mean I have got to cut some of this [crime] out. All of it, if possible . . . I am going to try very hard.' Others talked about going to college: anything to avoid jail.

The prison visit was recorded by Arnold Shapiro, a documentary maker. His film of the visit was later broadcast by KTLA, Channel 5 in Los Angeles and fronted by Peter Falk of *Colombo* fame. Viewers were riveted by the grim reality of prison life and by the seemingly incredible results of the Scared Straight programme. Falk revealed that of the seventeen youngsters, sixteen were still going straight three months later. He also reported that the wider programme had had a dramatic impact on reoffending rates. Falk said:

> Over 8,000 juvenile delinquents have sat in fear on these hard wooden benches and for the first time they really heard the brutal reality of crime and prison. The results of this unique programme are astounding. Participating communities report that 80 to 90 per cent of the kids that they send to Rahway go straight after leaving this stage. That is an amazing success story. And it is unequalled by traditional rehabilitation methods.

Politicians lined up to eulogise the programme. Newspaper columns were penned. Social commentators praised the approach of Scared Straight. Feckless kids were pushed into line and brought face to face with the consequences of their actions. It was the kind of short, sharp shock treatment that pundits had been crying out for. It was razor-edged deterrence.[3]

During the week of 5 March 1979 Shapiro's documentary was shown in two hundred major cities.[4] The following month it won the Oscar for best documentary feature at the Academy Awards. The Scared Straight programme was rolled out across the United States, Canada, the UK, Australia and Norway. Its effectiveness was attested to by judges, correction officers and other experts.

The data seemed remarkable. As George Nicola, a juvenile judge who worked in New Brunswick, a few miles from Rahway, put it: 'When you view the programme and review the statistics that have been collected, there is no doubt in my mind . . . that the juvenile awareness project at Rahway State prison is perhaps today the most effective, inexpensive deterrent in the entire correctional process in America.'[5]

But there turned out to be one rather large problem with Scared Straight. It didn't work. Rigorous testing would later prove that the kids who were taken on prison visits were *more likely* to commit offences in the future, not less – as we shall see. A more appropriate name for Scared Straight might have been Scared Crooked. It was an unequivocal failure. It damaged kids in a number of ways.

But first we will ask: how is this possible? How can something be a failure when the statistics seem to show that it is a success? How can it be failing when virtually every expert is lining up to endorse it? To answer that question we will examine one of the most important scientific innovations of the last two hundred years, and one that takes us to the heart of the closed-loop phenomenon – and how to overcome it.

The randomised control trial.

II

Closed loops are often perpetuated by people covering up mistakes. They are also kept in place when people spin their mistakes, rather than confronting them head on. But there is a third way that closed loops are sustained over time: through skewed interpretation.

That was the problem that bedevilled bloodletting, practised by medieval doctors. The doctors had what seemed like clear feedback on what worked and what didn't. Either the patient died in the aftermath of the procedure or did not. The evidence was there for all to see.

But how to interpret this evidence? As we've seen, doctors, already convinced of the wisdom of figures like Galen, trusted in the power of bloodletting. When a patient died, it was because they were so ill that not even bloodletting could save them. But when they lived, that confirmed the brilliance of the procedure.

Think of how many success stories must have been circulating around the medieval world: people who had been terribly ill, close to death perhaps, but bloodletting had been performed, and they had recovered. How persuasive their testimony would have sounded. 'I was on the brink of mortality, a doctor drained me of some blood, and now I am cured!'

Consider how they would have commended the procedure in market squares. Those who died on the other hand? Well, they would not be around to say anything, would they? Their testimony had vanished.

Now look at the diagram below.[6]

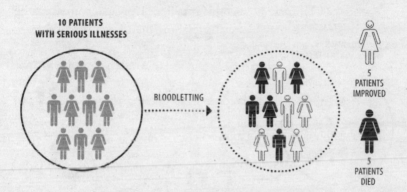

10 PATIENTS WITH SERIOUS ILLNESSES

BLOODLETTING

5 PATIENTS IMPROVED

5 PATIENTS DIED

Bloodletting without a control group

In this (hypothetical) example, a group of chronically ill people are given bloodletting. Some of them recover. This is the 'evidence' that justifies the treatment. People get better and they are understandably happy about it.

However, what the doctors don't see, and the patients don't see, is what would have happened if the treatment had *not been given*. In experiments this is commonly known as the 'counterfactual'. It is all the things that *could* have happened, but which, in everyday experience, we never observe, because we did something else.

We don't observe what would have happened if we had not got

married. Or see what would have happened if we had taken a different job. We can speculate on what would have happened, and we can make decent guesses. But we don't really know. This may seem like a trivial point, but the implications are profound.

Now look at another diagram, below. Here the patients have been randomly divided into two groups. Some of them get access to bloodletting while the others (called the control group) do not. This is known as a randomised control trial (RTC); in medicine it is called a clinical trial. We see from the diagram that many of the patients who receive bloodletting recover. It looks successful. The feedback is impressive.

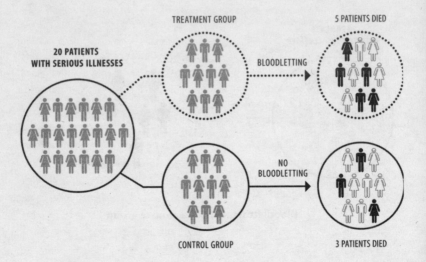

Bloodletting with a control group

But now look at the group who did not get the treatment. Many more have recovered than in the treated group. The reason is simple: the body has its own powers of recuperation. People recover naturally even without treatment. In fact, by comparing the two groups, it is possible to see that, far from saving people as medieval doctors sincerely believed, bloodletting, on average, kills them. This fact would have been invisible without the control group.* And this is why, as we noted in Chapter 1, bloodletting survived as a recognised treatment until the nineteenth century.

So far in this book we have examined cases of unambiguous error. When a plane crashes you know the procedures were defective. When DNA evidence shows that an innocent man is convicted, you know the trial or investigation was flawed. When a minimum viable product is rejected by early adopters, you can be sure the final product will bomb. When a nozzle is clogging up, you know it will cost you money. These examples gave us a chance to examine failure in the raw.

Much real-world failure is not like this. Often, failure is clouded in ambiguity. What looks like success may really be failure and vice versa. And this, in turn, represents a serious obstacle to progress. After all, how can you learn from failure if you are not sure you have actually failed? Or, to put it in the language of the last chapter, how can you drive evolution without a clear selection mechanism?

To take a concrete example, suppose you redesign your company website and that sales subsequently increase. That might lead you to believe that the redesign of the website caused the boost in sales. After all, one preceded the other. But how can you be sure? Perhaps sales went up not because of the new website, but because a rival went bust, or interest rates went down, or because it was a rainy month and more people shopped online. Indeed, it is entirely possible that sales would have gone up even more if you had *not* changed the website.

Looking at the sales statistics is not going to help you find an answer any more than looking at the number of people recovering from bloodletting will help you find out if the treatment is effective. The reason is simple: you can't observe the counterfactual. You don't know whether the change in sales was caused by something else; something, perhaps, you hadn't even considered.

---

* Random allocation (effectively flipping a coin) is important because it means that, providing the sample size is big enough, the two groups are likely to be similar. The only systematic difference between the groups is that one gets the treatment and the other does not.

RCTs solve this problem. In effect they provide a high-definition test. They turn shades of grey into something closer to black and white. By isolating the relationship between an intervention (blood-letting, a new website, etc.) and an outcome (recovery from illness, sales) without it being obscured by other influences, they clarify the feedback. Without such a test you could draw the wrong conclusions, not just once but potentially indefinitely.

RCTs have revolutionised pharmacology. Ben Goldacre, a doctor and writer who is an evangelist for evidence-based medicine, has said: 'This one idea has probably saved more lives, on a more spectacular scale, than any other idea you will come across this year.'[7] Mark Henderson, a former science editor of *The Times*, said: 'The Randomised Control Trial is one of the greatest inventions of modern science.'[8]

It is probably worth emphasising that RCTs are not a panacea. There are situations where they are difficult to use and where they might be considered unethical. And trials have often been rigged in subtle ways by pharmaceutical companies keen to come up with an answer that they have already prejudged.[9] But these are not arguments against randomised trials, merely against how they have been corrupted by people with dubious motives.

Another objection is that randomised trials neglect the holistic nature of a system. In medicine, for example, while a drug may cure a particular symptom, it may also have negative long-term effects on the rest of the body, or leave the underlying cause untreated. For example, prescribing a pill to combat a stomach complaint might cause damage to the immune system that could, in the long run, leave the patient worse off.

What this objection is saying, in effect, is that the measurement period for a clinical trial shouldn't be the immediate aftermath of administering a drug, but the entire life of the patient, and that the outcome shouldn't merely focus on a particular symptom, but the whole person. This shows that it is vital to keep an eye on the long-term consequences when conducting RCTs, something that has sometimes been overlooked in medicine.

But it is also worth noting that such considerations carry little weight when it comes to life-threatening conditions. If you find yourself in the middle of an epidemic of, for example, smallpox or Ebola you will want the vaccine even if there is a risk of complications in a few decades' time.[10]

With these caveats in mind, then, RCTs offer a powerful method of establishing rigorous tests in a complex world. Handled with care, they cut through the ambiguity that can play havoc with our interpretation of feedback. And they are often simple to conduct.

Take the example of the redesigned website mentioned earlier. The problem was in establishing whether the change in the design had increased sales, or was caused by something else. But suppose you randomly direct users to either the new or the old design. You could then measure whether they buy more goods from the former or the latter. This would filter out all the other influences such as interest rates, competition, weather and so on, and reveal the hidden counterfactual.

There have been around half a million RCTs in medicine since the 1950s. They have saved hundreds of thousands of lives. But the remarkable thing is that in many areas of human life RCTs have hardly been used at all. In the criminal justice system they are almost non-existent. In 2006, for example, there were almost 25,000 trials in medicine, but in crime and justice across the world there were only 85 between 1982 and 2004.[11]

David Halpern, one of the most respected policy analysts in the UK, has said: 'Many areas of government have not been tested in any form whatsoever. They are based on hunch, gut feel and narrative. The same is true of many areas outside government. We are effectively flying blind, without much of a clue as to what really works, and what doesn't. It is actually quite scary.'[12]

Closed loops are not merely an intellectual curiosity, they realistically describe the world we live in. They are small and large, subtle and intricate; they lurk in small companies, big companies, charities, corporations and governments. The majority of our assumptions have never been subject to robust failure tests. Unless we do something about it they never will be.

To glimpse the often mind-bending gulf between what we think we know, and what we really know, let us revisit the Scared Straight programme. It looked astonishingly effective. The observational statistics seemed compelling.* But we now know that the programme was increasing crime rather than reducing it.

In many ways, Scared Straight stands as a metaphor not merely for government policy (perhaps the closest thing in the twenti-eth-first century to bloodletting), but for the wider world. This programme could have continued on its merry way for decades, per-haps centuries, without a proper test.

Scared Straight is a metaphor, but above all, it is a warning.

III

In 1999 *Scared Straight! 20 Years Later* was broadcast in the United States. The documentary was fronted this time by Danny Glover rather than Peter Falk, and revisited those seventeen, scrawny teenagers who had appeared in the original film. The results were as seemingly mirac-ulous as the original programme had led audiences to believe.

Many of the interviewees talked about their new lives. Almost all credited the three-hour visit to Rahway two decades earlier as having turned their lives around. Terence, the young black kid who had once stolen cars and broken into stores, was now a part-time preacher at his local Baptist church, with a wife and two sons. 'Chances are, if I wouldn't have gone to Rahway, I would probably be locked up and could be in my grave,' he said.

Lori, the sixteen-year-old with the wide smile and big earrings, who had been dealing drugs, was now a thirty-six-year-old book-keeper and mother. 'I just thought it was a day away from school,' she said. 'I don't think I have ever been as afraid in my whole life . . . It made me not want to be an idiot any more . . . I started going to school more after that.'

---

* 'Observational statistics' is a phrase that encompasses all the statistics drawn from looking at what happened. Randomised control trials are different because they encompass not merely what happened, but also construct a counterfactual for comparison.

Angelo, the kid with the unkempt hair and wispy moustache, was now thirty-seven years old, tiled floors for a living and had three kids. He said 'If I didn't go to Rahway, I think I would have done hard time,' he said. 'If that one day didn't happen, I might not have my family. And my family to me right now is everything; it is the most beautiful experience in the world.'

This, then, is how the phenomenon of Scared Straight looked to millions of TV viewers. The statistics look good, too. This was a scheme, unlike most social programmes, that actually bothered to collect data. According to the evidence, around 80 to 90 per cent of people who attended the programme went straight. As stated in the documentary: 'That is an amazing success story. And it is unequalled by traditional rehabilitation methods.'

But if we rewind to the late spring of 1977, a rather different picture was starting to emerge. In April of that year, James Finckenauer, a professor at the Rutgers School of Criminal Justice, decided to test Scared Straight. He wasn't just interested in the observational statistics. As a scientist he knew that these could be misleading. He was not interested in hype or slickly presented documentaries either. He wanted to know if the scheme *really* worked. In short, he wanted to run an RCT.

Finckenauer has silver-white hair and enquiring eyes. He has published dozens of papers and won multiple awards for his research, but his most striking quality is his conversational style. He is cautious, considered and attentive. He also has a laser-like quality, as if he is trying to cut through the surface to find the truths lying beneath. These qualities would serve him well as he forensically unpicked the Scared Straight phenomenon.

Before starting the RCT, Finckenauer probed the existing evidence for Scared Straight. Where did the 80 to 90 per cent figure for kids going straight come from? He found that it was based on a questionnaire sent to the parents or guardians of children who had visited Rahway. (Another source of the data was letters of commendation sent in by the sponsoring agencies which brought kids to Rahway. These were not terribly reliable. These agencies may have had all sorts of hidden incentives to believe in the programme.).

There were four 'Yes or No' questions:

Have you noticed a marked change in your child's conduct since their visit to the prison?

Has there been a slight change in their behaviour since their visit to prison?

Do you think another visit is necessary for your son/daughter?

Are there any specific areas you think we might be of some assistance to you, or your son or daughter?

There was also space to write comments.[13]

But what did a 'marked' change actually mean? What did a 'slight' change mean? The questions were open to all kinds of interpretation. Finckenauer also discovered that many of the kids who visited Rahway had not been delinquent or even pre-delinquent in the first place. It hardly counts as a success that they didn't commit crime afterwards if they were already on the straight and narrow. Furthermore, the letters to parents were often sent within weeks of the prison visit. That was scarcely enough time to judge a change in behaviour.

And yet these were only minor quibbles. The deeper flaws go to the heart of what constitutes valid evidence. The first is that only those who responded to the questionnaire were included in the statistics. Those who didn't respond were entirely absent from the data. Consider how that might have distorted the result. It is possible that only the parents of children whose behaviour improved bothered to respond. Parents whose kids continued to behave badly might have thrown the questionnaire in the bin, or at least responded in fewer numbers. This could have skewed the stats beyond recognition.

This is a type of so-called 'selection bias' and it should sound familiar. It is pretty much the same problem that bedevilled medieval medicine when only those who recovered from bloodletting were able to testify to its effectiveness. The evidence sounded terrific but that is because it was dangerously incomplete. Those who did not recover from bloodletting were never given a chance to express an opinion. Why? Because they were already dead.

The deepest problem with the *Scared Straight* statistics, however, related to the counterfactual. Even if everyone *had* responded to the questionnaire (which they hadn't), we still wouldn't know whether the outcomes had been caused by the intervention, or by something else. Perhaps behaviour would have improved without the intervention. Perhaps it improved because the local economy was improving, or because of a new scheme at school, or some other factor. Perhaps the outcome would have been even better *without* the intervention.

In August 1978, Finckenauer divided a set of delinquent youths into two random groups.* One group attended the Scared Straight programme. The other group (the control group) did not. He then sat and waited to measure the results. Despite the hype, the stellar-looking stats, the slick PR, the Oscar-winning documentary, the commendations from politicians, the tributes from corrections officers, the widespread adoption of the scheme around the world, this was the first time the project had been subjected to the most rigorous kind of failure test.

And the results, when they finally arrived, were dramatic. Scared Straight didn't work. The children who attended Rahway were more likely to commit crimes than those who did not. 'The evidence showed that the kids who went on the programme were at greater risk of offending than those who didn't,' Finckenauer said. 'The data when you compared the treatment and control group was clear.'

This was, to many people, a surprise. The programme looked good. The logic seemed compelling. It had parents lining up to say that it had 'cured' their kids. The questionnaire data seemed solid, too. But all of these things were true of bloodletting. Only with an RCT could we cut through the ambiguity and see the real effect of the programme.

Finckenauer says:

---

* The process of conducting an RCT was much more difficult than Finckenauer thought possible. Advocates of Scared Straight didn't cooperate. Judge Nicola, a high-profile supporter, tried to halt the trial before it had even started. 'He saw no need for an evaluation since he had already collected hundreds of letters attesting to the success of the project,' Finckenauer says.

People were convinced of the success of Scared Straight because it seemed so intuitive. People loved the idea that kids could be turned around through a tough session with a group of lifers. But crime turns out to be more complex than that. Children commit offences for many different, often subtle reasons. With hindsight, a three-hour visit to prison was unlikely to solve the problem.

The intentions of the inmates were genuine: they really wanted the kids to go straight. But the programme was having unintended consequences. The experience of being shouted at seemed to be brutalising the youngsters. Many seemed to be going out and committing crime just to prove to themselves and their peers that they weren't really scared.[14]

Defenders of the scheme reacted angrily to Finckenauer's report. Judge Nicola, who had lavishly praised the programme in the documentary, said: '... the [Scared Straight] programme doesn't need defending'. Robert J. McAlesher, the staff adviser to Scared Straight, was even more blistering. 'We question the motives of dilettantes [i.e. Finckenauer] who compromise their intellectual integrity by thrusting themselves into the national limelight with meaningless statistics deceptively presented as the result of scientific study.'[15]

These responses were, in a sense, predictable. When we are presented with evidence that challenges our deeply held beliefs, we tend to reject the evidence or shoot the messenger rather than amend our beliefs. Indeed, many of the defenders of Scared Straight responded to the results of Finckenauer's RCT by saying that they had become *more convinced* of the efficacy of the programme, not less. This is precisely what the theory of cognitive dissonance would predict.

But even those with no prior commitment to Scared Straight continued to be attracted to the programme, like moths to a flame. The hard data showed that it was counterproductive, but the narrative of kids being deterred from crime by mean-talking inmates was too seductive to ignore. By the 1980s, Scared Straight-style programmes were in operation in Georgia, South Carolina and Wisconsin. Further programmes were set up in New York, Virginia, Alaska, Ohio and Michigan.[16]

It was as if the research conducted by Finckenauer had never happened.

By the 1990s similar programmes were burgeoning. The Los Angeles Police Department ran a scheme where one of the components was kids visiting the city prison to be 'shouted and screamed at' by convicts. At a programme in Carson City, Nevada, a youngster was reported as saying that the part of the tour that made the greatest impact was 'all the inmates calling us for sex and fighting for our belongings'. The idea was soon exported to the UK, Australia and Norway.

Meanwhile, the hard evidence against the scheme was multiplying. RCTs were conducted on Scared Straight-style programmes from the west to the east coast of America. They found the same thing: Scared Straight doesn't work. It often damages kids. One of the trials showed a 25 per cent increase in delinquency in the treatment group compared with the control group.

But none of this seemed to matter. The glitzy narrative was far more seductive than the boring old data.[17]

Even government officials eulogised the programme. In 1994, a Scared Straight-style scheme in Ohio was commended in the official publication of the US Office of Juvenile Justice and Delinquency Prevention. The experts had been bewitched by the narrative fallacy. In 1996, almost twenty years after Finckenauer's RCT, the *New York Times* reported that the original programme at Rahway was at the height of its popularity, hosting around ten groups per week or 12,500 kids per year.

But then in 2002 the Campbell Collaboration arrived on the scene. This is a global, non-profit organisation devoted to evidence-based policy. They conducted what is called a 'systematic review'. This is where the data from all the randomised trials are collated into a single spreadsheet. By pooling the results from all the individual trials (seven were used in the so-called meta-analysis), a systematic review represents the gold standard when it comes to scientific evidence. It is the ultimate failure test.[18]

Forgive me if you know what's coming, but the results were emphatic. Scared Straight doesn't work. It increases crime. Some research indicates that this increase can be as high as 28 per cent.[19] In exquisitely understated language, the authors effectively damned its entire rationale: 'We conclude that programmes like Scared Straight are likely to have a harmful effect and increase delinquency ... Doing nothing would have been better than exposing juveniles to the programme.'[20]

Scared Straight was, in many ways, ahead of its time. Unlike most social programmes, which collate no data whatsoever, it actually sent out questionnaires and gathered statistics. But, as with medieval bloodletting, observational stats do not always provide reliable data. Often, you need to test the counterfactual. Otherwise you may be harming people without even realising it.

And this is really the point. It doesn't require people to be actively deceitful or negligent for mistakes to be perpetuated. Sometimes it can happen in plain view of the evidence, because people either don't know how to, or are subconsciously unwilling to, interrogate the data.

But how often do we actually test our policies and strategies? How often do we probe our assumptions, in life or at work? In medicine, as we have seen, there have been almost one million randomised trials. In criminal justice, they scarcely exist. Policy, almost across the board, is run on narrative, hunch, untested ideology, and observational data skewed to fit predetermined conclusions.

Closed loops are not just an intellectual curiosity, they accurately (and sometimes terrifyingly) describe the world in which we live.

On 1 January 1982, an intruder broke into the home of a nineteen-year-old called Michele Mika. After rummaging through several rooms, he took a knife from the kitchen, entered Ms Mika's bedroom and murdered her. Michele's mother later found her face down in bed with an eight-inch carving knife in her back. After she was killed, Ms Mika was sexually assaulted for several hours. The motive was pure sexual gratification.[21]

More than twenty-five years later, on 17 March 2007, police arrested Angelo Speziale, a forty-five-year-old living in Hackensack, New Jersey. Speziale was one of the original seventeen youngsters profiled in Scared Straight. He was the kid with the unkempt hair and wispy moustache who had robbed shops in the neighbourhood. He had also been interviewed in the follow-up feature twenty years later, by which time he had three kids and a job tiling floors.

Like most of the people interviewed for the follow-up programme, Speziale claimed that the visit to Rahway had transformed his life. It sounded almost inspirational. 'If I didn't go to Rahway, I think I would have done hard time,' he said. Danny Glover, the narrator, said: 'Angelo, thirty-seven, is now a law-abiding family man.'

But the reality was rather different. In 2005, Speziale was arrested for shoplifting and police obtained a DNA sample. During routine testing they discovered that it matched the DNA of the sperm found in the corpse of Michele Mika. Mika and Speziale, it turned out, had lived on opposite sides of the same duplex on Teaneck Avenue at the time the murder had taken place.

The makers of the documentary did not deliberately mislead audiences about Speziale. They couldn't have known that he was deceiving them when he said he had 'gone straight'. They couldn't have realised that just three years after he had visited Rahway, he had raped and murdered an innocent nineteen-year-old. Only the test provided by DNA revealed the truth.

But the documentary makers did know by the early 1980s that Scared Straight was increasing crime. And yet they continued to make celebratory programmes on the project. A&E, an American cable and satellite channel, introduced *Beyond Scared Straight*, a new series, in 2011. By 2014 it was in its eighth season. Arnold Shapiro, the producer (who also made the original 1978 documentary), continues to defend the scheme, despite the overwhelming evidence against it. He argues that Scared Straight today involves more counselling and less shouting. But the logic of conducting the interventions in prisons has always relied on a confrontational component. As the *Daily Beast* put it:

> The episodes themselves do emphasize the horrors of prison life more than discussion. At the beginning of one filmed at Maryland's Jessup prison, a 50-year-old man convicted of first-degree murder

barks into a 17-year-old dropout's face, 'Don't smile at another man in prison, 'cause if you smile at another man in prison, that makes them think that you like them, and for you to like another man in prison, something seriously is wrong with you.'

In his three-hour visit to Rahway in 1978, Speziale endured a number of degradations, but one event is particularly chilling in hindsight. The youngster was forced to stand in front of the group and read out a newspaper report of a knife attack that had taken place in prison. 'Rahway inmate stabbed to death in cell block,' the sixteen-year-old read, voice trembling. 'He was stabbed about a dozen times in the neck, chest, head and back. Robinson was pronounced dead on arrival at Rahway General Hospital.'

There is no evidence of any connection between the fact that Speziale was humiliated into reading out loud the details of a savage knife attack on his visit to Rahway in 1978 and the fact that he perpetrated a similar crime a few years later. This is almost certainly a coincidence. But what we do know is that these visits, on average, damage the kids who are taken on them. We have known that for more than three decades.

In 2010, Speziale pleaded guilty to sexual assault and stabbing and was sentenced to twenty-five years.[22] He is now back in Rahway prison, where this story began. It is an endlessly disturbing and cautionary tale. But the deepest irony of all, and the one that takes us to the heart of the closed-loop phenomenon, is that Speziale might soon be delivering Scared Straight-style confrontations to the next generation of delinquents.*

---

* Eventually federal funding was withdrawn from schemes that used the *Scared Straight* methodology. But they still keep popping up, not just in the United States, but elsewhere in the world. Until data is taken more seriously than narrative, they always will.

PART 4

Small Steps and Giant Leaps

9

Marginal Gains

I

At around 9 a.m. the riders of Team Sky, the British professional cycling team, made their way out of a small hotel in Carcassonne, a beautiful town in the Languedoc-Roussillon region of southern France. It was a warm morning and the riders walked to the team bus in silence, contemplating the day to come.

They were about to start Stage 16 of the 2014 Tour de France, one of the sternest tests of endurance in the sporting world. They had already ridden 3,000 kilometres over the preceding fifteen stages and now faced a 237.5-kilometre ride culminating at the feared Port de Balès, a 19-kilometre climb into the Pyrenees. 'Here we go again,' Bernhard Eisel, one of the team members, said with a grim smile.

On the Team Sky bus there was a sense of anticipation. The riders were getting into their sports gear. The coaches were reviewing race plans. With thirty minutes to go, Nicolas Portal, one of Team Sky's sporting directors, began his pre-race briefing. He talked about the importance of the stage and alerted the riders to difficult sections along the route. As he did so photographs of tough corners and steep climbs were flashed onto a screen at the front of the bus.

As he finished his talk, a man towards the back, silent until that moment, started to speak. He had a shaved head, dark-rimmed glasses and an intense manner. He is the man who always has the final word before the race: the general manager of Team Sky, Sir David Brailsford.

'At the end of the day, success is about getting in the breakaway [where a group of cyclists ride away from the main pack],' he said.

'Let's not f*** about. Either we are in it or we are not. I know it is difficult. I know how hard it is. But everyone needs to buy into this. All focus on that. That is our goal for today. The rest will look after itself. Don't let anyone else make it happen; make it happen for yourselves . . . OK, hit it!'

A quiet buzz reverberated around the bus. Brailsford had struck the right note. All eight riders stood up and exchanged glances. They then made their way down the steps to the starting line of the sixteenth stage.

The previous evening Brailsford had given me a tour of the Team Sky operation. We looked at the trucks, the design of the team bus, and the detailed algorithms that are used to track the performance of each cyclist. It was an opportunity to glimpse behind the curtains of one of the most admired and tightly policed operations in all sport.

The success of Brailsford is legendary. When he joined British track cycling as an adviser in 1997, the team was behind the curve. In 2000 Great Britain won a single Olympic gold medal in the time trial. In 2004, one year after Brailsford was appointed performance director, Britain won two Olympic gold medals. In 2008 they won an astonishing eight gold medals and, at the London Olympics in 2012, repeated the feat.

Meanwhile, something even more remarkable was happening. Track cycling is competitive, but the most prestigious form of the sport is professional road cycling. Britain had never had a winner of the Tour de France since the race was established in 1903. British riders had won individual stages, but nobody had come close to winning the general classification.

But in 2009, even as the British track cycling team was preparing for the London Olympics, Brailsford embarked upon a new challenge. He created a road cycling team, Team Sky, while continuing to oversee the track team. On the day the new outfit was announced to the world, Brailsford also announced that they would win the Tour de France within five years.

Most people laughed at this aspiration. One commentator said: 'Brailsford has set himself up for an almighty fall.' But in 2012, two years ahead of schedule, Bradley Wiggins became the first-ever British rider to win the event. The following year, Team Sky triumphed again when Chris Froome, another Brit, won the general classification. It was widely acclaimed as one of the most extraordinary feats in British sporting history.

How did it happen? How did Brailsford conquer not one cycling discipline, but two? These were the questions I asked him over dinner at the team's small hotel after the tour of the facilities.

His answer was clear: 'It is about marginal gains,' he said. 'The approach comes from the idea that if you break down a big goal into small parts, and then improve on each of them, you will deliver a huge increase when you put them all together.'

It sounds simple, but as a philosophy, marginal gains has become one of the hottest concepts not just in sport, but beyond. It has formed the basis of business conferences, seminars and has even been debated in the armed forces. Many British sports now employ a director of marginal gains.

But what does this philosophy actually mean in practice? How do you deliver a marginal gains approach, not just in sport, but in other organisations? Most significantly of all, why does breaking a big project into smaller parts help you to tackle really ambitious goals?

To glimpse an answer, let us leave cycling for a moment and look at a very different area of life. For it turns out that the best way to grasp the meaning of marginal gains is to examine one of the most pressing issues facing the world today: global poverty.

II

Take a look at the graph on page 186.[1] It is reproduced from the work of Esther Duflo, one of the world's most respected economists, currently working out of MIT.

The vertical, light-grey bars show the amount of aid spending on Africa over the last thirty years. As you can see, the funding has gradually increased since the early 1960s, peaking at almost $800 million in 2006. The investment has a simple imperative: to improve the lives of the world's poorest. It is an important objective given that 25,000 children die of preventable causes every day.[2]

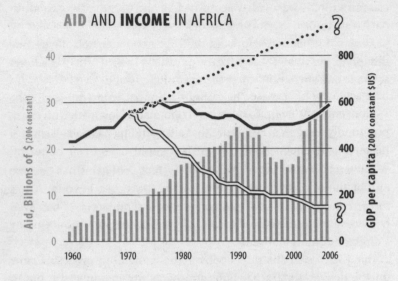

The key question here is: did the investment make a difference? Did it improve the lives of the people it was designed to help?

A sensible place to start when answering that question is with African GDP. In the diagram African GDP is shown by the solid black line. As you can see, this has stayed roughly constant over the period. This might lead one to the conclusion that all the aid spending hasn't done much good. It hasn't boosted economic activity. It hasn't raised the living standards of those living in Africa. In fact it all seems like an expensive waste of time.

But the insights from the previous chapter should urge a little caution. Why? Because the data doesn't give us an insight into the counterfactual. Perhaps the aid spending was incredibly successful. Perhaps, without it, GDP in Africa would have been far lower – the white line in the graph.

Of course, there is another possibility. Perhaps aid spending was even more detrimental than the solid black line might lead you to believe. Perhaps it was a disaster, destroying incentives, boosting corruption and lowering growth below what it would otherwise have been. Perhaps without it Africa would have actually surged ahead: as per the dotted line in the graph. How can we know either way?

Each of these two alternatives has high-profile supporters. Jeffrey Sachs, director of the Earth Institute at Columbia University, for example, is a vocal advocate of development spending. He argues that aid has benefited the lives of Africans and claims that more money could eradicate poverty altogether. *The End of Poverty*, his best-selling book, is based in part upon this premise.[3]

Conversely, William Easterly, an economist at New York University, profoundly disagrees. He argues that aid spending has had all sorts of negative side-effects, and that Africa would have been better off without it. His book *The White Man's Burden* presents this case with as much intellectual force as that of Sachs.[4]

The best way to adjudicate between these stances would be to conduct a randomised control trial. This would enable us to isolate the effect of development spending from all the other influences on African GDP. But there is a rather obvious problem. There is only one Africa. You cannot find lots of different Africas, randomly divide them into groups, give aid to some and not to others, and then measure the outcomes.

This may sound like a trivial point, but it has wider implications. When it comes to really big issues, it is very difficult to conduct controlled experiments. To run an RCT you need a control group, which is not easy when the unit of analysis is very large. This applies to many things beyond development aid, such as climate change (there is only one world), issues of war and peace, and the like.

But this takes us directly to the concept of marginal gains. If the answer to a big question is difficult to establish, why not break it down into lots of smaller questions? After all, aid spending has many sub-components. There are programmes on malaria, literacy, road-building, education and infrastructure, each of them constructed in different ways, with different kinds of incentives, and delivered by different organisations.

At this level of magnification, by looking at one programme at a time, it is perfectly possible to run controlled experiments. You try out the programme with some people or communities, but not with others, and then compare the two groups to see if it is working or not. Instead of debating whether aid is working *as a whole* (a debate that is very difficult to settle on the basis of observational data), you can find definitive answers at the smaller level and build back up from there.

To examine a concrete example, suppose you were trying to improve educational outcomes in Africa. One way to see if aid spending is working would be to look at the correlation between the quantity of spending and the average grade score across the continent. The problem is that this wouldn't give you any information about the counterfactual (what would have happened to scores without the funding).

But now suppose that instead of looking at the big picture, you examine an individual programme. That is precisely what a group of pioneering economists did in the impoverished Busia and Teso regions in the west of Kenya. As the author Tim Harford points out in his book *Adapt*, these economists wanted to know whether handing out free textbooks to schools would boost grades. Intuitively, they were pretty sure it would. In the past the observational data had been good. Schools that received books tended to improve their test scores.

But the economists wanted to be sure, so they performed an RCT. Instead of giving the textbooks to the most deserving schools, which is the common approach, they randomly divided a number of eligible schools into two groups: one group received free textbooks and another group did not. Now, the charity had a treatment group and a control group. They had a chance to examine whether the books were making a real difference.

The results, when they came in, were both emphatic and surprising. The students in the schools that received free textbooks didn't perform any better than those who did not. The test results in the two groups of schools were almost identical. This outcome contradicted intuition and the observational data. But then randomised trials often do.

The problem, it turned out, was not the books, but the language they were written in. English is the third language of most of the poor children living in remote Busia and Teso. They were struggling to grasp the material as it was presented. Researchers might not have realised this had they not run a trial. It pierced through to one of the untested assumptions in their approach.

Confronted with failure, the economists tried another approach. They conducted another randomised trial but instead of using textbooks they used visual aids. These were flipcharts with bold graphics that covered geography, maths, etc. Again, the economists expected them to boost test scores. Again, when they compared the test scores in the treatment group with those of the control group, the flipcharts were a failure. They led to no significant improvement in learning.

Undeterred, the economists started to think about the problem in a fresh way. They tried something completely new: a de-worming medication. This may seem like a curious way to improve education, but researchers were aware that these parasites stunt growth, cause children to feel lethargic, and lead to absenteeism. They disproportionately affect children in remote communities, just like those in Busia and Teso.

This time the results were excellent. They vastly exceeded the expectations of the researchers. As Tim Harford put it: 'The programme was a huge success, boosting children's height, reducing re-infection rates, and also reducing absenteeism from school by a quarter. And it was cheap.'[5]

This was a marginal gain. It was just one programme in one small region. But by looking at education at this level of magnification, it was possible to see what really works, and what doesn't. The economists had tested, failed and learned. They could now roll it out in other areas, while continuing to test, and iterate, and create yet more marginal gains.

This may sound like a gradual way to improve, but look at the alternative. Consider what would have happened if the economists had relied on intuition and observational data. They might have continued with free textbooks for ever, deluding themselves that they were making a difference, when they were doing virtually nothing at all.

This approach is now the focus of a crusading group of economists who have transformed international development over the last decade. They do not come up with grand designs; rather, they look for small advantages. As Esther Duflo, the French-born economist who is at the forefront of this approach, put it: 'If we don't know if we are doing any good, we are not any better than the medieval doctors and their leeches. Sometimes the patient gets better; sometimes the patient dies. Is it the leeches or something else? We don't know.'[6]

Critics of randomised trials often worry about the morality of 'experimenting on people'. Why should one group get X while another is getting Y? Shouldn't everyone have access to the best possible treatment? Put like this, RCTs may seem unethical. But now think about it in a different way. If you are genuinely unsure which policy is the most effective, it is only by running a trial that you can find out. The alternative is not morally neutral, it simply means that you never learn. In the long run this helps nobody.

Duflo, who is petite and dynamic, doesn't regard her work as lacking in ambition; rather, she regards these incremental improvements as pioneering. She told me:

It is very easy to sit back and come up with grand theories about how to change the world. But often our intuitions are wrong. The world is too complex to figure everything out from your armchair. The only way to be sure is to go out and test your ideas and programmes, and to realise that you will often be wrong. But that is not a bad thing. It leads to progress.

This links back to the work of Toby Ord, who we met in Chapter 7. He uses the data discovered by the likes of Duflo to advise private individuals on where to donate their money. He realised that relying on hunch and narrative can mean that millions of pounds are squandered on ineffective programmes. And this is why hundreds of controlled experiments are now being conducted across the developing world. Each test demonstrates whether a policy or programme works, or if it doesn't.

Each test provides a small gain of one kind or another (remember that failure is not inherently bad: it sets the stage for new ideas). By breaking a big problem into smaller parts, it is easier to cut through narrative fallacies. You fail more, but you learn more.

As Duflo puts it: 'It is possible to make significant progress against the biggest problem in the world through the accumulation of a set of small steps, each well thought out, carefully tested, and judiciously implemented.'[7]

III

And this takes us back to David Brailsford and British cycling. Note the similarity of the final quote of Duflo with that of Brailsford earlier in this chapter. 'The whole approach comes from the idea that if you break down a big goal into small parts, and then improve on each of them, you will gain a huge increase when you put them all together.'

Cycling is very different to international development, but the success of its most pioneering coach is based on the same conceptual insight. As Brailsford puts it: 'I realised early on that having a grand strategy was futile on its own. You also have to look at a smaller level, figure out what is working and what isn't. Each step may be small, but the aggregation can be huge.'

Running controlled trials in cycling is significantly easier than in development aid, not least because the aim of the sport is relatively simple: getting from A to B as quickly as possible. To obtain the most efficient bicycle design, for example, British cycling created a wind tunnel. This enabled them to isolate the aerodynamic effect, by varying the design of the bike and testing it in identical conditions. To discover the most efficient training methods, Brailsford created new data sets that enabled him to track every sub-component of physiological performance.

'Each gain on its own was small,' Brailsford said. 'But that doesn't really matter. We were getting a deeper understanding of each aspect of performance. It was the difference between trailing behind the rest of the world and coming first.'

In *Corporate Creativity*, the authors Alan Robinson and Sam Stern write of how Bob Crandall, the former chairman of American

Airlines, removed a single olive from every salad, and in doing so saved $500,000 annually.[8] Many seized on this as a marginal gain. But was it? After all, if removing an olive is a good idea, why not the lettuce too? At what point does an exercise in incremental cost-cutting start to impact on the bottom line?

Now we can see a clear answer. Marginal gains is not about making small changes and hoping they fly. Rather, it is about breaking down a big problem into small parts in order to rigorously establish what works and what doesn't. Ultimately the approach emerges from a basic property of empirical evidence: to find out if something is working, you must isolate its effect. Controlled experimentation is inherently 'marginal' in character.

Brailsford puts it this way: 'If you break a performance into its component parts, you can build back up with confidence. Clear feedback is the cornerstone of improvement. Marginal gains, as an approach, is about having the intellectual honesty to see where you are going wrong, and delivering improvements as a result.'

The marginal gains mentality has pervaded the entire Team Sky mindset. They make sure that the cyclists sleep on the same mattress each night to deliver a marginal gain in sleep quality; that the rooms are vacuumed before they arrive at each new hotel, to deliver a marginal gain in reduced infection; that the clothes are washed with skin-friendly detergent, a marginal gain in comfort.

'People think it is exhausting to think about success at such a high level of detail,' Brailsford says. 'But it would be far more exhausting, for me anyway, to neglect doing the analysis. I would much rather have clear answers than to delude myself that I have the "right" answers.'

Perhaps the most astonishing application of marginal gains is to be found not in cycling but in Formula One. In the closing weeks of the 2014 season I visited the Mercedes headquarters in Brackley, a few miles north of Oxford. It is a series of grey buildings on an industrial estate, with a stream running through it. It is populated with bright people, passionate about their sport – and whose attention to detail is staggering.

'When I first started in F1, we recorded eight channels of data. Now we have 16,000 from every single parameter on the car. And we derive another 50,000 channels from that data,' said Paddy Lowe, a Cambridge-educated engineer, who is currently the technical leader of Mercedes F1. 'Each channel provides information on a small aspect of performance. It takes us into the detail, but it also enables us to isolate key metrics that help us to improve.'

The most intuitive way to glimpse the relationship between marginal gains and big achievements is to examine the pit stop. This is one of thousands of different components which, collectively, determine whether an F1 team is successful or not. It is a marginal aspect of performance, but a crucial one. In order to gain a deeper insight I went out to the season-ending Grand Prix in Abu Dhabi and immersed myself within the Mercedes operation.

At the team's motorhome, a small, three-storey house within the Yas Marina Circuit, I talked to James Vowles, chief strategist for Mercedes F1. I asked him how the team went about developing the optimum pit-stop procedure. Vowles said:

We use the same method for everything, not just pit stops. First of all, you need a decent understanding of the engineering problem. So, with the pit stops we came up with a strategy based on our blue-sky ideas. But this strategy was always going to be less than optimal, because the problem is complex. So we created sensors so we could measure what was happening and test our assumptions.

But the crucial thing is what happened next. Once you have gone through a practice cycle with the initial strategy, you immediately realise that there are miscellaneous items that you are not measuring. Just doing a pit-stop practice-run opens your eyes to data points that are relevant to the task, but that were absent from the initial blueprint. So the second stage of the cycle is about improving your measurement statistics, even before you start to improve the pit-stop process.

Think about that for a moment. We have talked about the concept of an open loop. This is where a strategy is put in action, then tested to see if it is working. By seeing what is going wrong, you can then improve the strategy. Mercedes takes this one step further. They use the first test not to improve the strategy, but to create richer feedback. Only when they have a deeper understanding of all the relevant data do they start to iterate.

Vowles says:

> We have placed eight sensors on every single one of the wheel-nut guns in order to access the most systematic data. Just by looking at this data, without speaking to the human involved, I can ascertain exactly what has happened on each pit stop. When the gun operator initially connected to the wheel nut, I can tell that they, say, connected 20 degrees off the optimum angle. When they start rotating the gun, I can tell how long it has taken for the nut to physically loosen all its pre-loaded torque and for the wheel to start moving off the axle.
>
> I can tell how quickly the gun man has moved away; how quickly he has reconnected, how long it has taken for the tyre to be removed, the second tyre to be refitted to the axle, how clean the second connection was to it, and how long he was gunning on for. The precision of this information helps us to create an optimisation loop. It shows us how to improve every time-sensitive aspect.

This is marginal gains on turbocharge. 'You improve your data set before you begin to improve your final function; what you are doing is ensuring that you have understood what you didn't initially understand,' Vowles says. 'This is important because you must have the right information at the right time in order to deliver the right optimisation, which can further improve and guide the cycle.'

Later that evening I went to the pit-lane to watch the team practice. It was an astonishing feat of collective endeavour. The car of Lewis Hamilton, the top driver for Mercedes, was pushed into position by three runners, and then instantly pounced upon by a team of around sixteen people, all with clearly defined tasks and exquisitely coordinated procedures. Again and again they practised, dealing with every contingency that might arise in the race the next day. Every practice run was measured with the eight sensors, and videoed, so it could pass through another optimisation loop. One of the pit stops I witnessed was completed in an astonishing 1.95 seconds.*

Vowles said:

> The secret to modern F1 is not really to do with big ticket items; it is about hundreds of thousands of small items, optimised to the nth degree. People think that things like engines are based upon high-level strategic decisions, but they are not. What is an engine except many iterations of small components? You start with a sensible design, but it is the iterative process that guides you to the best solution. Success is about creating the most effective optimisation loop.

I also spoke to Andy Cowell, the leader of the team that devised the engine. His attitude was a carbon copy of that of Vowles.

> We got our development engine up and running in late December [2012]. We didn't design it to be car friendly. We didn't try and figure out the perfect weight and aerodynamic design. Rather, we got a working model out there early, so that we could test it, and improve. It was the process of learning in the test cell that enabled us to create the most thermally efficient engine in the world.

The marginal gains approach is not just about mechanistic iteration. You need judgement and creativity to determine how to find solutions to what the data is telling you, but those judgements, in turn, are tested as part of the next optimisation loop. Creativity not guided by a feedback mechanism is little more than white noise. Success is a complex interplay between creativity and measurement, the two operating together, the two sides of the optimisation loop.

---

* Doctors from Great Ormond Street Hospital for children visited a Formula 1 team to witness how a pit stop happens. They were seeking to learn how to improve the handover from operating room to the intensive care unit. The number of errors dropped significantly in the aftermath. See http://asq.org/healthcare-use/why-quality/great-ormond-street-hospital.html

We will examine the creative process in more detail in the next chapter, but Vowles and Cowell have described a compelling model. It is the model used by Brailsford and the latest generation of development economists. Mercedes clocks up literally thousands of tiny failures. As Toto Wolff, the charismatic executive director of the team, put it: 'We make sure we know where we are going wrong, so we can get things right.'

The basic proposition of this book is that we have an allergic attitude to failure. We try to avoid it, cover it up and airbrush it from our lives. We have looked at cognitive dissonance, the careful use of euphemisms, anything to divorce us from the pain we feel when we are confronted with the realisation that we have underperformed.

Brailsford, Duflo and Vowles see weaknesses with a different set of eyes. Every error, every flaw, every failure, however small, is a marginal gain in disguise. This information is regarded not as a threat but as an opportunity. They are, in a sense, like aviation safety experts, who regard every near-miss event as a precious chance to avert an accident before it happens.*

On the eve of the Grand Prix at the Yas Marina Circuit, qualifying took place. This is where the drivers compete to see who can post the fastest lap, with the winner taking pole position (the most advantageous place on the starting grid) for the Grand Prix. Nico Rosberg, a German driver for Mercedes, took first place on the grid and Lewis Hamilton, his British teammate, took second place.

Afterwards, I was given access to the highly secretive debriefing meeting. At a table in a room in the Mercedes garage, a few metres from the track, Hamilton and Rosberg sat facing each other. They

---

* We saw in the early part of this book how aviation learns from mistakes by studying accidents and near-miss events. These adverse events are used to generate hypotheses about what went wrong, and possible ways of amending the system. But these are not the final word. After all, the proposed changes, however intuitive, might cause unforeseen dangers. Instead, proposed changes are always trialled in simulators, under different conditions and with different pilots, before being incorporated into the real-world system. In other words, aviation uses learning from error at multiple levels to drive progress.

were flanked by their respective race engineers. On the left was Paddy Lowe, the technical boss, and on other tables were experts in different aspects of performance.

Everybody wore headsets with microphones and scrutinised data on computer screens. On a big screen in the corner of the room was the team back in the UK, all hooked into the conversation. Much of the meeting was confidential. But the process was fascinating. Hamilton and Rosberg were taken through each dimension of performance: tyres, engine, the helmet, whether the drinks provided during qualifying were at the right temperature.

Each observation from the two drivers was then double-checked against the hard data, and possible improvements noted. After the meeting, the next stage of the optimisation loop was already underway, with analysts creating new marginal gains. I couldn't help contemplating the contrast between the spirit of this approach and that of other areas of our world.

The following day I observed the race from the Mercedes garage. Hamilton made a blistering start from second position on the grid and went on to win the race. The points from his victory propelled him to the overall driver's championship. Rosberg came second in the overall classification. Mercedes won the constructors championship: the most successful team in F1.

Afterwards, champagne bottles were uncorked in the garage as mechanics, engineers, pit-stop operators and the two drivers finally let their hair down. 'I drive the car, but I have an incredible operation behind me,' Hamilton said. Vowles added: 'We will enjoy tonight, but tomorrow we will feed what we learned today into the next stage of the optimisation loop.'

Paddy Lowe, the man responsible for the technical operation, looked on from the back of the garage. 'F1 is an unusual environment because you have incredibly intelligent people driven by the desire to win,' he said. 'The ambition spurs rapid innovation. Things from just two years ago seem antique. Standing still is tantamount to extinction.'

IV

Google had a decision to make. Jamie Divine, then one of the company's top designers, had come up with a new shade of blue to use on the Google toolbar. He reckoned it would boost the number of click-throughs.

The narrative surrounding the new shade sounded very good. The colour was enticing; it meshed with what was known about consumer psychology. Divine, after all, was one of the top designers at the company. But how could Google be sure that he was right?

The conventional way would have been to change the colour on the Google toolbar and see what happened. The obvious problem with this approach should, by now, be obvious. Even if clicks increased, Google could not be certain if the increase was caused by the colour change or by something else. Perhaps the number of clicks would have gone up *even more* if the colour had stayed the same.

And this is why, even as executives were debating Divine's shade, a product manager decided to conduct a test. He picked a slightly different shade of blue (one with a hint of green) and put it into a contest with the shade selected by Divine. In effect, users clicking on the Google website were randomly assigned to one of the two shades and their behaviour monitored. It was an RCT. The result of the experiment was clear: more people clicked through on the blue with a hint of green.

There was no room for spin or bluster of the kind that often accompanies business decisions. There was just a flip of a coin, a random assignment, and a precise measurement.* The fact that Divine's shade lost out in this trial didn't mean he was a poor designer. Rather, it showed that his considerable knowledge was insufficient to predict how a tiny alteration in shade would impact upon consumer behaviour. But then nobody could have known that for sure. The world is too complex.

---

* In order to conduct RCTs effectively, it is important to create the right methodology including a large enough sample size. See http://www.evanmiller.org/how-not-to-run-an-ab-test.html

But this was just the start. Google executives realised that the success of the greeny-blue shade was not conclusive. After all, who's to say that this particular shade is better than all other possible shades? Marissa Mayer, of Yahoo!, then a vice president at Google, came up with a more systematic trial. She divided the relevant part of the colour spectrum into forty constituent shades and then ran another test.

Users of Google Mail were randomly grouped into forty populations of 2.5 per cent and, as they visited the site at different times, were confronted with different shades, and tracked. Google were thus able to determine the optimal shade, not through blue-sky thinking or slick narratives, but through testing. They determined the optimum shade through trial and error.

This approach is now a key part of Google's operation. As of 2010, the company was carrying out 12,000 RCTs every year. This is an astonishing amount of experimentation and it means that Google clocks up thousands of little failures. Each RCT may seem like nitpicking, but the cumulative effect starts to look very different. According to Google UK's managing director, Dan Cobley, the colour-switch generated $200 million in additional annual revenue*.

Perhaps the company most associated with randomised trials, however, is Capital One, the credit card provider. The business was created by Rich Fairbank and Nigel Morris, two consultants with backgrounds in evidence-based research. They created the company with one objective in mind: to test as widely and as intelligently as possible.

When sending out letters to solicit new clients, for example, they could have gone to a number of different experts who would doubtless have come up with different templates and colours. Should the colour be red or blue? Should the font be Times New Roman or Calibri?

Instead of debating the questions, however, Fairbank and Morris

---

* This should be taken as an estimate rather than a definitive amount since many variables will have affected revenues following the implementation of the new colour.

tested them. They sent out 50,000 letters to randomly selected households with one colour and 50,000 with another colour, and then measured the relative profitability from the resulting groups. Then they tested different fonts, and different wording, and different scripts at their call centres.[9]

Every year since it was founded Capital One has run thousands of similar tests. They have turned the company into a 'scientific laboratory where every decision about product design, marketing, channels of communication, credit lines, customer selection, collection policies and cross selling decisions could be subjected to systematic testing and using thousands of experiments'.[10]

As of 2015, Capital One was valued at around £45 billion.

Jim Manzi, an American entrepreneur and author who helps companies to run randomised trials, estimates that 20 per cent of all retail data is now put through his software platform. This hints, more than anything else, at how far the marginal gains approach has travelled in the corporate world. 'Businesses now execute more RCTs than all other kinds of institutions combined,' he told me. 'It is one of the biggest changes in corporate practice for a generation.'[11]

Harrah's Casino Group is symbolic of the quiet revolution that has been taking place. The brand, which operates casinos and resorts across America, reportedly has three golden rules for staff: 'Don't harass women, don't steal, and you've got to have a control group.'

RCTs, whether in business or beyond, are often very dependent on context. A trial that improves, say, educational outcomes in Kenya has no claim to improve outcomes in London.* This is both the beauty of the social world, and its challenge. We need to run lots of trials, lots of replications, to tease out how far conclusions can be

---

* This is sometimes called the problem of 'external validity': it is about the extent to which the results of one RCT can be applied to new contexts. Pharmacogenetics is a field based on this realisation: the efficacy of many drugs depends on the genotype (and hence, often the ethnic origin) of patients. Consequently most drugs currently prescribed work well for Europeans and white Americans, because they formed the majority of test groups.

extended from one trial to other contexts. To do this we need to create the capacity for running experiments at scale and at a lower unit cost.

But this doesn't mean that we cannot draw big conclusions from RCTs. Perhaps the most ambitious use of randomised trials in public policy took place in regard to employment policy. In America in the 1980s, how to get people off welfare and into work was one of the most pressing issues of the day. Policy would conventionally have been decided by the top-down deliberations of presidents and congressmen in collaboration with advisers and pressure groups.

Instead, it was determined by experimentation. As Jim Manzi details in his excellent book *Uncontrolled*, states were given waivers to depart from federal policy on the proviso they used randomised trials to evaluate the changes. The results were dramatic. The trials revealed that financial incentives don't work. Time limits don't work.

The only thing that worked? Mandatory work requirements. This paved the way for Bill Clinton's highly successful workfare programme, secured with the backing of a Republican Congress.

V

Marginal gains may seem like an approach that only big corporations, governments and sports franchises can hope to adopt. After all, running controlled experiments requires expertise and, often, sizeable budgets. But a willingness to test assumptions is ultimately about a mindset. It is about intellectual honesty and a readiness to learn when one fails. Seen in this way, it is relevant to any business; in fact to almost any problem.

Take Takeru Kobayashi. At one time, he was an impoverished economics student, struggling to pay the electricity bill of the apartment he shared with his girlfriend in Yokkaichi, on the eastern coast of Japan. Then he heard about a televised speed-eating contest in the area that had a first prize of $5,000. He entered the competition, did a bit of serious practice, and won.[12]

Intrigued, he discovered that speed-eating is a globally competitive sport, with serious rewards. This was a possible route out of poverty. So, as documented in the excellent book *Think Like a Freak*, Kobayashi targeted the world's biggest competition – Nathan's Hot Dog Eating Contest, which takes place every 4 July in Coney Island, New York.

The rules are straightforward: eat as many hot dogs and buns as you can in twelve minutes. You are allowed to drink anything you like, but you are not allowed to vomit significantly (a problem known in the sport as a 'reversal of fortune').

Kobayashi approached the contest with a marginal gains mindset. First, instead of eating the hot dog as a whole (as all speed-eating champions had done until that point), he tried breaking it in half. He found that it gave him more options for chewing, and freed his hands to improve loading. It was a marginal gain. Then he experimented with eating the dog and the bread separately rather than at once. He found that the dogs went down super-fast, but he still struggled with the chewy, doughy buns.

So he experimented by dipping the buns in water, then in water at different temperatures, then with water sprinkled with vegetable oil, then he videotaped his training sessions, recorded the data on spreadsheets, tracked slightly different strategies (flat out, pacing himself, sprint finishing), tested different ways of chewing, swallowing and various 'wriggles' that manipulated the space in his stomach in order to avoid vomiting. He tested each small assumption.

When he arrived at Coney Island he was a rank outsider. Nobody gave him a chance. He was slight and short, unlike many of his super-sized competitors. The world record was 25.125 hot dogs in twelve minutes, an astonishing total. Most observers thought this was close to the upper limit for humans. Kobayashi had other ideas. The student smashed the competition to pieces. He ate an eye-watering 50 hot dogs, almost doubling the record. 'People think that if you have a huge appetite, then you'll be better at it,' he said. 'But, actually, it's how you confront the food that is brought to you.'

Kobayashi had eaten more than any competitor in history not because he had a surgically enlarged stomach or an extra oesophagus (as some competitors alleged); rather, he triumphed via the aggregation of marginal gains. By failing in all sorts of small, well-measured, rigorously tested ways, he iterated his way to success. It was bottom-up rather than top-down, if you'll forgive the expression.

And if this approach can be applied to eating salty tubes of sandwiched meat, it can be applied to almost anything.

VI

To conclude this chapter, let's examine the concept of marginal gains in visual form. The process of optimisation can be compared to trying to get to the top of a summit. Suppose you start from a position below the summit of the smaller of two hills, Point A, and take a tiny step in a particular direction. You then test to see if you have gone up and, if you have, you take another small step, and test again.

In this way, by taking lots of small steps, each rigorously examined to see if it is taking you in the right direction, you will eventually end up at the smaller summit. Indeed, this method is so powerful that it will work even if you are wearing a blindfold, as the business expert Eric Ries has written in an excellent essay on the art of optimisation.[13]

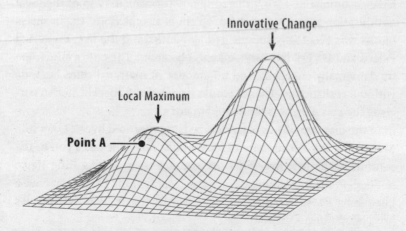

This is the potency of marginal gains. By dividing a big challenge into small parts, you are able to create rigorous tests, and thus deliver incremental improvements. Each may seem small or, as Brailsford often says, 'virtually negligible', but over time, and with discipline, they accumulate. You eventually reach the optimum point, the summit of the smaller hill. This is the Local Maximum[14]. It is often the difference between winning and losing, whether in sport, business or speed-eating hot dogs.

But this visualisation also reveals the inherent limitations of marginal gains. Often in business, technology and life, progress is not about small, well-delivered steps, but creative leaps. It is about acts of imagination that can transform the entire landscape of a problem. Indeed, these are sometimes the most important drivers of change in the modern world.

To see this difference, take Blockbuster. This was a business based around the renting of videos and later DVDs. As a concept it fared well for more than two decades, delivering an impressive rate of return. You can imagine a manager at the company using a marginal gains approach: altering the company's logo, tweaking the design of the shelving at the stores, trialling different discount approaches like two-for-one, and so on.

Each of these tests would have been useful. Over time they would have accumulated, taking the company towards the top of the local optimisation summit. But the problem is also obvious: the business model was eventually superseded by Netflix and the like, rendering videos and DVDs, to a large extent, obsolete.* The entire landscape fundamentally changed. And no amount of marginal gains (at least within a realistic timeframe) would have helped Blockbuster to survive. The company was liquidated in 2013.†

In the diagram, the new landscape is represented by the taller hill. Marginal gains is a strategy of local optimisation: it takes you to the summit of the first hill. But once you are there, taking little steps,

---

* Blockbuster turned down a chance to purchase the then fledgling Netflix for $50 million in 2000.

† In many cases genetic evolution is also a strategy for local optimisation. Many optimisation algorithms – computer programmes that broadly mimic the evolutionary process – have steps where large changes are made at regular intervals to explore distant parts of the parameter space, and thus move away from the local optimum towards a higher peak.

however well tested, runs out of traction. To have stayed ahead of the competition, Blockbuster would have needed to move into an entirely new space, leveraging new technology and fresh insights.

There is an ongoing debate in the political, scientific and business world about whether to focus on the bold leaps that lead to new conceptual terrain, or on the marginal gains that help to optimise one's existing fundamental assumptions. Is it about testing small assumptions or big ones; is it about transforming the world or tweaking it; is it about considering the big picture (the so-called *gestalt*) or the fine detail (the margins)?

The simple answer, however, is that it has to be both. At the level of the system and, increasingly, at the level of the organisation, success is about developing the capacity to think big and small, to be both imaginative and disciplined, to immerse oneself in the minutiae of a problem and to stand beyond it in order to glimpse the wider vista.

In this chapter we have looked at small steps and found that they are driven by discovering little failures. Marginal gains, as a philosophy, absolutely depends on the ability to detect and learn from small, often latent weaknesses. Now we are going to look at giant leaps, the audacious changes in technology, design and science that transform our world.

And we will see that beneath the inspirational stories told about these shifts, the deepest and most overlooked truth is that innovation cannot happen without failure. Indeed, the aversion to failure is the single largest obstacle to creative change, not just in business but beyond.

10

How Failure Drives Innovation

I

The headquarters of Dyson are in a futuristic building about forty miles west of Oxford. Outside the front entrance is a Harrier jump jet – not a replica, a real one – and a high-speed landing craft. They both hint at the unconventionality of what goes on inside.

James Dyson, the chairman and chief engineer of the company, works in a glass-fronted office just above the entrance. Along the back wall are the beautifully conceived products that have turned him into an icon of British innovation: super-efficient vacuum cleaners, futuristic hand dryers, and other devices yet to roll off the production line. In all, he has applied for more than four thousand patents.[1]

Progress is often driven not by the accumulation of small steps, but by dramatic leaps. The television wasn't an iteration of a previous device, it was a new technology altogether. Einstein's General Theory of Relativity didn't tinker with Newton's Law of Universal Gravitation, it replaced it in almost every detail. Likewise Dyson's dual-cyclone vacuum cleaner was not a marginal improvement on the conventional Hoover that existed at the time, it represented a shift that altered the way insiders think about the very problem of removing dust and hair from household floors.

Dyson is an evangelist for the creative process of change, not least because he believes it is fundamentally misconceived in the world today. As we talk in his office, he darts around picking up papers, patents, textbooks, and his own designs to illustrate his argument. He is tall, bright-eyed and restless. A conversation scheduled for half an hour continues late into the evening, so that by the end the sun has gone down, and his expressive face is lit only by a table lamp (designed, incidentally, by his son: it contains an LED light that lasts for 160,000 hours rather than the usual 2,000).

He says:

> People think of creativity as a mystical process. The idea is that creative insights emerge from the ether, through pure contemplation. This model conceives of innovation as something that happens to people, normally geniuses. But this could not be more wrong. Creativity is something that has to be worked at, and it has specific characteristics. Unless we understand how it happens, we will not improve our creativity, as a society or as a world.

Dyson's journey into the nature of creativity started while vacuuming his own home, a small farmhouse in the west of England, on a Saturday morning in his mid-twenties. Like everyone else he was struck by just how quickly his cleaner lost suction. 'It was a top of the range Hoover,' he says. 'It had one of the most powerful vacuum motors in the world. But it lost its suction within minutes. It started to let out this high-pitched scream. I had faced the problem before Growing up, it had been my chore to vacuum the family home and the suction was a constant bugbear. But this time I just snapped.'

Dyson strode into his garden and opened up the device. Inside he could see the basic engineering proposition of the conventional vacuum cleaner: a motor, a bag (which also doubled as a filter) and a tube. The logic was simple: dust and air is sucked into the bag, the air escapes through the small holes in the lining of the bag and into the motor, while the dust (thicker than the air) stays in the bag. He says:

> The bag was full of dust and so I assumed this was the reason that it had lost suction. So I ripped open the bag, emptied out the dust and Sellotaped it back up again. But when I went back to vacuum in the house, the efficiency was no better. The screaming started straight away. There was no suction.
>
> I suddenly realised that the real problem was not that the bag was

full; it was the thin lining of dust on the inside of the bag. The walls of the bag were clogged. The fine dust was blocking the filter. And that is why performance in conventional vacuum cleaners dips so rapidly; it is the very first dust that blocks them up.

This realisation triggered a new thought: what if there were no bag? What if you could make an entirely bag-less vacuum cleaner? 'If you could find a way of removing the dust from the air another way, without using a conventional bag, you would no longer lose suction because of a blocked filter,' he says. 'It would revolutionise vacuum cleaning.'

This idea percolated in Dyson's mind for the next three years. A graduate of the Royal College of Art, he was already a qualified engineer and was helping to run a local company in Bath. He enjoyed pulling things apart and seeing how they worked. He was curious, inquisitive and willing to engage with a difficulty rather than just accepting it. But now he had a live problem, one that intrigued him.

It wasn't until he went to a timber merchant that the solution powered into his mind like a thunderbolt.

Nowadays you pick up wood from a merchant and just walk out. In the old days, they virtually had to cut and plane it for you. There was a lot of hanging about. As I stood there waiting I noticed this ducting going off the machines. It travelled along to this thing on the roof, thirty or forty foot tall.

It was a cyclone [a cone-shaped device that changes the dynamics of the airflow, separating the dust from the air via centrifugal force]. It was made of galvanised steel. And although a ton of dust was coming off the machines as they cut the wood, there was no dust coming out of the chimney at the top. I was intrigued. This thing was collecting fine dust all day long and it didn't look as though it was blocking at all.

Dyson rushed home. This was his moment of insight. 'I vaguely knew about cyclones, but not really the detail. But I was fascinated to see if it would work in miniature form. I got an old cardboard box and made a replica of what I had seen with gaffer tape and cardboard. I then connected it via a bit of hose to an upright vacuum cleaner. And I had my cardboard cyclone.'

His heart was beating fast as he pushed it around the house. Would it work? 'It seemed absolutely fine,' he says. 'It seemed to be picking up dust, but the dust didn't seem to be coming out of the chimney. I went to my boss and said: "I think I have an interesting idea."'

This simple idea, this moment of insight, would ultimately make Dyson a personal fortune in excess of £3 billion.

II

A number of things jump out about the Dyson story. The first is that the solution seems rather obvious in hindsight. This is often the case with innovation, and it's something we will come back to.

But now consider a couple of other aspects of the story. The first is that the creative process started with a *problem*, what you might even call a failure, in the existing technology. The vacuum cleaner kept blocking. It let out a screaming noise. Dyson had to keep bending down to pick up bits of rubbish by hand.

Had everything been going smoothly Dyson would have had no motivation to change things. Moreover, he would have had no intellectual challenge to sink his teeth into. It was the very nature of the engineering problem that sparked a possible solution (a bag-less vacuum cleaner).

And this turns out to be an almost perfect metaphor for the creative process, whether it involves vacuum cleaners, a quest for a new brand name, or a new scientific theory. Creativity is, in many respects, a *response*.

Relativity was a response to the failure of Newtonian mechanics to make accurate predictions when objects were moving at fast speeds.

Masking tape was a response to the failure of existing adhesive tape, which would rip the paint off when it was removed from cars and walls.

The collapsible buggy was a response to the impracticality of unwieldy prams (Owen Maclaren, the designer, came up with the idea after watching his daughter struggling with a pram while out with his granddaughter).

The wind-up radio was a response to the lack of batteries in Africa, something that was hampering the spread of educational information (Trevor Baylis came up with the idea after watching a television programme on AIDS).

The ATM was a response to the problem of getting hold of cash outside opening hours. It was invented by John Shepherd-Barron while lying in the bath one night, worrying because he had forgotten to go to the bank.

Dropbox, as we have seen, was a response to the problem of forgetting your flash drive and thus not having access to important files.

This aspect of the creative process, the fact that it emerges in response to a particular difficulty, has spawned its own terminology. It is called the 'problem phase' of innovation. 'The damn thing had been bugging me for years,' Dyson says of the conventional vacuum cleaner. 'I couldn't bear the inefficiency of the technology. It wasn't so much a "problem phase" as a "hatred phase".'

We often leave this aspect of the creative process out of the picture. We focus on the moment of epiphany, the detonation of insight that happened when Newton was hit by the apple or Archimedes was taking a bath. That is perhaps why creativity seems so ethereal. The idea is that such insights could happen anytime, anywhere. It is just a matter of sitting back and letting them flow.

But this leaves out an indispensable feature of creativity. Without a problem, without a failure, without a flaw, without a frustration, innovation has nothing to latch on to. It loses its pivot. As Dyson puts it: 'Creativity should be thought of as a dialogue. You have to have a problem before you can have the game-changing riposte.'

Perhaps the most graphic way to glimpse the responsive nature of creativity is to consider an experiment by Charlan Nemeth, a psychologist at the University of California, Berkeley, and her colleagues.[2] She took 265 female undergraduates and randomly divided them into five-person teams. Each team was given the same task: to come up with ideas about how to reduce traffic congestion in the San Francisco Bay Area. These five-person teams were then assigned to one of three ways of working.

The first group were given the instruction to brainstorm. This is one of the most influential creativity techniques in history, and it is based on the mystical conception of how creativity happens: through contemplation and the free flow of ideas. In brainstorming the entire approach is to *remove* obstacles. It is to minimise challenges. People are warned not to criticise each other, or point out the difficulties in each other's suggestions. Blockages are bad. Negative feedback is a sin.

As Alex Faickney Osborn, an advertising executive who wrote a series of bestselling books on brainstorming in the 1940s and 1950s, put it: 'Creativity is so delicate a flower that praise tends to make it bloom, while discouragement often nips it in the bud.'[3]

The second group were given no guidelines at all: they were allowed to come up with ideas in any way they thought best.

But the third group were actively encouraged to point out the flaws in each other's ideas. Their instructions read: 'Most research and advice suggests that the best way to come up with good solutions is to come up with many solutions. Free-wheeling is welcome; don't be afraid to say anything that comes to mind. However, in addition, most studies suggest that *you should debate and even criticise each other's ideas* [my italics].'

The results were remarkable. The groups with the dissent and criticise guidelines generated 25 per cent more ideas than those who were brainstorming (or who had no instructions). Just as striking, when individuals were later asked to come up with more solutions for the traffic problem, those with the dissent guidelines generated twice as many new ideas as the brainstormers.

Further studies have shown that those who dissent rather than brainstorm produce not just more ideas, but more productive and imaginative ideas. As Nemeth put it: 'The basic finding is that the encouragement of debate – and even criticism if warranted – appears to stimulate more creative ideas. And cultures that permit and even encourage such expression of differing viewpoints may stimulate the most innovation.'

The reason is not difficult to identify. The problem with brainstorming is not its insistence on free-wheeling or quick association. Rather, it is that when these ideas are not checked by the feedback of criticism, they have nothing to respond to. Criticism surfaces problems. It brings difficulties to light. This forces us to think afresh. When our assumptions are violated we are nudged into a new relationship with reality. Removing failure from innovation is like removing oxygen from a fire.

Think back to Dyson and his Hoover. It was the flaw in the existing technology that forced Dyson to think about cleaning in a new way. The blockage in the filter wasn't something to hide away from, or pretend wasn't there. Rather, the blockage, the failure, was a gilt-edged invitation to re-imagine vacuum-cleaning.

Imagination is not fragile. It feeds off flaws, difficulties and problems. Insulating ourselves from failures – whether via brainstorming guidelines, the familiar cultural taboo on criticism or the influence of cognitive dissonance* – is to rob one of our most valuable mental faculties of fuel.

'It always starts with a problem,' Dyson says. 'I hated vacuum cleaners for twenty years, but I hated hand dryers for even longer. If they had worked perfectly, I would have had no motivation to come up with a new solution. But more importantly I would not have had the context to offer a creative solution. Failures feed the imagination. You cannot have the one without the other.'

Perhaps the most eloquent testimony to the creative power of error comes from a different experiment by Nemeth and a colleague.[4] In a typical free association study, we are given a word and have to respond with the first word that pops into our heads.

The problem is that when many of us free associate, we come up

---

* Think, for example, of economists who reframe their predictions, so that they never actually fail. This systematically undermines the creative process. For without the failure, without the flaw, without the frustration, they are deprived not just of the motivation but also the conceptual fuel to reimagine their models. Their considerable intellectual brilliance is directed at defending their ideas rather than revolutionising them.

with rather boring associations. If someone says 'blue', most people reply 'sky'. If someone says 'green', we say 'grass'. This is hardly the stuff of inspiration. In her free association experiment, Nemeth showed slides to volunteers. As expected, they came up with conventional, banal associations.

But then she had a lab assistant call out the wrong colour as part of the experiment. When a blue slide was shown, the assistant called out 'green'. And this is when something odd happened. When Nemeth then asked these volunteers to free associate on the colours that had been wrongly identified, they suddenly became far more creative. They came up with associations that reached way beyond tired convention. Blue became 'jeans' or 'lonely' or 'Miles Davis'.[5]

What was going on? We should now be able to glimpse an answer. Contradictory information *jars*, in much the same way that error jars. It encourages us to engage in a new way. We start to reach beyond our usual thought processes (why would you think differently when things are going just as expected?). When someone shouts out the wrong colour, our conventional mental operations are disrupted. That is when we find associations, connections, which might never have occurred to us.

And this takes us to the second crucial aspect of the Dyson story. You'll remember that in his moment of insight he essentially brought two disparate ideas together: a vacuum cleaner and a sawmill. These were two different things. They existed in two different places of vastly different scale: in the home and in the sawmill. You could almost say that they inhabited separate conceptual categories.

Dyson's innovation, stripped down to its essentials, was to merge them. He was a *connecting agent*. The act of creativity was an act, above all, of synthesis. 'I think the fact that I had so many years of frustration probably made me the perfect person to glimpse a possible solution,' he says. 'But the solution was really about combining two existing technologies.'

And it turns out that this act of connectivity is another central feature of innovation. Johannes Gutenberg invented mass printing by applying the pressing of wine (which, as a technology, had existed for many centuries) to the pressing of pages.[6]

The Wright brothers applied their understanding of manufacturing bicycles to the problem of powered flight.

The rank algorithm behind the success of Google was developed by Sergey Brin and Larry Page from an existing method of ranking academic articles.

Sellotape, a staggeringly successful commercial innovation, was developed by merging glue and cellophane.

The collapsible buggy was created by fusing the folding undercarriages for Spitfires in the Second World War with an existing technology for transporting children.

Little wonder that Steve Jobs, a master in the art of merging concepts, once said: 'Creativity is just connecting things.'

If failure sparks creativity into life, the moment of insight invariably emerges from the attempt to bridge the problem with previously unconnected ideas or technologies. It is about finding a hidden connection in order to solve a problem with meaning. But the crucial point to realise is that these processes are intimately intertwined. It is precisely because we have been hit by jarring information that we are nudged into looking for unusual connections, as we saw in the free association experiment.

To put it simply, failure and epiphany are inextricably linked. When we come up with a brilliant idea, when it pops into our mind, it has often emerged from a period of gestation. It is a consequence of engaging with a problem, sometimes, as in the case of Dyson, for many years.

As the neuroscientist David Eagleman says in his book *Incognito: The Secret Lives of the Brain*: 'When an idea is served up from behind the scenes, the neural circuitry has been working on the problems for hours or days or years, consolidating information and trying out new combinations. But you merely take credit without further wonderment at the vast, hidden political machinery behind the scenes.'[7]

Much of the literature on creativity focuses on how to trigger these moments of innovative synthesis; how to drive the problem phase towards its resolution. And it turns out that epiphanies often happen when we are in one of two types of environment.

The first is when we are switching off: having a shower, going for a walk, sipping a cold beer, daydreaming. When we are too focused, when we are thinking too literally, we can't spot the obscure associations that are so important to creativity. We have to take a step back for the 'associative state' to emerge. As the poet Julia Cameron put it: 'I learned to get out of the way and let that creative force work through me.'[8]

The other type of environment where creative moments often happen, as we have seen, is when we are being sparked by the dissent of others. When Kevin Dunbar, a psychologist at McGill University, went to look at how scientific breakthroughs actually happen, for example (he took cameras into four molecular biology labs and recorded pretty much everything that took place), he assumed that it would involve scientists beavering away in isolated contemplation.

In fact, the breakthroughs happened at lab meetings, where groups of researchers would gather around a desk to talk through their work. Why here? Because they were forced to respond to challenges and critiques from their fellow researchers. They were jarred into seeing new associations.

As the author Steven Johnson puts it: 'Questions from colleagues forced researchers to think about their experiments on a different scale or level. Group interactions challenged researchers' assumptions about their more surprising findings . . . The ground zero of innovation was not the microscope. It was the conference table.'[9]

And this helps to explain why cities are so creative, why atriums are important; in fact why any environment which allows disparate people, and therefore ideas, to bump into each other, is so conducive. They facilitate the association of diverse ideas, and bring people face to face with dissent and criticism. All help to ignite creativity.

This brief jaunt through the literature on creativity reveals one thing above all else: innovation is highly *context-dependent*. It is a response to a particular problem at a particular time and place. Take away the context, and you remove both the spur to innovation, and its raw material.

The best way to see this truth is through the phenomenon of *the multiple*. Steven Johnson runs through an entire list of breakthroughs that were conceived by different people, working independently, at almost precisely the same time.[10]

Sunspots, for example, were discovered by four scientists in four different countries in 1611. The mathematical calculus was developed by both Sir Isaac Newton and Gottfried Leibniz in the 1670s. The fore-runner to the first electric battery was invented by Ewald Georg von Kleist in 1745 and Andreas Cuneus of Leyden in 1746.

Four people independently proposed the law of the conservation of energy in the 1840s. The theory of evolution through natural selection was proposed independently by Charles Darwin and Alfred Russel Wallace (an extraordinary, unsung polymath) in the mid-nineteenth century.[11] S. Korschinsky in 1889 and Hugo de Vries in 1901 independently established the significance of genetic mutation.

Even Einstein's pioneering work has echoes in the work of his contemporaries. The French mathematician Henri Poincaré wrote about the 'Principle of Relativity' in 1904, a year before Einstein published his landmark paper on the Special Theory.

In the 1920s William Ogburn and Dorothy Thomas, two academics from Columbia University, found as many as 148 examples of independent innovation. Multiples are the norm; not the exception. They entitled their paper 'Are Inventions Inevitable?'.*

The reason harks back to the 'responsive' nature of creativity. The failures of Newton's Laws created a specific problem. It invited particular solutions. It wasn't just Einstein and Poincaré, but also Hendrik Lorentz and David Hilbert who were working on a possible remedy.[12] Indeed, the so-called 'Relativity priority dispute' is about who invented what, when.[13]

---

* There is a fascinating, related literature on how innovators have fought over the credit for particular breakthroughs. Some of these battles have been fierce, as between Newton and Leibniz, who argued over who had first thought of mathematical calculus. Less often, these disputes are resolved amicably, as between Wallace and Darwin. As one author put it: Wallace, 'admirably free from envy or jealousy', was content to remain in Darwin's shadow (Tori Reeve, *Down House: The Home of Charles Darwin*).

And that is why the seductive idea that if Einstein had been born three hundred years earlier, we could have had the benefit of the Theory of Relativity in the seventeenth century is so flawed. Relativity *couldn't* have happened back then, largely because the problems that it responded to were not yet visible.

Einstein may have seen further and deeper than his contemporaries (there is still a large role for individualism: Einstein really was a creative genius), but he wasn't pulling insights out of the ether. As Johnson writes: 'Good ideas are not conjured out of thin air.'

Dyson is well aware of this aspect of creativity. 'Every time I have gone for a patent in a particular field, someone else has got there first,' he says. 'I don't think there has been a single time in all the thousands of patents we have applied for where we were the first. With the vacuum cyclone, there were already a number of patents lodged.'

But this raises a rather obvious question. Why didn't the person who came up with the original idea for a vacuum cyclone go on to make a fortune (the first cyclone vacuum-cleaner patent was lodged as early as 1928[14])? Why did Dyson, rather than his predecessors, change the world of domestic cleaning?

We noted earlier that we tend to overlook what happens *before* the moment of epiphany. But, if anything, we are even more neglectful of what happens afterwards. This is a serious oversight because it obscures the reason why some people change the world while others are footnotes in the patent catalogue.

The eureka moment is not the endpoint of innovation, it is the start of perhaps the most fascinating stage of all.

III

Dyson strode into his workshop. He had come up with his big idea: a bag-less vacuum cleaner where dust is removed from the air by the geometry of the airflow rather than a filter. But he was pretty much alone. The directors at his company didn't back his idea (the response he received was: 'If that is such a good concept, how come Hoover and Electrolux aren't doing it already?'), so he started his own business along with a silent partner, who had provided half the capital.

Dyson's workshop was a tiny, former coach house. It had no windows and no heating. At the beginning he had no tools and precious little money. He also had huge debts, having remortgaged his house in order to start the business. But the then thirty-three-year-old (who also had three young children – and a very understanding wife) was nothing if not determined.

His first prototype, as we have seen, was the cardboard-and-gaffer-tape cyclone that he made after returning from the wood merchants. It seemed to work well. But although no dust was visible to the naked eye coming out of the top of the makeshift cyclone, he had to check whether he was getting rid of *all* the dust.

This was one of his first post-epiphany tasks. He bought some black cloth and obtained a quantity of fine white dust. Then he placed the cloth above his makeshift cyclone, vacuumed the dust and noticed that some of it was, indeed, getting through. He could see white residue on the cloth.

So he altered the dimensions of the cyclone to see if it would improve the efficiency. He tried new sizes, new shapes. Each time he would note how a small change in one dimension would impact the overall engineering solution. The key challenge was to balance airflow with separation efficiency.

With each iteration he was learning new things. He was seeing what worked. Most of the time he was failing. 'A cyclone has a number of variables: size of entry, exit, angle, diameter, length: and the trying thing is that if you change one dimension, it affects all the others.'

His discipline was astonishing. 'I couldn't afford a computer, so I would hand-write the results into a book', he recalls. 'In the first year alone, I conducted literally hundreds of experiments. It was a very, very thick book.'

But as the intensive, iterative process gradually solved the problem of separating ultra-fine dust, Dyson came up against another problem: long pieces of hair and fluff. These were not being separated from the airflow by the cyclone dynamics. 'They were just coming out of the top along with the air', he says. 'It was another huge problem and it didn't seem as if a conventional cyclone could solve it.'

The sheer scale of the problem set the stage for a second eureka moment: the dual cyclone. 'The first cyclone gets rid of the awkward strands of cotton or hair, before the air is pushed into the second cyclone, which gets rid of the finer dust,' he went on. 'You need both to make the device work properly.'

In all, it took an astonishing 5,127 prototypes before Dyson believed the technology was ready to go in the vacuum cleaner. The creative leap may have been a crucial and precious thing, but it was only the start of the creative process. The real hard yards were done patiently evolving the design via bottom-up iteration. To put it another way, with the epiphany he had vaulted onto a taller mountain in a new landscape; now he was systematically working towards this new summit.

According to Dyson:

When you file a patent, somebody is almost always there before you. A lot of your argument with the patent examiner is to say: 'Look, they may have had the eureka moment when they came back from the timber yard. They may even have created an early prototype.' But none of my forebears had made their prototypes work. Mine is statistically different. That was my decisive advantage.

Creativity, then, has a dual aspect. Insight often requires taking a step back and seeing the big picture. It is about drawing together disparate ideas. It is the art of *connection*. But to make a creative insight work requires disciplined focus. As Dyson puts it: 'If insight is about the big picture, development is about the small picture. The trick is to sustain both perspectives at the same time.'

And this turns out to be the very cornerstone of understanding how creative success happens in the world today, as alluded to at the end of the last chapter. It is often said that in a rapidly changing world innovative companies will dominate. But this is, at best, only partly true. In their book *Great by Choice*, Jim Collins and Morten Hansen show that innovation may indeed be a *necessary* condition for success, but it is by no means sufficient.[15]

Genentech, the US-based biotechnology corporation, for example, outpaced Amgen, a major competitor, by more than two times in patent productivity between 1983 and 2002 (they also outpaced

Amgen in terms of the impact of their patents as measured by the number of citations) but Amgen's financial performance outperformed that of Genentech by more than thirty to one.

This finding is by no means unusual. In their book *Will and Vision*, Gerard J. Tellis and Peter N. Golder looked at the relationship between long-term market leadership and pioneering innovation in sixty-six different commercial sectors. They found that only 9 per cent of the pioneers ended up as the final winners. They also found that 64 per cent of pioneers failed outright.[16]

Jim Collins writes: 'Gillette didn't pioneer the safety razor, Star did. Polaroid didn't pioneer the instant camera, Dubroni did. Microsoft didn't pioneer the personal computer spreadsheet, VisiCorp did. Amazon didn't pioneer online bookselling and AOL didn't pioneer online internet service.'[17]

What was the key ingredient that characterised the winners, the companies that may not have come up with an idea first, but who made it work? The answer can be conveyed in one word: *discipline*. This is not just the discipline to iterate a creative idea into a rigorous solution; it is also the discipline to get the manufacturing process perfect, the supply lines faultless, delivery seamless.[*]

Dyson was not the first to come up with the idea of a cyclone vacuum cleaner. He was not even the second, or the third. But he was the only one with the stamina to 'fail' his concept into a workable solution. And he had the rigour to create an efficient manufacturing process, so he could sell a consistent product.

His competitors confronted the same problem and had the same insight. But they didn't have the same resilience to make their idea work, let alone take it on to a working production line.

Collins takes the battle between Intel and Advanced Memory

---

[*] Getting the manufacturing process running seamlessly is often about ironing out unwanted deviations. It is about using process controls and the like to reduce variation. Creative change is often about experimentation; in other words, increasing variation. For more on this distinction, and how to reconcile them, see: http://www.forbes.com/sites/ricksmith/2014/06/11/is-six-sigma-killing-your-companys-future/

Systems as symbolic of this crucial distinction. Intel was months behind its fierce competitor in the race for the 1,000-bit memory chip. In the rush to introduce the 1103 chip, it hit major problems, including one that could actually erase data from the chip. It was so far behind the game that the outcome seemed like a forgone conclusion.

And yet Intel destroyed Advanced Memory Systems in the marketplace. They worked around the clock, creating new prototypes, iterating the chip into a workable solution. But they also ensured that they nailed all the surrounding supply issues crucial for success. As Collins puts it: 'Intel obsessed over manufacturing, delivery and scale.'

By 1973, everyone was using Intel. Its slogan is not 'Intel Creates', it is 'Intel Delivers'.

Dyson says:

It is no good creating the most beautiful products if you produce them shoddily. It is no good having the most innovative engineering solution if the consumers can't be certain it will be delivered on time. It is no good if inconsistent production means that a great idea is not translated into a polished product. The original idea is only 2 per cent of the journey. You mustn't neglect the rest.

Collins writes:

We concluded that each environment has a level of 'threshold innovation' that you need to meet to be a contender in the game ... Companies that fail even to meet the innovation threshold cannot win. But – and this surprised us – once you're above the threshold, especially in a highly turbulent environment, being more innovative doesn't seem to matter very much.[18]

Winners require innovation *and* discipline, the imagination to see the big picture and the focus to perceive the very small. 'The great task, rarely achieved, is to blend creative intensity with relentless discipline so as to amplify the creativity rather than destroy it,' Collins writes. 'When you marry operating excellence with innovation, you multiply the value of your creativity.'[19]

IV

Let us conclude our study of creativity by looking at Pixar, an animation company that draws together many of these strands. As an institution it has almost no peers in its reputation for innovation. When Ed Catmull, the company's long-serving president, wrote his autobiography he entitled it *Creativity Inc.*

Pixar blockbusters include *Toy Story*, *Monsters, Inc.* and *Finding Nemo*. The films have generated an average worldwide gross of over $600 million. They have been critical successes, too, winning Oscars in multiple categories. *Toy Story* and *Toy Story 2* both received 100 per cent scores on Rotten Tomatoes.

Naturally Pixar has a lot of clever, creative people working in its offices. Lead authors come up with terrific storylines for the latest film. They are presented to the wider group at large meetings. They are often applauded afterwards. A good storyline is an act of creative synthesis: bringing disparate narrative strands together in novel form. It is a crucial part of the Pixar process.

But now consider what happens next. The storyline is pulled apart. As the animation gets into operation, each frame, each strand of the story, each scene is subject to debate, dissent and testing. All told, it takes around twelve thousand storyboard drawings to make one ninety-minute feature, and because of the iterative process, story teams often create more than 125,000 storyboards by the time the film is actually delivered.

Monsters, Inc. is a perfect illustration of a creative idea adapted in the light of criticism. It started off with a plot centred on a middle-aged accountant, who hates his job and who is given a sketchbook by his mum. As a child he had drawn some monsters in the sketchbook and that night they turn up in his bedroom, but only the accountant can see them. These monsters become the fears he had never engaged with, and over time he learns to understand them, and thus overcome them.

The final version, which would wow the world (and take $560 million at the box office), is rather different. It tells the story of Sulley, a rather unkempt monster, and his unlikely friendship with a little girl

nicknamed Boo. Over the period of the film's development it was
altered in the light of criticism and the testing of ideas. Even after the
main protagonist had changed to a little girl rather than a middle-
aged accountant, the plot continued to evolve. Catmull has
written:

> The human protagonist was a six-year-old named Mary. Then she
> was seven, named Boo, and bossy – even domineering. Finally Boo
> was turned into a fearless, preverbal toddler. The idea of Sulley's
> buddy character – the round, one-eyed Mike, voiced by Billy Crystal
> – wasn't added until more than a year after the first treatment was
> written. The process of determining the rules of the incredibly intri-
> cate world Pete [the director of the film] created also took him down
> countless blind alleys – until eventually those blind alleys converged
> on a path that led the story where it needed to go.[20]

Toy Story 2 is another archetype of the Pixar creative process. Just
a year out from its theatrical release, the narrative was not right. The
story is about whether Woody, a toy cowboy, will leave the pampered
life he enjoys on the shelf of a collector to go back to Andy, who he
loves. The problem is that this is a Disney movie, and so the audience
knows at the outset that it will have a happy ending: Woody will
reunite with Andy.

'What the film needed were reasons to believe that Woody was
facing a real dilemma, and one that viewers could relate to. What it
needed, in other words, was drama,' Catmull writes in his memoir.
With the clock ticking, the process of iteration took on an urgent
feel. People were working overtime, late into the night, testing ideas.

One artist turned up at work with his small child, intending to
take him to nursery, but forgot. After he had been at work a couple
of hours, his wife phoned to ask how the drop-off had gone. Suddenly
he realised that he'd left the child in the boiling hot car park. They
rushed out and poured cold water on the unconscious child.
Thankfully he was OK, but the episode revealed how stretched the
staff had become.

Hundreds of small changes were made to the film. Dozens of

larger changes were made too. There was also one major alteration to the plot: the story had always started with Woody suffering
a rip in his arm that meant Andy left him behind when going to
cowboy camp. At this point there was a decision to add a new
character.

'[We] added a character named Wheezy the penguin, who tells
Woody that he has been on that same shelf for months because of a
broken squeaker,' Catmull says. 'Wheezy introduces the idea early on
that no matter how cherished, when a toy gets damaged, it is likely to
be shelved, tossed aside – maybe for good. Wheezy, then, establishes
the emotional stakes of the story.'

The plot now had real tension. Will Woody stay with someone he
loves, knowing he will eventually be discarded, or choose a world
where he can be pampered forever? It is a theme with high crossover
and moral seriousness. Ultimately, Woody chooses Andy but in the
foreknowledge that the decision will lead to future unhappiness. 'I
can't stop Andy from growing up,' he says to Stinky Pete. 'But I
wouldn't miss it for the world.'

Catmull says:

> Early on, all of our movies suck. That's a blunt assessment, I know, but
> I . . . choose that phrasing because saying it in a softer way fails to
> convey how bad the first versions of our films really are. I'm not trying
> to be modest or self-effacing by saying this. Pixar films are not good at
> first, and our job is to make them go . . . from suck to non-suck . . .
>
> We are true believers in the power of bracing, candid feedback
> and the iterative process – reworking, reworking and reworking
> again, until a flawed story finds its throughline or a hollow character
> finds its soul.

Does this sound familiar? It is an almost perfect description of the
dissent guidelines in the Nemeth experiment.

It is sometimes said that testing may be important for engineers
and hard items like vacuum cleaners, nozzles and curtain rails, but it
doesn't apply to soft, intangible problems like writing novels or
scripts for children's animations. In fact, iteration is vital for both. It

is not an optional extra; it is an indispensable aspect of the creative process.

Consider what happened when Pixar considered abandoning its iron discipline; when they tried to go from epiphany to final product in one large, mystical leap. 'This then became our goal – finalise the script *before* we start making the film,' Catmull writes about *Finding Nemo*. 'We were confident that locking in the story early would yield not just a phenomenal movie but a cost-efficient production.'

It didn't work. The initial idea by Andrew Stanton, one of Pixar's most respected directors, was about an overprotective clownfish called Marlin, looking for his son. His pitch to the team was superb. 'The narrative, as he described it, would be intercut with a series of flashbacks that explained what had happened to make Nemo's father such an overprotective worrywart when it came to his son,' Catmull writes. 'He seamlessly wove together two stories: what was happening in Marlin's world, during the epic search after Nemo is scooped up by a scuba diver, and what was happening in the aquarium in Sydney, where Nemo had ended up with a group of tropical fish called "the Tank Gang".'

The response in the room was one of stunned admiration. But once the creative blueprint was put into production, flaws began to emerge. The flashbacks proved confusing to test audiences. Marlin seemed unlikable because it took so long to see why he had been so overprotective. When Michael Eisner of Disney saw the rough cut he was not impressed. 'Yesterday we saw for the second time the next Pixar movie *Finding Nemo*. It's OK, but nowhere near as good as their previous films.'

At this point Pixar reverted to disciplined iteration. First they adapted the narrative to a more chronological approach – and it began to align. The tale of the Tank Gang became a subplot. Other changes, smaller, but cumulatively significant, began to emerge. By the end, the film had gone from suck to non-suck. Catmull writes:

> Despite our hopes that *Finding Nemo* would be the film that changed the way we did business, we ended up making as many adjustments

during production as we had on any other film we had made. The result, of course, was a movie we're incredibly proud of, one that went on to become the highest grossing animated film ever.

The only thing it didn't do was transform our production process.[21]

V

Dyson, Catmull and the other innovators we have encountered offer a powerful rebuke to the way we conventionally think about creativity. To spark the imagination and take our insights to their fullest expression, we should not insulate ourselves from failure; rather, we should engage with it.

This perspective does not only have large implications for innovation, it also has direct implications for the way we teach. Today education is conceived as providing young people with a body of knowledge. Students are rewarded when they apply this knowledge correctly. Failures are punished.

But this is surely only one part of how we learn. We learn not just by being correct, but also by being wrong. It is when we fail that we learn new things, push the boundaries, and become more creative. Nobody had a new insight by regurgitating information, however sophisticated.

Dyson says:

> We live in a world of experts. There is nothing particularly wrong with that. The expertise we have developed is crucial for all of us. But when we are trying to solve new problems, in business or technology, we need to reach beyond our current expertise. We do not want to know how to *apply* the rules; we want to *break* the rules. We do that by failing – and learning.

Dyson advocates that we provide children with the tools they need not just to answer questions, but to ask questions. 'The problem with academia is that it is about being good at remembering things like chemical formulae and theories, because that is what you have to regurgitate. But children are not allowed to learn through experimenting and experience. This is a great pity. You need both.'

One of the most powerful aspects of the Dyson story is that it evokes a point that was made in Chapter 7; namely, that technological change is often driven by the synergy between practical and theoretical knowledge. One of the first things Dyson did when he had the insight for a cyclone cleaner was to buy two books on the mathematical theory of how cyclones work. He also went to visit the author of one of those books, an academic called R. G. Dorman.[22]

This was hugely helpful to Dyson. It allowed him to understand cyclone dynamics more fully. It played a role in directing his research and gave him a powerful background on the mathematics of separation efficiency. But it was by no means sufficient. The theory was too abstract to lead him directly to the precise dimensions that would deliver a functional vacuum cleaner.

Moreover, as Dyson iterated his device, he discovered that the theory had flaws. Dorman's equation predicted that cyclones would only be able to remove fine dust down to a lower limit of 20 microns. But Dyson quickly broke through this theoretical limit. By the end, his cyclone could separate dust smaller than 0.3 microns (this is approximately the size of the particles in cigarette smoke). Dyson's practical engagement with the problem had forced a change in the theory.

And this is invariably how progress happens. It is an interplay between the practical and the theoretical, between top-down and bottom-up, between creativity and discipline, between the small picture and the big picture. The crucial point – and the one that is most dramatically overlooked in our culture – is that in all these things, failure is a blessing, not a curse. It is the jolt that inspires creativity and the selection test that drives evolution.

Failure has many dimensions, many subtle meanings, but unless we see it in a new light, as a friend rather than a foe, it will remain woefully underexploited. Andrew Stanton, director of *Finding Nemo* and *WALL-E*, has said:

My strategy has always been: be wrong as fast as we can . . . which basically means, we're gonna screw up, let's just admit that. Let's not be afraid of that. But let's do it as fast as we can so we can get to the answer. You can't get to adulthood before you go through puberty. I won't get it right the first time, but I will get it wrong really soon, really quickly.

As our conversation draws to a close, I wonder why Dyson still comes into his office every day, rather than enjoying his wealth. 'A lot of people ask me that. They seem to assume that I spend my life with my feet up,' he says, smiling.

But the answer is simple: I love the creative process. I love coming in here every day and testing new ideas. We have plans for many new products in the coming years.

But we are also still developing the vacuum cleaner. We didn't stop at the 5,127th prototype, you know. Today, we have forty-eight cyclone technology, which spins the dust at 200,000 Gs. It exerts a huge centrifugal force, which is why it can separate the tiniest particles. But even this isn't the end. What excites me most is that we are still only at the beginning.

PART 5

The Blame Game

11

Libyan Arab Airlines Flight 114

I

It is February 1973. The atmosphere in the Middle East is like a tinder-box. More than five years earlier in the Six Day War between Israel and forces from Egypt, Jordan and Syria there were more than 20,000 fatalities, mostly on the Arab side. In just eight months' time, the Yom Kippur War will take place, leading to another 15,000 deaths. Tensions are on a hair-trigger.

Just weeks earlier, Israel has received intelligence that Arab terrorists are planning to hijack a commercial airliner in order to crash it into a densely populated area, probably Tel Aviv, or into the nuclear installation at Dimona. The Israeli Air Force is on high alert.

At 13.54 on 21 February a commercial airliner is picked up by Israeli radar crossing the Gulf of Suez into the Israeli war zone. It is following a 'hostile' trajectory, the same as the one flown by Egyptian warplanes. Is it merely off course? This is possible, given that Egypt and the Sinai peninsula have been engulfed by a sandstorm, reducing external visibility. But Israeli commanders want to be sure. At 13.56, Israeli F-4 Phantoms are dispatched to intercept the airliner.[1]

Three minutes later the Phantoms reach the plane and confirm that it is a Libyan airliner. Flying alongside the jet they can see the Libyan crew through the window of the cockpit. The commanders at base are immediately suspicious. If the plane was destined for Cairo, it is more than 100 miles off course. Moreover, the Libyan state is a well-known sponsor of international terrorism. Could this be a hostile threat?

The Israelis are concerned about something else too. When flying towards Sinai, the airliner crossed some of the most sensitive areas of Egyptian airspace, and yet wasn't intercepted by Egyptian MiG fighter aircraft. Why? Egypt has a highly efficient early warning system. They, like Israel, are acutely sensitive about their airspace being breached. Just a few months earlier, an Ethiopian passenger jet that had inadvertently veered into their war zone, was shot down and destroyed. Why has there been no response from the Egyptians?

The commanders in Tel Aviv become ever more confident that this is not an ordinary passenger jet, but is flying a military mission with the explicit consent of their enemies in Cairo. Tensions at the command centre are starting to rise.

The Israeli pilots are ordered to instruct the Libyan airliner to land at the Rephidim airbase (today called the Bir Gifgafa airfield) before it can reach the heart of Israel. The Phantoms do this by rocking their wings and communicating the instruction by radio. The Libyan crew should acknowledge the request by rocking their wings in response and opening radio channels. They do neither. Instead they continue on their course towards Israel.

The Phantoms are in no doubt that the instruction was received. One Israeli pilot flew to within a few metres of the airliner and looked directly into the eyes of the co-pilot. He hand-gestured for the plane to land and the co-pilot responded with hand signals of his own, indicating that he had understood the instruction. And yet now the airliner is continuing on its trajectory towards Israel.

It doesn't make sense, unless . . .

At 14.01 the Phantoms are ordered to fire tracer shells in front of the nose of the airliner to force it to land. At last the airliner responds. It turns towards the Rephidim airbase, descends to 5,000 feet and lowers its landing gear. But then, without warning, it suddenly turns back towards the west, as if trying to escape. It revs up its engines and begins to ascend.

The Israelis are baffled. The first duty of a captain is to ensure the safety of his passengers. Surely, if that is his objective, he *must* land the plane.

The Israelis now suspect that the airliner is trying to escape at any cost. They begin to wonder if there are any passengers actually on board the jet. At 14.05 the Israeli pilots are instructed to look through the windows of the passenger cabin. They report that all the window shades are down. But this is strange too. Even when a movie is playing, some of the shades are usually up.

The Israelis are now near-certain that this is a hostile plane, probably without passengers on board. It must be forced to land, not least to deter future incursions of the same kind.

At 14.08 shots are fired at the wing tips of the airliner and yet it still defies the instruction to land. Finally, at 14.10, the Phantoms shoot at the base of the wings, forcing it down. The pilot very nearly makes a successful crash-landing in the desert below, but after skidding for 600 metres the plane hits a sand dune and explodes.

Libyan Arab Airlines Flight 114 is, in fact, a perfectly ordinary passenger flight from Benghazi to Cairo, which has veered off course, inadvertently flying into the Israeli warzone. Of the 113 passengers and crew 108 die in the fireball.

The following day there is understandable outrage around the world. How could the Israelis (who initially denied responsibility) have shot down an unarmed civilian plane? How dare they massacre so many innocents? What on earth were they thinking? The Israeli military leadership are blamed for a terrible tragedy.

The Israelis, for their part, are perplexed when they discover that Libyan Arab Airlines Flight 114 was a routine flight from Benghazi to Cairo with no terrorist agenda. The Egyptian state was not involved. It was a plane full of innocent travellers and holidaymakers. The Israeli Air Force have been involved in a devastating tragedy.

But from their perspective, which the rest of the world has not yet had access to, there was an equal and opposite response: to blame the crew of the airliner. After all, why didn't they land? They had come within a few thousand feet of the Rephidim runway. Why did they turn west? Why did they keep going even after having their wing tips shot at by the Phantoms?

Were they mad? Or just criminally negligent?

This is a chapter about the psychology of blame. We will see that this is an all-too-common response to failures and adverse events of all kinds. When something goes wrong, we like to point the finger at *someone else*. We like to collapse what could be a highly complex event into a simple headline: 'Israeli murderers kill 108 innocents' or 'negligent crew wilfully ignore instruction to land.'

For the most part in this chapter, we will look at how blame attaches to the failures that occur in safety critical industries such as aviation and healthcare, before extending this analysis to other organisations and contexts. We will see that blame is, in many respects, a subversion of the narrative fallacy: an oversimplification driven by biases in the human brain. We will also see that it has subtle but measurable consequences, undermining our capacity to learn.

A quick recap. We have seen that progress is driven by learning from failure and, in the previous two sections, looked at the evolutionary framework that underpins this idea. We also looked at organisations that have harnessed the evolutionary mechanism to drive progress, and confronted failure to inspire creative leaps. But we have also seen that an evolutionary system on its own is not enough. When we looked at the Virginia Mason Health System in Chapter 3, we noted that a new system created to learn from mistakes initially made no difference because professionals didn't make any reports. The information was suppressed due to a fear of blame and cognitive dissonance.

If the previous two sections of the book were about systems that institutionalise the evolutionary mechanism, the next two sections will look at the psychological and cultural conditions that enable it to flourish. In Part 5 we will return to our study of cognitive dissonance, which can be thought of as the internal anxieties that cause us to squander the information provided by failure. And we will look at how to combat this tendency, thus unleashing openness, resilience and growth. In this chapter and the next, we will look at the *external* pressures that lead people to suppress the information vital for adaptation: namely the fear of blame. The instinct to blame creates powerful and often self-reinforcing dynamics within organisations and cultures which have to be addressed if meaningful evolution is going to take place.

Think of it like this: if our first reaction is to assume that the person

closest to a mistake has been negligent or malign, then blame will
flow freely and the *anticipation* of blame will cause people to cover
up their mistakes. But if our first reaction is to regard error as a
learning opportunity, then we will be motivated to investigate what
really happened.

It may be that after proper investigation we discover the person
who made the error really has been negligent or malign, in which
case blame will be fully justified. But we may find that the error was
caused not by negligence, but by a systemic defect – just as with the
B-17 bombers in Chapter 1, where identical levers side by side in
the cockpit (one linked to the flaps and the other to the landing gear)
were causing accidents during landing.

Proper investigation achieves two things: it reveals a crucial learning opportunity, which means that the systemic problem can be
fixed, leading to meaningful evolution. But it has a cultural consequence too: professionals will feel empowered to be open about
honest mistakes, along with other vital information, because they
know that they will not be unfairly penalised – thus driving evolution still further.

In short, we have to engage with the complexity of the world if we
are to learn from it; we have to resist the hardwired tendency to
blame instantly, and look deeper into the factors surrounding error if
we are going to figure out what really happened and thus create a
culture based upon openness and honesty rather than defensiveness
and back-covering.

With this in mind, let us return to Libyan Arab Airlines Flight 114
and try to figure out what actually happened on the afternoon of 21
February 1973. In revisiting the tragedy we will return to the work
of Zvi Lanir, a decision-researcher whose influential article 'The
Reasonable Choice of Disaster', published in the *Journal of Strategic
Studies*, must rate as among the most gripping academic papers ever
written.

Why, he asks, did the airliner keep flying when it had been confronted by Israeli Phantom jets? Why did it try to escape back towards
Egypt? If it was a passenger jet, why did the crew endanger the lives
of their passengers, as well as their own lives?

We only have the answers to these questions for a simple but profound reason: the black box survived the fireball. This provides us with the opportunity for a proper investigation, and therefore to do something that the emotionally driven, often self-serving blame game, with its crude simplifications, can never achieve: reform of the system.

II

Libyan Arab Airlines Flight 114 is on a routine flight from Benghazi to Cairo. The captain, in the front left of the cockpit, is French, as is the flight engineer, who is sitting behind him. The co-pilot, front right, is Libyan. There has been a sandstorm across Egypt, reducing visibility.

The pilot and flight engineer are chatting amiably. The co-pilot, who is not proficient in French, is not taking part in the conversation. All three are oblivious to the fact that the aircraft has drifted more than sixty miles off course, and has been flying over Egyptian military installations.

This deviation should have been picked up by the Egyptian military's early warning system, but because of the sandstorm and other subtleties associated with the set-up of the system, it is not. The airliner is now about to enter the Israeli warzone over Sinai.

It is not until 13.44 that the pilot begins to have doubts about their position. He raises his concerns with the engineer, but not with the co-pilot. At 13.52, he receives permission from Air Traffic Control at Cairo Approach to begin his descent.

At 13.56 the pilot tries to pick up the radio transmitter signal from Cairo airport, but it is in a different position from where he was expecting. His confusion mounts. Are they off course? Is that the correct signal? He continues to fly 'as scheduled' but he is now losing situational awareness. Cairo Approach has not yet indicated that he is now more than eighty miles off course.

At 13.59 Cairo Approach finally informs the pilot that the airliner is deviating from the airport. They tell him to 'stick to BEACON and report position', but the Libyan co-pilot indicates that they are struggling to receive the signal from the radio beacon. A couple of minutes later Cairo Approach ask the pilot to start communicating directly with Cairo Control at the airport, indicating that they believe he is nearing his destination.

The confusion in the cockpit mounts. Are they near Cairo? Why is that beacon signal so far to the west? But even as they are trying to figure out their position, they are startled by something completely unexpected: the roar of fighter jets. They are now surrounded by high-speed military aircraft.

Crucially, the co-pilot misidentifies the aircraft as Egyptian MiGs rather than Israeli F-4 Phantoms, despite the highly visible Shield of David on their bodies. 'Four MiGs behind us,' he says.

Given the good relationship between Libya and Egypt, the crew assume that these planes must be friendly. They assume that they have come to guide the plane, which they now accept must be off course, to Cairo airport. The captain informs Cairo Control: 'I guess we have some problems with our heading and we now have four MiGs trying to get behind us.'

But one of the 'MiGs' pulls up alongside the cockpit and starts to gesticulate. He seems to be ordering them to land. Why the aggression? They are friendly, aren't they? The pilot, clearly now in a state of bewilderment, reacts vocally. 'Oh, no! I don't understand such language,' he says (in other words 'that's no way for the MiGs to behave!'), but he is still communicating in French, and the co-pilot doesn't understand.

The crew are beginning to panic. Perception is narrowing. What on earth do these jets want?

Between 1406 and 1410 Cairo Control is silent but the crew are no longer focused on their position. Tracer shells are fired in front of the nose of the aircraft. The crew are becoming frantic. Why are they firing at us?

They know that there are two airports in the Egyptian capital: Cairo West, the civilian airport, and Cairo East, a military airport. Could it be that they have over-flown Cairo West and veered into the territory of Cairo East? If so, perhaps the MiGs are trying to chivvy the airliner back to the civilian airport. Perhaps that is where they want them to land.

They turn the plane towards the west and start to descend. The captain drops the landing gear into place. But now they notice that they are not at Cairo West after all. They can see military aircraft and hangars below. This is not a civilian airport at all. Where are they? (In fact, they are now descending towards the Israeli Rephidim airbase, more than 100 miles from the Egyptian capital.)

Their confusion escalates even more. They make the logical decision to ascend and turn west once again, seeking out Cairo West, when the fatal end-game commences. To their horror, the MiGs start to shoot at their wing tips. They are seized by panic. Why are Egyptians firing at a Libyan aircraft? Are they mad?

At 14.09 the pilot radios to Cairo Control: 'We are now shot by *your* fighter [my italics].' Cairo Control answers: 'We are going to tell them [the military authorities] that you are an unreported aircraft . . . and we do not know where you are.' But the call to the military authorities merely adds to the bewilderment. The Egyptian military has no MiGs currently in the air.

The crew are straining their eyes out of the window of the cockpit. They are desperately trying to make sense of a situation that has grown to Kafkaesque proportions. But it is too late. They are hit by direct fire to the base of their wings. The plane is crippled. They are going down.

Too late, the co-pilot notices a sign that had been there all along, and which could have solved the entire mystery: the Shield of David on the body of the jet fighters. They are not MiGs after all. They are Israeli Phantoms. They are not in Egyptian airspace. They are over occupied Sinai. If they had known that, they would have landed at Rephidim, and everything would have been solved.

The crew lose control as the plane careers down into the desert.

Now, who is to blame? The Israeli Air Force command, which shot down a commercial jet? The crew of the Libyan airliner, who flew off course and were unable to understand what the Phantoms were trying to tell them? Egyptian air traffic control, who were not quick enough to alert Flight 114 as to how far they had drifted off course? All three?

What should be crystal clear is that a desire to apportion blame, before taking the time to understand what really happened, is senseless. It may be intellectually satisfying to have a culprit, someone to hang the disaster on. And it certainly makes life simple. After all, why get into the fine print? It was *clearly* the fault of Israel/the crew/ Egypt Control. What else needs saying?

Instant blame often leads to what has been called a 'circular firing squad'. This is where everyone is blaming everyone else. It is familiar in business, politics and the military. Sometimes, this is a mutual exercise in deflecting responsibility. But often everyone in a circular firing squad is being sincere. They all really think that it is the other guy's fault.

It is only when you look at the problem in the round that you glimpse how these contradictory perspectives can be reconciled and you can attempt something that an instantaneous blame game can never achieve: reform of the system. After all, if you don't know what went wrong, how can you put things right?

In the aftermath of the shooting down of Libyan Arab Airlines Flight 114, new laws and protocols were developed in an attempt to reduce the number of inadvertent attacks on civilian aircraft by military forces. An amendment to the Chicago Convention governing the problem of aerial intrusions into theatres of war was signed by an extraordinary session of the International Civil Aviation Organization on 10 May 1984. The black box analysis helped to make future tragedies less likely.[2] *

It set the stage for evolution.

III

Let us move away from the high altitude misunderstandings that caused Libyan Arab Airlines Flight 114 to crash and focus, instead,

---

* One issue that was never fully resolved with Libyan Arab Airlines Flight 114 is why, according to the pilot of one of the Israeli Phantoms, all the window shades were down. It seems almost certain that, in high pressure circumstances and with limited time, the pilot did not notice that some of the shades were, in fact, up.

on the kinds of errors that blight major organisations. Mistakes are made at businesses, hospitals and government departments all the time. It is an inevitable part of our everyday interaction with a complex world.

And yet if professionals think they are going to be blamed for honest mistakes, why would they be open about them? If they do not trust their managers to take the trouble to see what really happened, why would they report what is going wrong, and how can the system adapt?

And the truth is that companies blame *all the time*. It is not just because managers instinctively jump to the blame response. There is also a more insidious reason: managers often feel that it is expedient to blame. After all, if a major company disaster can be conveniently pinned on a few 'bad apples', it may play better in PR terms. 'It wasn't us; it was them!'

There is also a widespread management view that punishment can exert a benign disciplinary effect. It will make people sit up and take notice. By stigmatising mistakes, by being tough on them, managers think that staff will become more diligent and motivated.

Perhaps these considerations explain the sheer pervasiveness of the blame game. According to one report by Harvard Business School, it was found that executives believe that around 2 to 5 per cent of the failures in their organisations were 'truly blameworthy'. But when asked how many of these mistakes were *treated* as blameworthy, they admitted that the number was 'between 70 to 90 per cent'.

This is one of the most pressing cultural issues in the corporate and political world today.[3]

In 2004, Amy Edmondson, a professor at Harvard Business School, and colleagues conducted an influential study into the consequences of a blame culture. Her particular focus was on drug administration errors at two hospitals in the United States (she calls them University Hospital and Memorial Hospital to protect anonymity), but the implications reached far wider.[4]

Drug administration errors are alarmingly common in healthcare. Edmondson cites the example of a nurse reporting for duty at 3 p.m.

and noticing that a bag hanging upside down on an Intensive Care drip was not heparin, a blood thinner used routinely to prevent clotting after surgery, but lidocaine, a heart rhythm stabiliser. The absence of heparin could have been fatal, although on this occasion the error was addressed before the patient suffered ill effects.

Sadly, as we know from the first part of the book, medical errors are often much more serious. According to a paper published by the US Food and Drug Administration, errors in drug administration, just one type of medical error, injure approximately 1.3 million patients each year in the United States. Edmondson cites evidence that the average patient can expect between one and two medication errors during *every hospital stay*.

In her six-month investigation Edmondson focused on eight different units in Memorial and University hospitals. She found that some of these units, across both hospitals, had tough, disciplined cultures. In one unit, the nurse manager was 'dressed impeccably in a business suit' and she had tough discussions with the nurses 'behind closed doors'. In another the manager was described as 'an authority'.

Blame in these units was common. Nurses said things like: 'The environment is unforgiving; heads will roll', 'You get put on trial' and 'You're guilty if you make a mistake'. The managers thought they had their staff on a tight leash. They thought they had a disciplined, high-performance culture. Mistakes were penalised. The managers believed they were on the side of patients, holding the clinicians to account.

And, at first, it seemed as if these managers were right. Blame seemed to be having a positive impact on performance. Edmondson was amazed to discover that the nurses in these units were hardly ever reporting mistakes. Remarkably, at the toughest unit of all (as determined by a questionnaire and a subjective survey undertaken by an independent researcher), the number of errors reported was less than 10 per cent of another unit.

But then Edmondson probed deeper with the help of an anthropologist and found something curious. These nurses in the so-called disciplined cultures may have been reporting fewer errors, but they were making more errors. In the low-blame teams, on the other hand, this finding was reversed. They were reporting more errors, but were making fewer errors overall.*

What was going on? The mystery was, in fact, easy to solve. It was precisely because the nurses in low-blame teams were reporting so many errors that they were learning from them, and not making the same mistakes again. Nurses in the high-blame teams were not speaking up because they feared the consequences, and so learning was being squandered.

This reflects the point about the Virginia Mason Health System. It was only when professionals believed that reports on errors and near-misses would be treated as learning opportunities rather than a pretext to blame that this crucial information started to flow. Managers were initially worried that reducing the penalties for error would lead to an increase in the number of errors. In fact, the opposite happened. Insurance claims fell by a dramatic 74 per cent. Similar results have been found elsewhere. Claims and lawsuits made against the University of Michigan Health System, for example, dropped from 262 in August 2001 to 83 following the introduction of an open and disclose policy in 2007. The number of lawsuits against the University of Illinois Medical Center fell by half in two years after creating a system of open reporting.

'Holding people accountable and [unfairly] blaming people are two quite different things,' Sidney Dekker, one of the world's leading thinkers on complex systems, has said. 'Blaming people may in fact make them less accountable: They will tell fewer accounts, they may feel less compelled to have their voice heard, to participate in improvement efforts.'[5]

In a simple world, blame, as a management technique, made sense. When you are on a one-dimensional production line, for example, mistakes are obvious, transparent and are often caused by a lack of focus. Management can reduce them by increasing the penalties for

---

* As estimated by how often the nursing units were intercepting errors before they became consequential, and other key variables governing self-correction and learning.

non-compliance. They can also send a motivational message by getting heavy once in a while. People rarely lose concentration when their jobs are on the line.

But in a complex world this analysis flips on its head. In the world of business, politics, aviation and healthcare, people often make mistakes for subtle, situational reasons. The problem is often not a lack of focus, it is a consequence of complexity. Increasing punishment, in this context, doesn't reduce mistakes, it reduces openness. It drives the mistakes underground. The more unfair the culture, the greater the punishment for honest mistakes and the faster the rush to judgment, the deeper this information is buried. This means that lessons are not learned, so the same mistakes are made again and again, leading to more punitive punishment, and even deeper concealment and back-covering.

Consider the case of a major financial institution, which sustained heavy losses after a problem emerged in an automated trading program (I cannot name the bank for legal reasons). The chief technology officer (CTO) admitted that nobody fully understood the IT system that had been created.[6] This is entirely normal: major IT systems are invariably complex beyond the understanding of their designers.

He therefore recommended to the board that the engineers should *not* be fired. He didn't think it would be fair. They had done their best, the program had been stress-tested, and it had operated perfectly for a number of months. But he was overruled. The board, which had not engaged in any systematic attempt to understand what had happened, thought that it was 'just obvious' that the IT staff were to blame. After all, they had been closest to the system.

The board had other concerns, too. The failure had cost millions of dollars and had been widely reported in the press. They were worried the event might 'contaminate the franchise'. They thought that acting decisively would play better in PR terms. They also argued that it would send a resolute message to staff about the company's sharp-edged attitude towards failure.

All this sounds plausible, but now think of the cultural ramifications. The board thought they had sent a strong signal that they were tough on mistakes; they had, in fact, sent a chilling message to their staff. If you fail, we will blame you. If you mess up, you will be scapegoated. They had told their staff, with an eloquence that no memo could ever match: 'act defensively, cover your backs, and cover up the precious information that we need to flourish'.

The IT department changed rather a lot after the firings, according to the CTO. Meetings became more fraught, colleagues stopped coming up with new ideas, the flow of information dried up. The board felt that they had protected the brand, but they had, in reality, poisoned it. They had destroyed much of the data crucial to successful adaptation. They have had more than a dozen major IT incidents since the initial failure.[7]

In management courses today, a contrast is often offered between a 'blame culture' and an 'anything goes' culture. In this conception, the cultural challenge is to find a sensible balance between these two, seemingly competing objectives. Blame too much and people will clam up. Blame too little and they will become sloppy.

But judged from a deeper level, these are not in conflict after all. The reconciliation of these seemingly contradictory objectives (discipline and openness) lies in black box thinking. A manager who takes the time to probe the data and who listens to the various perspectives has a crucial advantage. Not only does he figure out what really happened in the specific case, he also sends an empowering message to his staff: if you make an honest mistake we will not penalise you.

This doesn't mean that blame is never justified. If, after investigation, it turns out that a person was genuinely negligent, then punishment is not only justifiable, but imperative. Professionals themselves demand this. In aviation, for example, pilots are the most vocal in calling for punishments for colleagues who get drunk or demonstrate gross negligence. They don't want the reputation of their profession undermined by irresponsible behaviour.

But the crucial point here is that justifiable blame does not undermine openness. Why? Because management has taken the time to find out what really happened rather than blaming pre-emptively, giving professionals the confidence that they can speak up without being penalised for honest mistakes. This is what is sometimes called a 'just culture'.

The question, according to Sidney Dekker, is not: who is to blame? It is not even: where, precisely, is the line between justifiable blame and an honest mistake? because this can never be determined in the abstract. Rather, the question is: do those within the organisation *trust* the people who are tasked with drawing that line? It is only when people trust those sitting in judgement that they will be open *and* diligent.[8]

The nurses in the high-blame unit at Memorial Hospital didn't trust their manager. To the hospital bosses, the manager doubtless looked like a no-nonsense leader, the kind of person who instilled toughness and discipline, someone who ensured that nurses were held accountable for their mistakes. It looked as if she was on the side of the most important people of all: patients.

In reality, however, she was guilty of a distinctive kind of laziness. By failing to engage with the complexity of the system she managed, she was blaming pre-emptively and thus undermining openness and learning. She was weakening the most important accountability of all: what the philosopher Virginia Sharpe calls 'forward looking accountability'. This is the accountability to learn from adverse events so that future patients are not harmed by avoidable mistakes.

The nurse managers in the low-blame units did not lack toughness. In many ways, they were the toughest of all. They didn't wear suits; they wore scrubs. They got their hands dirty. They understood the high-pressure reality of those they managed. They were intimately aware of the complexity of the system and were therefore far more willing to engage with the demanding work of learning from mistakes. They were black box thinkers.

Here is the summary of the findings for Memorial Nurse Unit 3, rated as the least open culture. Espoused attitude: blame. Nurse manager: hands off. Nurse manager attire: business suit. Nurse manager attitude towards staff: views residents as kids needing discipline, treats nurses in the same way, pays careful attention to reporting structures. Staff's view of nurse manager: 'Treats you as guilty if you make a mistake.' Staff's view of errors: 'You get put on trial.'

Here is the summary of the findings for Memorial Nurse Unit 1, rated as the most open culture of all. Espoused attitude: learn. Nurse manager: hands on. Nurse manager attire: scrubs. Nurse manager attitude towards staff: 'They are capable and seasoned.' Staff's view of manager: 'A superb leader and nurse.' Staff's view of errors: normal, natural, important to document.

This is not just about healthcare; it is about organisational culture in general. When we are dealing with complexity, blaming without proper analysis is one of the most common as well as one of the most perilous things an organisation can do. And it rests, in part, on the erroneous belief that toughness and openness are in conflict with each other. They are not.

This analysis is not just true of learning from the mistakes that emerge from complex systems. It is also about the risk-taking and experimentation vital for innovation. Think back to the biologists at Unilever who tested rapidly to drive learning. In all they made 449 'failures'. This kind of process cannot happen if mistakes are regarded as blameworthy. When we are testing assumptions, we are pushing out the frontiers of our knowledge about what works and what doesn't. Penalising these mistakes has a simple outcome: it destroys innovation and enlightened risk-taking.

In short, blame undermines the information vital for meaningful adaptation. It obscures the complexity of our world, deluding us into thinking we understand our environment when we should be learning from it.

As Amy Edmondson of Harvard Business School put it:

Executives I've interviewed in organisations as different as hospitals and investment banks admit to being torn. How can they respond constructively to failures without giving rise to an anything-goes attitude? If people aren't blamed for their failures, what will ensure they try as hard as possible? But this concern is based on a false dichotomy. In actuality, a culture that makes it safe to admit and report on failure can – and in some organisational contexts must – coexist with high standards for performance.[9]

It is worth noting here, if only briefly, the link between blame and cognitive dissonance. In a culture where mistakes are considered blameworthy they are also likely to be dissonant. When the external culture stigmatises mistakes, professionals are likely to internalise these attitudes. Blame and dissonance, in effect, are driven by the same misguided attitude to error, something we will return to in Part 5.

IV

The blame response can be observed in the laboratory. When volunteers are shown a film of a driver cutting across lanes, for example, they will almost unanimously apportion blame. They will infer that he is selfish, impatient and out of control. And this inference may turn out to be true. But the situation is not always as cut-and-dried as it first appears.

After all, the driver may have had the sun in his eyes. He may have been swerving to avoid a car that had veered into his lane. In fact, there are many possible mitigating factors. To most observers looking from the outside in, these do not register. It is not because they don't think such possibilities are irrelevant, it is that often they don't even consider them. The brain just plumps for the simplest, most intuitive narrative: 'He's a homicidal fool!' This is sometimes called by the rather inelegant name of the fundamental attribution error.

It is only when the question is flipped – 'What happened the last time *you* last jumped lanes?' – that volunteers pause to consider the situational factors. 'Oh, yeah, that was because I thought a child was about to run across the street!' Often these excuses are self-serving. But they are not always so. Sometimes there really are wider issues that lead to mistakes – but we cannot even see them if we do not consider them, still less investigate them.

Even in an absurdly simple event like this, then, it pays to pause, to look beneath the surface, to challenge the most obvious, reductionist narrative. This is not about being 'soft', but about learning what really went wrong. How much more important to engage in this kind of activity in a complex, interdependent system, like a hospital or business?

It is noteworthy that even experienced aviation investigators fall prey to the fundamental attribution error. When they are first confronted with an accident, the sense-making part of the brain is already creating explanations before the black box has been discovered. This is why studies have shown that their first instinct is almost always (around 90 per cent of the time) to blame 'operator error'.

As one airline investigator told me: 'When you see an incident, your brain just seems to scream out: "What the hell was the pilot thinking!" It is a kneejerk response. It takes real discipline to probe the black box data without prejudging the issue.'*

In a sense, blame is a subversion of the narrative fallacy. It is a way of collapsing a complex event into a simple and intuitive explanation: 'It was his fault!'

Of course, blame can sometimes be a matter not of cognitive bias, but of pure expediency. If we place the blame on someone else it takes the heat off ourselves. This process can happen at a collective as well as at an individual level.

Take, for example, the credit crunch of 2007. This was a disaster involving investment bankers, regulators, politicians, mortgage brokers, central bankers and retail creditors. But the public (and many politicians) chose to focus the blame almost exclusively on bankers.

Many bankers did indeed behave recklessly. Some would argue that they should have been penalised more severely. But the narrow focus on bankers served to obscure a different truth. Many people

---

* 'Hindsight bias', another well-studied psychological tendency, also plays a role here. Once we know the outcome of an event – a patient has died, a plane has crashed, an IT system has malfunctioned – it is notoriously difficult to free one's mind from that concrete eventuality. It is tough to put oneself in the shoes of the operator, often acting in high-pressure circumstances, trying to reconcile different demands, and unaware of how a particular decision might pan out.

As Anthony Hidden QC, the man who investigated the Clapham Junction Rail Disaster, which killed thirty-five people in 1988, put it: 'There is almost no human action or decision that cannot be made to look flawed and less sensible in the misleading light of hindsight.'

had taken out loans they couldn't afford to repay. Many had maxed out their credit cards. To put it simply: the public had contributed to the crisis too.

But if we can't accept our own failures, how can we learn from them?

Overcoming the blame tendency is a defining issue in the corporate world. Ben Dattner, a psychologist and organisational consultant, tells of an experience when he was working at the Republic National Bank of New York. He noticed a piece of paper that a co-worker had stapled to his cubicle wall. It read: 'The six phases of a project: 1. Enthusiasm 2. Disillusionment 3. Panic 4. Search for the guilty 5. Punishment of the innocent 6. Rewards for the uninvolved.'

Dattner writes: 'I have yet to come across a more accurate description of how most dramas play out in our working lives.'[10]

His point is that you do not need to examine a high-profile failure to glimpse the dangers of blame; they can be seen in the most conventional of office environments.

And this is the real problem. The evolutionary process cannot function without information about what is working, and what isn't. This information can come from many sources, depending on the context (patients, consumers, experiments, whistleblowers, etc). But professionals working on the ground have crucial data to share in almost any context. Healthcare, for example, cannot begin to reform procedures if doctors do not report their failures. And scientific theories cannot evolve if scientists cover up data that reveals the weaknesses in existing hypotheses.

That is why openness is not an optional extra, a useful cultural add-on. Rather, it is a pre-requisite for any adaption worthy of the name. In a complex world, which we cannot fully understand from above, and must therefore discover from below, this cultural requirement trumps almost every other management issue.

A transparent approach should not merely determine the response to failures; it should infiltrate decisions on strategy and preferment. Meritocracy is synonymous with forward accountability.

The alternative is not just that people will spend their time shielding themselves from blame and deflecting it onto others. They will also spend huge amounts of time trying to take credit for other people's work. When a culture is unfair and opaque, it creates multiple perverse incentives. When a culture is fair and transparent, on the other hand, it bolsters the adaptive process.

Our public culture is, if anything, the most blame-orientated of all. Politicians are vilified, sometimes with justification, often without. There is little understanding that the mistakes committed in public institutions are precious opportunities to learn. They are just taken as evidence that political leaders are incompetent, negligent, or both. This adds to the wider phobia towards error, and increases the dissonance of mistakes. It inexorably leads to a culture of spin and subterfuge.

It might be expedient to condemn newspapers for the tendency to blame public figures, but this would be to miss the point. The reason that it is commercially profitable for papers to run stories that apportion instant blame is because there is a ready market for them. After all, we prefer easy stories; we all have an inbuilt bias towards simplicity over complexity. These stories are, in effect, mass-printed by-products of the narrative fallacy.

In a more progressive culture, this market would be undermined. Such stories would be met with incredulity. Newspapers would have an incentive to provide deeper analysis before apportioning blame. This may sound like wishful thinking, but it indicates a direction of travel.

The impetus that drives learning from mistakes is precisely the same as the one that aims at a just culture. Forward looking accountability is nothing more and nothing less than learning from failure. To generate openness, we must avoid pre-emptive blaming. All these things interlock in a truly adaptive system.

As the philosopher Karl Popper put it: 'True ignorance is not the absence of knowledge, but the refusal to acquire it.'

12

The Second Victim

I

To glimpse the full consequences of a blame culture, let us examine one of the defining British tragedies of recent years: the death of Peter Connelly, a seventeen-month-old baby in Haringey, North London, in 2007. During the course of his trial, to protect his anonymity, he was referred to in the British press as 'Baby P'.[1]

Little Peter died at the hands of his mother, Tracey, her boyfriend, Steven Barker, and Barker's brother, Jason Owen. He had suffered terrible abuse and neglect over the course of his short lifetime. Fifteen months after the tragedy the three perpetrators were found guilty of 'causing or allowing the death of a child'. They were sentenced to prison.

But the very next day the media focused its outrage on a very different group of people. The *Sun* newspaper ran a front-page headline with the words: 'Blood on their Hands'. Other media outlets vented similar outrage. Was their anger directed at accessories to the murder who had not yet been prosecuted? Were there other shadowy figures in the background who had been involved in Peter's tragic death?

In fact, the outrage was aimed at those who had been responsible for protecting Peter: mainly his social worker, Maria Ward, and Sharon Shoesmith, director of children's services for the area. The *Sun* created a petition calling for their sacking and ran photos of them asking 'Do you know them?' with a number to ring.[2] The petition was signed by 1.6 million people.[3]

The local council offices were almost immediately surrounded by a crowd holding placards. Shoesmith received death threats. Ward had to leave her home out of fear for her life. Shoesmith's daughter was threatened with murder, and had to go into hiding.[4]

To those at the receiving end the experience felt like something close to the Salem witch trials. Something terrible had happened. The instinct was to ensure that something equally terrible happened to someone else. It was the blame game at its most vivid and destructive.

Many were convinced that the social work profession would improve its performance in the aftermath of the furore. This is what people think accountability looks like: a muscular response to failure. The idea is that even if the punishment is over the top in the specific instance, it will force people to sit up and take responsibility. As one pundit put it: 'it will focus minds'.

But what really happened? Did social workers become 'more accountable'? Were children better protected?

In fact, social workers started leaving the profession en masse. The numbers entering the profession also plummeted. In one area the council had to spend £1.5 million on agency social work teams because it didn't have enough permanent staff to handle a jump in child protection referrals.[5] By 2011 there were 1,350 reported vacancies in child protection work.[6]

Those who stayed in the profession found themselves with bigger caseloads. This meant they had less time to look after the interests of each child. They also started to intervene more aggressively, terrified of the consequences if a child under their supervision was harmed. The number of children removed from their families soared. The cost of missing a signal was just too high. The court system sagged under the weight of new cases and an estimated £100 million was needed to cope with the increase in child protection orders.

There were non-financial consequences too. The children taken from their homes were placed into care and with foster families. This meant that the state had to accept a lower quality of foster families to meet demand. Children are often damaged by leaving their own families. Soon, the media had moved into reverse, running stories about the horrors of loving parents having their kids forcibly removed. One headline was: 'In hiding, the mother accused of abuse for cuddling her child'.[7]

In Haringey, North London, the situation was even worse. The number of health visitors almost halved. The workload for those who stayed in the profession, already high, escalated. The number of care applications increased by an astonishing 211 per cent between 2008 and 2009.[8] The British Association for Adoption and Fostering warned that the continuing increase in care applications by England's local authorities following the Baby P case 'could cause a catastrophe in children's services'.[9]

Crucially, defensiveness started to infiltrate every aspect of social work. Social workers became cautious about what they documented, in case it came back to destroy them. The bureaucratic paper trails got longer, but the words were no longer about conveying information, they were about back-covering. Precious information was concealed out of sheer terror of the consequences. The amount of activity devoted to protecting themselves from future bloodletting undermined attention to the actual task of social work.*

Almost every respected commentator and academic estimates that the harm done to children following the media-driven attempt to 'increase accountability' was high indeed.[10] Forward-looking accountability collapsed. The number of children killed at the hands of their parents *increased* by more than 25 per cent in the year following the outcry and remained higher for every one of the next three years.[11]

When a public inquiry finally reported on the death of Baby Peter, there were allegations that its findings were prejudged and subject to political manipulation. Even the authors of the report seemed to feel that they could not stand in the way of public anger. They worried what might happen to *them* if they didn't appease the appetite for a scapegoat. This is what happens in a blame culture.[12]

None of this is to assert that blame was not justified in the Baby P case. Like many public institutions in the UK, the social work system

---

* This has a rather obvious analogue with what is sometimes called 'defensive medicine' where clinicians use a host of unnecessary tests that protect their backs, but massively increase healthcare costs.

would benefit from a vast cultural change directed at it becoming a truly adaptive organisation with forward-looking accountability. This book has looked at what such a system looks like, and how it can be achieved. Once a high-performance culture is in place, increasing discipline and accountability is both positive and, indeed, warmly welcomed by most professionals.

But trying to increase discipline and accountability in the absence of a just culture has precisely the opposite effect. It destroys morale, increases defensiveness and drives vital information deep underground. It is like trying to revive a stricken patient by hammering him over the head with a mallet.

Blame has other, more personal consequences, too, particularly in safety-critical industries. Many professionals involved in a tragedy, such as clinicians or social workers, often suffer from post-traumatic stress disorder, even when they are not to blame. They are emotionally scarred by their involvement in a tragedy. This is a very human response and one that needs sensitive handling.

But when feelings of guilt are compounded by unjustified accusations of criminality, individuals can be pushed over the edge. This phenomenon is now so prevalent that it has led to the coining of a new term: the 'second victim'. Studies show that professionals suffer feelings of distress, agony, anguish, fear, guilt and depression.[13] Other studies reveal the prevalence of suicidal thoughts.[14]

Sharon Shoesmith was so terrified by the effect of the Baby P affair on her daughters that she contemplated taking not just her own life but those of her entire family. This was a woman described as strong and resolute before she was engulfed in the blame game. 'For a moment you can understand how people wipe out their whole family,' she said. 'Your pain is their pain and their pain is your pain. And you just want to get rid of the pain for everybody.'[15]

In his seminal book *Just Culture* Sidney Dekker writes: 'the question is whether we want to fool ourselves that we can meaningfully wring such accountability out of practitioners by blaming them, suing them, or putting them on trial. No single piece of evidence so far seems to demonstrate we can.'[16]

It is time to stop fooling ourselves.

II

To conclude our study of blame let us take one final incident, perhaps the most notorious aviation near-miss of the twentieth century. Aviation doesn't normally penalise mistakes, as we noted in Part 1. The industry has created a culture where errors are not stigmatised, but viewed as learning opportunities. Indeed, aviation is often held up as an industry leader in terms of its culture.

But on this occasion the industry turned on the professionals. The so-called November Oscar incident was the first time in history that a British pilot was put on trial for doing what he believed to be his duty in high-pressure circumstances.

What makes the case so fascinating is that it highlights the temptation of the blame game, even in an industry that understands its dangers. And it reveals, once again, how a simple incident can look very different when you look beyond the superficial explanations.

William Glen Stewart, who had first flown a Tiger Moth as a nineteen-year-old at the RAF base at Leuchars on the east coast of Scotland,[17] was one of the most experienced pilots in the British Airways fleet. On 21 November 1989, he was in command on a routine flight from Bahrain to London Heathrow. Also in the cabin were Brian Leversha, the flight engineer, and Timothy Luffingham, the twenty-nine-year-old first officer.

The short version of the case against Stewart was simple. Flight B747-136 G-AWNO (codename November Oscar) had taken off from Bahrain and, as the flight reached European airspace, the crew had been informed that the weather at Heathrow was dire. Thick fog had reduced external visibility to a just a few feet.

Stewart would have to make what is called an 'instrument landing'. This is where the lack of visibility obliges the crew to rely on various gauges inside the aircraft to bring the plane safely onto the runway. The procedure, which requires the use of autopilot and other internal systems, is far from easy, although not beyond the competence of Stewart.

Because of the difficulty of the procedure, however, there are a number of safety protocols that have to be followed on approach, rules and regulations that ensure that the captain does not take undue risks under the pressure of a tricky landing. The allegation was simple: Stewart had wilfully ignored these rules.

As they came into land, the aircraft's autopilot wasn't picking up the two radio signals being beamed from the end of the Heathrow runway. These are crucial to a successful instrument landing. The beacons guide the plane on to the correct lateral and vertical course. Without them you could be coming in off-kilter. You could be too high, too low, or too far to the left or right.

If the plane has not captured these beams, the approach must be abandoned no later than 1,000 feet above the ground. A 'go-around' must be initiated, which involves discarding the landing and going back into a holding pattern so that the problem can be fixed or an alternative destination with less severe weather conditions selected. Stewart, however, continued with the descent below 1,000 feet, dropping lower and lower in defiance of the rules.

By the time November Oscar, which had 255 passengers on board, had descended to 750 feet, the plane was so far to the right of the runway that it was actually outside the perimeter fence and flying parallel to the A4 Bath Road. The crew couldn't see this deviation because the fog was so thick. The plane was now on a collision course with the line of hotels that run alongside the A4.

Only at 125 feet did Stewart finally order the go-around, but he was a fraction slow. Even as he was revving the engines and pitching up the nose, the plane sank another fifty feet. So close did it come to the roof of the Penta Hotel that it set off the fire sprinklers in the corridors, something the press would latch on to in the aftermath. The undercarriage of the plane was visible to bystanders through the fog as it reached its lowest point, before thundering back into the sky.

Car alarms started to whoop in the hotel car park. Guests dozing in the hotel were rudely awoken. People on the streets scattered as the plane, its bottom half peeping through the mist, reached its lowest point. Up in the cockpit, Luffingham glimpsed the runway lights way off to the left through the mist as November Oscar regained altitude. After the go-around, the plane landed safely, to the applause of the passengers in the cabin.

An investigation was quickly initiated. A jumbo jet had come within touching distance of what would almost certainly have been the most devastating accident in British aviation history. Had the plane dropped another 60 inches it would have connected with the Penta Hotel, and almost certainly destroyed it.

To many of the public Stewart's culpability seemed obvious. Although he had ultimately averted a major disaster, he *had* disobeyed protocol. His hands had been on the controls when it flew under the mandatory minimum.

With this in mind one can see why it would have been tempting to pin the incident on Stewart. The heat was on British Airways and the Civil Aviation Authority, the regulator. By pinning it on the pilot they may have hoped to escape censure for poor oversight and procedure.

Eighteen months later, on 8 May 1991, Stewart was convicted at Isleworth Crown Court in south-west London. The jury decided that he had been guilty of breaking regulations and almost bringing destruction on south-west London. An experienced pilot had become a criminal.[18]

But what really happened on that flight? Was Stewart culpable? Was he negligent? Or was he merely responding to a chain of unforeseen events that could have led almost anyone towards disaster?

In investigating the incident in depth, we will draw upon the seminal report by the journalist Stephan Wilkinson[19] and unpublished papers from the trial, as well as confidential documents from the British Airways internal investigation and interviews with eyewitnesses.

For the deeper story, it turns out, doesn't begin as a Boeing 747 approaches Heathrow, or even the moment it took off from Bahrain. Rather, it starts two days earlier, as the crew enjoyed a Chinese meal during a stopover in Mauritius.

III

It had been a long trip. The crew had been involved in a series of flights in the days before landing in Mauritius and decided it might be nice to unwind by sharing dinner. William Stewart sat alongside Tim Luffingham, the first officer. Engineer Brian Leversha and his wife, Carol, who had also come on the trip, were also there. It was an agreeable evening.

But by the time the crew arrived in Bahrain for the next leg of the trip, almost everyone had been struck down with gastroenteritis. Carol Leversha had the worst symptoms of all. Brian had called the local British Airways approved doctor while they were still in Mauritius, but he had been unavailable. Instead, the doctor had recommended a colleague who, although not on the BA roster, was about to be added to the approved list. He dispensed painkillers to Carol and suggested that she give them to anyone else who started to feel ill.

Two days later, the flight from Bahrain to London was scheduled for 00.14. The so-called 'slip time' (the gap between landing on the previous flight and departure for the next) added to the difficulties of the crew. They had arrived in Bahrain late at night and had gone to sleep. But they had had a full day, and would normally be getting ready for bed again. Instead, they were to fly an overnight into Heathrow. They were also suffering the after-effects of gastroenteritis. It was far from ideal.

But the crew were professional. They were not going to allow a stomach-bug or tiredness to ground a flight containing 255 passengers. As Leversha (now seventy-five) told me when I met him at his home in rural Hampshire: 'Some of the crew had suffered worse than others, but there was a consensus that we had gotten over the worst effects. We all felt that it would have been unprofessional to force BA to send out a replacement crew, with all the disruption that would have caused. We wanted to get the job done.'

The flight itself was gruelling from the start. Strong headwinds shrank the fuel reserves. Soon after taking off, Luffingham, the co-pilot, started to feel unwell. It seemed that the gastroenteritis had returned. He borrowed some pills from Carol Leversha, who was in the jump seat, and asked for permission to leave the cockpit. Stewart agreed. Luffingham made his way back into the First Class cabin to get some sleep and use the facilities, leaving Stewart to fly the plane with just the engineer.

Stewart considered bringing the plane onto the ground at this stage. He and Leversha debated landing at Tehran, one of the only viable stopping points, but they were worried about the fraught political situation in the Iranian capital. Flying on seemed like the prudent thing to do. After all, it wasn't unusual for a pilot to fly unaided by a co-pilot if the latter had been taken ill.

By the time November Oscar reached the skies above Frankfurt, however, the situation took a severe turn for the worse. They were informed that the weather conditions at Heathrow were appalling. Low fog had destroyed external visibility. It was close to zero-zero conditions. They would have to land on instruments in what is called Category 3 conditions (the most demanding kind of landing).

This posed an immediate problem. Stewart was qualified to fly a Category 3 approach, as was Leversha. But Luffingham, relatively new with British Airways, was not. As they flew over Germany, Stewart radioed to the British Airways office in Frankfurt to ask for a dispensation for Luffingham: essentially, a verbal waiver that would allow the aircraft to land at Heathrow. Frankfurt made the call to London to find out.

Somewhere in south-west England in the early hours the British Airways duty pilot was awoken by phone. He agreed to a verbal ispensation. It was not considered a significant risk to agree to the dispensation, given that Stewart was fully qualified to make a Category 3 landing. Indeed, these waivers were handed out as a matter of routine.

By the time November Oscar had reached British airspace, Luffingham was back in his seat. The plane was put into a holding pattern over Lambourne, to the north-east of London. Leversha, from his position behind the captain, was a tad uneasy. Stewart had been flying virtually solo in the dark for more than five hours, with only a fifteen-minute rest. The weather conditions were dire. Fuel was low. He wondered if they should reroute to Manchester, where the weather was better. 'Come on, Glen,' he said. 'Let's shove off to Manchester.'

Stewart considered it. He asked for weather conditions in Manchester, as well as at London Gatwick, and the crew discussed the options. Stewart was on the point of rerouting when Heathrow finally cleared November Oscar for its approach.

But suddenly there was another complication. They had been due to approach Heathrow from the west, flying out past Windsor before turning around, and landing in an easterly direction. They had the loose-leaf file with the charts of the required route ready at hand in the cockpit. But now Air Traffic Control told them that the fog had lifted ever so slightly, the weather conditions had changed, and that they should therefore land in a westerly direction.

This was challenging, but by no means disastrous. Up at 8,000 feet, planes are typically travelling at around 240 knots. At touch-down, this has to be reduced to around 140 knots, otherwise the brakes would not be able to prevent the plane piling through the end of the runway. Speed is steadily reduced during the approach by taking off the thrust from the engine and using the flaps. This takes a certain number of 'track miles' to complete.

But the distance had now been shortened by 25 miles. The work-load in the cabin had ramped up significantly. They had to retrieve new graphs from the loose-leaf file and create a new mental model of their approach. There was also a 10-knot tailwind, putting even more pressure on time. The smooth interaction of the crew was becoming strained.

And then there was another unexpected problem. Outside Heathrow there are colour-coded approach lights that appear like a Christmas tree on the ground, guiding the pilot visually towards the touchdown zone. ATC radioed to say that some of these lights were not functioning. This hardly mattered, given that there was no external visibility anyway. But protocol demanded that Leversha go through the checklist at the very moment he was reaching overload.

Then yet another problem: they were cleared to land dangerously late. The thick fog meant that an unusual number of planes were circling above Heathrow, reducing the distance between aircraft coming into land. Air Traffic Control was under pressure. They were making the best of an increasingly fraught situation. It was later established that clearance for November Oscar was given *later* than regulations permitted. A hurried landing was being pushed to its absolute limits.

But probably none of this would have mattered except for the last problem in a long chain of unforeseen events. Stewart, exhausted and under mounting pressure, unable to see anything but white fog outside his windows, focused his eyes on the instruments. The two radio beams at the far end of the runway were now sending out lateral and vertical guidance, crucial for November Oscar to calibrate its approach onto the correct path.

But the autopilot didn't seem to be capturing the lateral signal. It is almost certain that an Air France plane, still on the runway at Heathrow due to the squeezed distance between incoming aircraft, was deflecting the beam. Stewart, who had a low opinion of the Boeing 747 automatic functions, was straining his eyes at the localiser and glidescope, the internal instruments that should have been picking up the signals.

The flight was now dropping through the London sky at 700 feet per minute. It was travelling at close to 200mph. The tension in the cockpit was intense. But the autopilot was not locking on to the radio signal; instead it was 'hemstitching'. As the journalist Stephan Wilkinson wrote in his report on the incident, the plane was 'trundling back and forth through the localizer beam like a clumsy bloodhound not quite able to catch the scent'.

The plane had now gone through the 1,000-foot legal minimum. Technically, Stewart was outside regulations. Nobody in the cockpit knew it, but the plane was deviating out beyond the perimeter fence, and was rapidly converging with the long line of hotels that run alongside the Bath Road. According to protocol, Stewart should have been ordering a go-around.

But he was exhausted. Fuel was critical. His first officer was still dazed with illness and, besides, was not qualified to assist. A go-around itself was not a risk-free option. Air Traffic Control had earlier indicated that the fog was lifting, causing Leversha to later argue that this entitled Stewart to wait a crucial few heartbeats to see if the plane broke out of the fog, allowing him to target the runway visually.

Moments later, the plane was at 250 feet. The roof of the Penta Hotel was less than six seconds from impact. Stewart was straining his eyes through the cockpit window, frantically seeking out the white lights of the runway through the morning mist. The 255 passengers were oblivious to the looming catastrophe. Even Carol Leversha, reading a novel by Dean Koontz in the jump seat of the cockpit, hadn't grasped the peril of the situation, or how close they were to disaster.

At 125 feet above the ground Stewart finally ordered a go-around. Protocols dictate that he should have pulled up as rapidly as possible (insiders call this the 'minimum height loss technique'), but he was a little slow. The plane dropped another 50 feet as the engines revved into life. Investigators would later establish that the undercarriage of the 200 tonne jet, travelling at close to 200mphthrough the London fog, came within 5 feet of the roof of the Penta Hotel.

After the go-around the plane, as we now know, landed safely and smoothly. The passengers, as already noted, applauded. Luffingham noticed that Stewart's hands were trembling. They were just a few minutes behind schedule. Stewart, who sincerely believed that he had done his best in the most trying conditions he had ever experienced as a pilot, breathed deeply and closed his eyes for a moment or two as if in prayer.

Now, was Stewart to blame? Was he culpable? Or was he reacting to a series of difficulties that nobody could have anticipated in advance?

In the summary version of the incident, Stewart *seemed* blameworthy. After all, he did fly the plane below the height required in the regulations. But when we explore the context with a little more tenacity, a new perspective emerges. We see the subtle factors lurking in the background. We get a sense of the high-pressure reality faced by Stewart as he confronted a series of unforeseen incidents. Suddenly he seems like a pilot doing his best in testing circumstances. He may not have acted perfectly, but he certainly doesn't seem to have acted like a criminal either.

I have spoken to dozens of pilots, investigators and regulators about the November Oscar incident and, although perspectives vary, there is a broad consensus that it was a mistake to pin the blame on Stewart. It was wrong of British Airways to censure him and for the lawyers at the CAA to put him on trial. Why? Because if pilots anticipate being blamed unfairly, they will not make the reports on their own mistakes and near-misses, thus suppressing the precious information that has driven aviation's remarkable safety record. This is why blame should never be apportioned for reasons of corporate or political expediency, but only ever after a proper investigation by experts with a ground-level understanding of the complexity in which professionals operate.

The jury did their best to make up their minds on the facts, but it is not easy while sitting in a staid courtroom to make a judgement about split-second decisions made in the cockpit of a 200 tonne jumbo jet flying through thick fog at nearly 200mph.

But if the Oscar November incident shows anything, it is just how easy it is to engage in the blame game. A tragedy very nearly happened, therefore someone had to be punished. Aviation is generally an industry with an empowering attitude towards error, and is rightly considered a leader when it comes to having a just culture. It rarely engages in blame and uses mistakes to drive learning. This is worth re-emphasising because the case of William Glen Stewart should not obscure the lessons we learned from aviation in Part 1 of the book.

But what the Oscar November incident reveals is that even a pioneering industry like aviation is not *completely* immune from the blame tendency. And perhaps it exposes, more than anything, just how far we need to travel to eradicate the blame instinct once and for all.

On a cold winter morning, I visited Brian Leversha, the flight engineer, and his wife Carol. Leversha had left British Airways in the aftermath of the event out of sadness for the way he and his fellow crew members had been treated. The couple have lived for the last three decades in a rural retreat, forty miles from London.

Leversha has had more than twenty years to reflect on the most infamous near-miss event in British aviation history. He spent much of our time together talking about his friend William Glen Stewart, the pilot who had been criminalised. 'Such a lovely guy, so decent and thoughtful,' Leversha said. 'He was old school in his manners and his sense of duty.'

In his sentencing the trial judge had given Stewart a choice between a £2,000 fine or 45 days in prison: he took the former. 'The leniency of the sentence reflected the fact that the judge didn't think the case should ever have been brought to trial,' Leversha said. 'But Glen was deeply hurt by the affair. He was humiliated by the trial and the conviction. He was such a gracious man. Just three days after the incident, he wrote to me and the co-pilot taking full responsibility.'

Leversha passed me a cardboard box, ten inches thick with papers, notes and reports relating to the incident. Over the next few weeks, I delved into the paperwork, which included internal British Airways reports, correspondence with the legal teams, and technical data relating to the incident. About three-quarters of the way down, I found the letter that Stewart wrote to Leversha. It revealed the sense of honour of the man who had faced prosecutors at Isleworth Crown Court, standing in a dock usually reserved for murderers, thieves and conmen. It read:

> Dear Brian,
>   I would like to state that during the recent trip . . . you carried out your duties in the manner I have come to expect from experienced flight engineers, but which I also know is far beyond what is written in official manuals. Your help makes my job easier . . . Regarding the go-around incident my opinion is that you behaved and called every standard and non standard action as written in all manuals, plus the welcome extras. Well done, I could not have asked for better.

Leversha said:

> If he made a mistake, it was in not fully cooperating with the airline investigation, but then he sensed that they were out to get him from the start. He was a family man, loved by his wife, Samantha, and their children. And, you know, he just loved flying. He got into it as a boy, watching the Tiger Moths up at RAF Leuchars, just over the

bay from St Andrews golf club. That place must have meant so much to him. It was where his love of flying was born.

Stewart's final journey took place on 1 December 1992, three years and nine days after B747-136 caused the fire sprinklers to activate in the corridors of the Penta Hotel. It is retold with telling sparseness by the journalist Stephan Wilkinson:

He left his small house in Wokingham without a word to his wife. He drove some nine hours to a beach ten miles from his birth place in Scotland, near RAF Leuchars.

Stewart attached a hose to the exhaust pipe, led it into the car through a nearly closed window and in moments had asphyxiated himself. He did not leave a letter or any explanation for his action.

PART 6

Creating a Growth Culture

13

The Beckham Effect

I

David Beckham is one of England's finest modern footballers. He holds the record number of caps for an outfield player with the England team with 115 appearances. He captained England for six years and fifty-nine games, and scored goals in three World Cups.

As a club player he won the Premier League title six times, the FA Cup twice and the UEFA Champions League once with Manchester United. He also won La Liga with Real Madrid, the Major League Soccer Cup twice with LA Galaxy and made contributions to A.C. Milan during two loan spells.

Beckham's forte was as a free-kick taker and crosser. For a time he was arguably the finest dead-ball specialist in the world. Perhaps his most famous strike was two and a half minutes into stoppage time in England's crucial game against Greece in 2001, a match his team had to at least draw to guarantee qualification for the 2002 World Cup. They were trailing 2–1 at the time.

A foul had been committed ten yards outside the Greece box. Beckham placed the ball down on the turf and then stepped back to size up the challenge. He took his run-up, and, with an effortlessness that remains mesmerising on YouTube more than ten years later, bent the ball around a four-man wall and into the top corner of the goal more than thirty yards away, the trajectory describing a parabola of pure artistry. It was virtually the last kick of the game.

In all, Beckham scored from an astonishing 65 free kicks during his career: 29 for Manchester United, 14 for Real Madrid, 12 for LA Galaxy, 7 for England's national team, 2 for Preston North End and 1 for A.C. Milan. When you factor in his contributions from open play, his defensive stamina, and his capacity to create scoring opportunities for his teammates, it is some track record.

It is intriguing, then, to rewind to Beckham's youth to see how he built up this mastery. As a six-year-old he would spend afternoons practising keep-me-ups in his tiny back garden in East London. This is the way that most youngsters develop ball control: trying to keep the ball in the air by kicking, kneeing and heading. It is one of the most popular training techniques in the game.

At first little David was pretty average. He could do five or six before the ball would elude his control and land on the ground. But he stuck at it. He spent afternoon after afternoon, slipping up again and again, but with each mistake learning how to finesse the ball, sustain his concentration, and get his body back into position to keep the sequence going.

Sandra, his mother, who would watch him through the kitchen window as she cooked dinner, told me: 'I was amazed at how devoted he was. He would start when he got back from school and then continue until his dad got back from work. Then they would go down to the park to practise some more. He was such an amazing kid when it came to his appetite for hard work.'

Slowly, Beckham improved. After six months, he could get up to 50 keep-me-ups. Six months after that he was up to 200. By the time he got to the age of nine, he had reached a new record: 2,003. In total the sequence took around fifteen minutes and his legs ached at the end of it.

For an outsider looking in this sequence would have seemed miraculous. It would have unfolded like a chain of logic. Two thousand and three touches of the ball without it even touching the ground! It would have seemed like a revelation of genius.

But to Sandra, who had watched for three years through the kitchen window, it looked very different. She had seen the countless failures that had driven progress. She had witnessed all the frustrations and disappointments. And she had seen how young David had learned from every one.

Only after getting to 2,003 did Beckham conclude that he had mastered the art of keep-me-ups so he focused his attention on something new. You guessed it: free kicks. He spent afternoon after afternoon with Ted, his father, aiming at the wire meshing over the window of a shed at the local park.

His dad would often stand in between Beckham and the target, forcing him to bend the ball around him. Over time the ball was taken farther and farther back, encouraging Beckham to deliver with greater power and velocity. Just like his keep-me-ups, he improved with every attempt.

'After a couple of years, people would stop and stare,' Ted told me. 'He must have taken more than 50,000 free kicks at that park. He had an incredible appetite.'

In the spring of 2014, I went to Paris to interview Beckham. He was in his final year at Paris Saint-Germain and living in the Hôtel Le Bristol, near the Champs-Elysées. 'When people talk about my free kicks they focus on the goals,' he said. 'But when I think about free kicks I think about all those failures. It took tons of misses before I got it right.'

Beckham, relaxing in a beige beanie, ripped jeans and a white T-shirt, sustained this work ethic throughout his career. As England captain he was well known for staying behind after practice to work on his free kicks. The day before my visit he had remained an extra two hours at the Paris Saint-Germain training ground to work on his technique and accuracy.

He was still working out how to improve, learning from his mistakes, into the twilight of his career. 'You have to keep pushing yourself, if you want to improve . . . Without that journey I would never have succeeded.'

It is striking how often successful people have a counter-intuitive perspective on failure. They strive to succeed, like everyone else, but they are intimately aware of how indispensable failure is to the overall process. And they embrace, rather than shy away from, this part of the journey.

Michael Jordan, the basketball great, is a case in point. In a famous Nike commercial, he said: 'I've missed more than nine thousand shots. I've lost almost three hundred games. Twenty-six times I've been trusted to take the game-winning shot and missed.'

For many the ad was perplexing. Why boast about your mistakes? But to Jordan it made perfect sense. 'Mental toughness and heart are a lot stronger than some of the physical advantages you might have,' he said. 'I've always said that and I've always believed that.'

James Dyson embodies this perspective, too. He was once called 'an evangelist for failure'. 'The most important quality I look for in people coming to Dyson is the willingness to try, fail and learn. I love that spirit, all too rare in the world today,' he says.

In the previous section we looked at how blame can undermine openness and learning, and how to address it. But in Part 2, we noted that there is a different and altogether more subtle barrier to meaningful evolution: the internal fear of failure. This is the threat to ego; the damage to our self-esteem; the fact that many of us can't admit our mistakes even *to ourselves* – and often give up as soon as we hit difficulties.

In this section we are going to look at how to overcome both tendencies which undermine learning in so many ways. We will examine why some people and organisations are able to look failure squarely in the face; how they learn from mistakes rather than spinning them; how they avoid the instinct to blame. We will also look at how they sustain their motivation through multiple set-backs and challenges rather than fizzling out.

In short: if learning from failure is vital to success, how do we overcome both the internal as well as the external barriers that prevent this from happening?

II

In 2010 Jason Moser, a psychologist at Michigan State University, and colleagues took a group of volunteers and gave them a test.[1] As part of the set-up, an electroencephalography (or EEG) cap was placed on their heads. This consists of a number of electrodes, which measure the voltage fluctuations in the brain.

In effect Moser wanted to see what was happening at a neural level when the volunteers made mistakes. He was interested in two brain signals in particular. One is called Error Related Negativity, or ERN. This was discovered simultaneously (yet another example of multiple independent discovery) by two research teams in 1990, and is a negative signal, originating in the anterior cingulate cortex, a brain area that helps to regulate attention. This reaction is largely involuntary and is the inevitable brain response to making a mistake.

The second signal under investigation was Error Positivity, or Pe. This is observed 200–500 milliseconds after the mistake and is associated with heightened awareness. It is a separate signal from ERN, emerges from a different part of the brain, and happens when we are focusing on our mistakes.

Moser was aware that previous studies had shown that people tend to learn more rapidly when their brains exhibit two responses. Firstly, a larger ERN signal (i.e. a bigger reaction to the mistake) and secondly a steady Pe signal (i.e. people are paying attention to the error, focusing on it, so they are more likely to learn from it).

Before beginning the experiment Moser divided the students into two groups according to how they answered a pre-set questionnaire. The questions were designed to elicit something called 'mindset'. People in a Fixed Mindset tend to believe their basic qualities, like their intelligence or talent, are largely fixed traits. They strongly agree with statements like 'You have a certain amount of intelligence, and you can't really do much to change it.'

People in a Growth Mindset, on the other hand, tend to believe that their most basic abilities can be developed through hard work. They do not think that innate intelligence is irrelevant, but believe that they can become smarter through persistence and dedication. As a group they tend to *disagree* with statements such as: 'Your intelligence is something about you that you can't change very much.'

Mindset is not quite as binary as it might sound. After all, most people tend to think that success is based on a combination of talent *and* practice. But the questionnaire forces volunteers to rate on a scale how we think about these issues. It drills down into our implicit beliefs and assumptions, the thoughts that often drive our behaviour when we haven't got time to think.

Once Moser had divided the volunteers into two groups and had placed the EEG cap on their heads, he began the experiment. The test was simple, if dull. The students had to identify the middle letter of a five-letter sequence such as BBBBB or BBGBB. Sometimes the letter was the same as the other four, sometimes it was different, and volunteers would make mistakes from time to time as they lost focus.

As he looked at the electrical activity in the brain, however, Moser started noticing a dramatic difference in how the two groups responded to their mistakes. Both those in the Fixed and Growth Mindset groupings exhibited a strong ERN signal. Of course they did. Speaking metaphorically, the brain sits up and pays attention when things go wrong. Nobody likes to mess up, particularly on something as simple as identifying a letter.

Yet, when it came to the Pe signal, the two groups were strikingly different. Those in a Growth Mindset recorded a signal that was vastly higher than those in a Fixed Mindset. Indeed, compared with those at the extreme end of the fixed spectrum, those in the Growth Mindset had a Pe signal *three times larger* (an amplitude of 15 compared to only 5). 'That is a huge difference,' Moser has said.

It was as if the brain in Fixed Mindset people was ignoring the mistakes; it was not paying attention to them. On the other hand, for those in the Growth Mindset, it was as if the mistake was of great interest; attention was directed towards it. What's more, the size of the Pe signal was directly correlated with improvement in performance in the aftermath of mistakes.

Moser's experiment is fascinating because it provides a metaphor for many of the insights of this book. When we engage with our errors we improve. This is true at the level of systems, as we saw when we compared healthcare and aviation (or science and pseudo-science), and at the level of individuals, if we think back to prosecution lawyers in the aftermath of DNA exonerations. It is also true, in a manner of speaking, at the level of the brain.

But it also explains why some people learn from their mistakes, while others do not. The difference is ultimately about how we conceptualise our failures. Those in the Growth Mindset, by definition, *think* about error in a different way from those in the Fixed

Mindset. Because they believe that progress is driven, in large part, by practice, they naturally regard failure as an inevitable aspect of learning.

Is it any wonder they pay attention to their mistakes and extract the learning opportunities? Is it any wonder they are not crushed by failure? And is it any wonder they are sympathetic to bottom-up iteration?

Those who think that success emerges from talent and innate intelligence, on the other hand, are far more likely to be threatened by their mistakes. They will regard failures as evidence that they don't have what it takes, and never will: after all, you can't change what you were born with. They are going to be more intimidated by situations in which they will be judged. Failure is dissonant.

Dozens of experiments have now established the broad behavioural consequences of this crucial dichotomy. In one experiment by the psychologist Carol Dweck and a colleague, eleven- and twelve-year-olds were given eight easy tests, then four very difficult ones. As they worked, the two groups exhibited startlingly different responses.[2]

Here are the children in the Fixed Mindset grouping being described by Dweck: 'Maybe the most striking thing about this group was how quickly they began to denigrate their abilities and blame their intelligence for the failures, saying things like "I guess I am not very smart", "I never did have a good memory" and "I'm no good at things like this". Two-thirds of them showed a clear deterioration in their strategies, and more than half of them lapsed into completely ineffective strategies.

And the kids in the Growth Mindset? Here is Dweck again:

> They didn't even consider themselves to be failing ... In line with their optimism, more than 80% maintained or improved the quality of their strategies during the difficult problems. A full quarter of the group actually improved. They taught themselves new and more sophisticated strategies for addressing the new and more difficult problems. A few of them even solved the problems that were supposedly beyond them.

These differences are, on the face of it, remarkable. These were children who had been matched for ability. Dweck ensured that they were all equally motivated by offering toys that the children had personally selected. And yet some persevered as the going got tough while others wilted.

Why the stark difference? It hinged on mindset. For the kids in the Fixed Mindset group, with a static attitude to intelligence, failure is debilitating. It shows not just that you are not up to the job, but that you might as well give up. After all, you cannot change how much talent you have.

For the kids in the Growth Mindset, everything changed. For them intelligence is dynamic. It is something that can grow, expand and improve. Difficulties are not regarded as reasons to give up, but as learning opportunities. The children in this group spontaneously said things like 'I love a challenge' and 'mistakes are our friend'.

This is not just about ten- and eleven-year-olds, however, it is about the basic contours of human psychology. Let us move, for a moment, from the classroom to a two-year investigation into Fortune 1000 companies. Two psychologists conducted interviews with staff in seven top firms in order to probe their respective mindsets. The results were aggregated for each company to determine whether the overall culture had a growth or a fixed orientation.[3]

They then looked at the attitudes in these firms. The differences were stark. Those in the Fixed Mindset companies were worried about mistakes, feared being blamed and felt that errors were more likely to be concealed. They tended to agree with statements like 'In this company there is a lot of cheating, taking shortcuts, and cutting corners' or 'In this company people often hide information and keep secrets'.

For those in Growth Mindset cultures, everything changed. The culture was perceived as more honest, collaborative and the attitude to errors was far more robust. They tended to agree with statements like: 'This company genuinely supports risk-taking and will support me even if I fail' or 'When people make mistakes, this company see the learning that results as "value added"' or 'People are encouraged to be innovative in this company – creativity is welcomed'.

It hardly needs stating that these are precisely the kinds of behaviour that predict adaptation and growth. They are an almost perfect summary of the cultures of the successful institutions covered in the preceding chapters. Indeed, when it came to the question of whether an organisation was rife with unethical or underhand behaviour, those in Growth Mindset companies disagreed 41 per cent more strongly than those in Fixed Mindset organisations.

This evokes the intimate interrelationship between cognitive dissonance, blame and openness, as mentioned in Chapter 11. It is when a culture has an unhealthy attitude to mistakes that blame is common, cover-ups are normal and people fear to take sensible risks. When this attitude flips, blame is less likely to be pre-emptive, openness is fostered, and cover-ups are seen for what they are: blatant self-sabotage.

In an email from the head of HR in one of the most prestigious financial institutions in the world, I learned of the lengths that some of the most talented people can go to in order avoid failure.

> When someone is given a new challenge, like giving a major presentation to clients, it is inevitable that they will be less than perfect first time around. It takes time to build expertise, even for exceptional people.
>
> But there are huge differences in how individuals respond. Some love the challenge. They elicit feedback, talk to colleagues, and seek out chances to be involved in future presentations. Always – and I mean always – they improve. But others are threatened by the initial 'failure'. In fact, they engage in astonishingly sophisticated avoidance strategies to ensure they are never put in that situation ever again. They are sabotaging their progress because of their fear of messing up.

III

West Point is a training academy for aspiring army officers in the United States. Situated on high ground fifty miles to the north of New York City, it is regarded as one of the most formidable educational institutions in the world. In 2009 it was rated the top college in America by *Forbes* magazine.[4]

The campus is legendary, with neo-gothic buildings hewn from black and grey granite. It hosts the oldest museum in the US Army and the Patton monument, a bronze statue of the famous American cavalryman. Each year it also houses 1,200 new recruits, known as cadets, who hope to graduate into the officer class of the most powerful army in the world.

Just to make it into the academy is tough. Aspiring cadets must receive a personal nomination from a congressman or another high-ranking member of the American establishment and must also excel on a battery of cognitive and physical tests. But once the cadets walk through the fabled gates of the academy, the real struggle begins.

They have to undergo a super-tough initiation, a six-and-a-half-week regime known as cadet basic training. This is to examine not just the intellectual and physical prowess of new recruits, but also their resolve. According to one academic paper, it is 'deliberately engineered to test the very limits of cadets' physical, emotional, and mental capacities'. West Point insiders call cadet basic training 'Beast Barracks' or simply 'The Beast'.

The cadets live in spartan conditions and are woken at 5 a.m. every morning. They have to complete physical exercises between 5.30 and 6.55 a.m., engage in a series of morning classes to test intellect and reasoning before a new set of classes in the afternoon. In the late afternoon, there is organised athletics, before the cadets get ready for yet more training in the evening. They go to bed at 10 p.m.

Trials include 'ruck' marches, ten miles at a time up steep hills, while carrying loads of between 35 and 50 kilograms. Then there is the so-called 'chamber' where cadets don gas masks and then enter a hut filled with tear gas. They have to remove their gas masks, read aloud the information on a sign on the wall, then take a breath before leaving the chamber. It is far from pleasant.

Around fifty cadets drop out of West Point each year during Beast Barracks. This is unsurprising. The initiation is tough. As the official prospectus for students puts it: 'This is the most physically and emotionally demanding part of the four years at West Point, and is designed to help you make the transition from new cadet to Soldier.'[5]

For a long time the military regarded Beast Barracks as a way of separating the best from the rest. Indeed, they had a scientific measure of talent, called the Whole Candidate Score. This quantifies the attributes that are vital to getting through the initiation process. It measures physical prowess through such things as the maximum number of push-ups. It measures intelligence through SATs (a standard test). It measures educational ability through the Grade Point Average. It measures leadership potential. These, plus many other ingredients of talent, are then pulled together into a weighted average.

These qualities are, of course, important. They doubtless reveal some of the attributes that are required to get through Beast Barracks. But they also seem to leave something out. What if the aspiring army officer has wonderful abilities, and huge reserves of physical strength, but lacks staying power? What if he drops out as soon as the going gets tough, or when he endures failure, despite being both incredibly strong and intelligent?

In 2004, Angela Lee Duckworth, an American psychologist, approached military chiefs to ask if she could measure the 'grit' of aspiring candidates at West Point.[6] Her questionnaire had little of the sophistication of the Whole Candidate Score. It was just a five-minute survey asking respondents to rate themselves from 1 to 5 according to twelve basic statements such as 'setbacks don't discourage me' and 'I finish whatever I begin'.

Duckworth wanted to find out if these aspects of character – in particular the willingness to persevere through failure – would prove to be a stronger predictor of who would make it through Beast Barracks than the army's sophisticated Whole Candidate Score. The results were clear. When the test scores came back, the grit rating was a significantly superior predictor of success than the Whole Candidate Score. Duckworth carried on giving out the grit questionnaire for the next five years. It proved to be a more powerful predictor in every single year.

Duckworth also approached the national director of the American

Spelling Bee in 2005, and asked if she could test competitors. Spelling Bees are competitive tournaments in which youngsters have to spell increasingly difficult words. In the final round of the American Spelling Bee competition in 2013, for example, contestants had to spell words such as 'kaburi' (a land crab); 'cipollino' (a variety of marble) and 'envoûtement' (a magical ritual).

Again, the results were clear. Those with above-average grit scores were 40 per cent more likely to advance to further rounds than their same age peers. Indeed, a key advantage of those who excelled, according to Duckworth, was that 'they were not studying the words they already know . . . [rather] they isolate what they don't know, identify their own weaknesses, and work on that.'

Duckworth also found that the same analysis applies in bigger, less selective settings. In one study, she and her colleagues looked at college résumés of aspiring teachers for evidence of grit. She then looked at how effective these people turned out to be as teachers in under-resourced communities. Grit, once again, was the key factor driving long-term success.

The reason is not difficult to see: if we drop out when we hit problems, progress is scuppered, no matter how talented we are. If we interpret difficulties as indictments of who we are, rather than as pathways to progress, we will run a mile from failure. Grit, then, is strongly related to the Growth Mindset; it is about the way we conceptualise success and failure.

One of the problems in our culture is that success is positioned as something that happens quickly. Reality television, for example, suggests or leads us to believe that success can happen in the time it takes to impress a whimsical judge or audience. It is about overnight stardom and instant gratification. This is one of the reasons why such programmes are so popular with audiences.

But success in the real world rarely happens in this way. When it comes to creating a dual cyclone vacuum cleaner, learning how to take a world-class free kick or becoming an expert chess player or military leader, success requires long application. It demands a willingness to strive and persevere through difficulties and challenges.

And yet if young people think success happens instantly for the truly talented, why would they persevere? If they take up, say, the violin and are not immediately playing like a virtuoso, they are going to assume they don't have what it takes – and so they will give up. In effect, the mistaken idea that success is an instant phenomenon destroys resilience.

It is worth pointing out here that giving up is not always a bad thing. If you spend your life trying to build the Tower of Babel, you will waste your life. At some point you have to make a calculation as to whether the costs of carrying on are outweighed by the benefits of giving up and trying something new. These are some of the most important decisions we have to make.

But this takes us to a prevailing misconception about the Growth Mindset. Won't people in the Growth Mindset persevere in a futile task for too long, it is sometimes asked? Won't they waste their lives on challenges they will never really accomplish?

In fact, the truth is quite the reverse. It is those with a Growth Mindset who are more capable of making a rational decision to quit. As Dweck puts it: 'There is nothing in the growth mindset that prevents students from deciding that they lack the skills a problem requires. In fact, it allows students to give up without shame or fear that they are revealing a deep and abiding deficiency.'

Think back to the disposition effect covered in Chapter 5. A rational financial trader should keep shares that are most likely to appreciate in the future while selling those likely to depreciate. But traders are actually more likely to keep the shares that have lost money, regardless of future prospects. Why? Because they hate to crystallise a loss. This is why people hold on to losing stocks for far too long, desperately hoping they will rebound. Even professional stock pickers are vulnerable, holding losing stocks twice as long as winning stocks.

Now think about the Growth Mindset: it is about being able to see failure in a clear-eyed way; not as an indictment of one's judgement, but as a learning opportunity. This is why evidence suggests that traders in a Growth Mindset are *less inclined* to the disposition effect; less inclined to blindly persevere with a losing stock. When we see failure without its related stigma, the point is not that we commit to futile tasks, but that we are more capable of meaningful adaptation: whether that means quitting and trying something else or sticking – and growing[7].

But now suppose that we have already made a rational decision to persevere: the Growth Mindset now has an additional significance. It helps us to deal with challenges and setbacks. It is no good spending an entire career cowering in fear of negative feedback, avoiding situations in which you might be judged, and thus scuppering any chance of improvement. You haven't given up; but you haven't progressed, either.

James Dyson worked his way through 5,127 prototypes while his competitors didn't get through the first 100, not because he was more intelligent, but because he was more resilient. Likewise, Beckham and Jordan may have been born with admirable sporting qualities, but these would have meant little without a Growth Mindset.

And this is really the point. A growth-orientated culture is not a happy-clappy, wishy-washy, we-are-all-winners approach to business or life. And it is certainly not a trope to egalitarian sensibilities. Rather, it is a cutting-edge approach to organisational psychology based upon the most basic scientific principle of all: we progress fastest when we face up to failure – and learn from it.

14

Redefining Failure

I

We have arrived at a conclusion that was hinted at in the opening pages: if we wish to fulfil our potential as individuals and organisations, we must redefine failure. In many ways, that has been the purpose of this book. We have taken a journey through the rich and diverse literature on failure in an attempt to offer a new perspective on what it means, and how it should be handled.

At the level of the brain, the individual, the organisation and the system, failure is a means – sometimes the only means – of learning, progressing and becoming more creative. This is a hallmark of science, where errors point to how theories can be reformed; of sport, where practice could be defined as the willingness to clock up well-calibrated mistakes; of aviation, where every accident is harnessed as a means of driving system safety.

Errors have many different meanings, and call for different types of response depending on context, but in all of their guises they represent invaluable aids with the potential to help us learn.

Can so much turn on the basis of a reinterpretation of error? Can a new approach to success emerge by flipping the way we think about failure? The evidence for such a claim is contained in every example we have looked at: the contrast between science and pseudoscience, between healthcare and aviation, between centrally planned and well-regulated market systems. It is revealed, too, in the differences that emerge from the Fixed and Growth Mindsets.

When we see failure in a new light, success becomes a new and exhilarating concept. Competence is no longer a static phenomenon, something reserved for great people and organisations on the basis of fixed superiority. Rather, it is seen as dynamic in nature: something that grows as we strive to push back the frontiers of our knowledge. We are motivated not to boast about what we currently know, and to get defensive when people point to gaps in our knowledge.

Rather, we look in wonder at the infinite space beyond the boundaries of what we currently understand, and dare to step into that unbounded terrain, discovering new problems as we find new solutions, as great scientists do. As the philosopher Karl Popper put it: 'it is part of the greatness and beauty of science that we can learn through our own critical investigations that the world is utterly different from what we ever imagined – until our imagination was fired by the refutation of our earlier theories.'[1]

Many progressive institutions have attempted to inspire precisely this kind of redefinition of failure. James Dyson spends much of his life working to reform educational culture. He wants students to be equipped with a new way of thinking about the world. He rails against the prevailing conception of education as about exam perfection, about avoiding mistakes. He worries that this leads to intellectual stagnation. The Dyson Foundation works, above all, to de-stigmatise failure. He wants youngsters to experiment, to try new things, to take risks.

Innovative head teachers are engaged in precisely the same terrain. Heather Hanbury, the former headmistress of Wimbledon High School in south-west London, for example, created an annual event for her students called 'failure week'. She was aware that her students were performing well in exams, but she also realised that many were struggling with non-academic challenges, and not reaching their creative potential, particularly outside the classroom.

For one week she created workshops and assemblies where failure was celebrated. She asked parents and tutors and other role models to talk about how they had failed, and what they had learned. She showed YouTube clips of famous people practising: i.e. learning from their own mistakes. She told students about the journeys taken by the likes of David Beckham and James Dyson so they could have a more authentic understanding of how success really happens.

Hanbury has said:

You're not born with fear of failure, it's not an instinct, it's something that grows and develops in you as you get older. Very young children have no fear of failure at all. They have great fun trying new things and learning very fast. Our focus here is on failing well, on being good at failure. What I mean by this is taking the risk and then learning from it if it doesn't work.

There's no point in failing and then dealing with it by pretending it didn't happen, or blaming someone else. That would be a wasted opportunity to learn more about yourself and perhaps to identify gaps in your skills, experiences or qualifications. Once you've identified the learning you can then take action to make a difference.[3]

Other organisations have undertaken similar projects of redefinition. W. Leigh Thompson, the chief scientific officer at pharmaceutical giant Eli Lilly, initiated 'failure parties' in the 1990s to celebrate excellent scientific work that nevertheless resulted in failure. It was about de-stigmatising failure and liberating staff from the twin dangers of blame and cognitive dissonance.

But can these kinds of interventions have real effects? Do they really change behaviour and boost performance and adaptation?

Consider an experiment involving a group of schoolchildren who had shown difficulty in dealing with failure. In that respect they were like many of us. Half of these students were then given a course where they experienced consistent success. The questions posed during these sessions were easy and the students were delighted to ace them. They began to develop intellectual self-confidence, as you would expect.

The second group were not given successes, but training in how to reinterpret their failures. They were sometimes given problems that they couldn't solve, but they were also taught to think that they could improve if they expended effort. The failures were positioned not as indications of their lack of intelligence, but as opportunities to improve their reasoning and understanding.

At the end of these training courses, the two groups were tested

on a difficult problem. Those who had experienced consistent success were as demoralised by failing to solve this problem as they had
been before the training. They were so sensitive to failure that their
performance declined and it took many days for them to recover.
Some were even more afraid of challenges and didn't want to take
risks.

The group that had been taught to reinterpret failure were quite
different. They significantly improved in their ability to deal with the
challenging task. Many actually demonstrated superior performance
after failure and when they went back to class began asking their
teachers for more challenging work. Far from ducking out of situations where they might fail, they embraced them.

This hints at one of the great paradoxes about school and life.
Often it is those who are the most successful who are also the most
vulnerable. They have won so many plaudits, been praised so lavishly for their flawless performances, that they haven't learned to
deal with the setbacks that confront us all. This has been found to
be particularly true of young girls. Female students who go through
primary school getting consistently high grades, and who appear to
their teachers as highly capable, are often the most devastated by
failure.[3]

In one famous experiment a group of schoolgirls were measured
for their IQ and then given a task that began with a really challenging
section. You might have expected the girls with the higher IQs to
perform better on the test. In fact, the results were the other way
around. The high IQ girls, who had always succeeded in life, were so
flustered by the initial struggle that they became 'helpless'. They
hardly bothered with the later problems on the test. The relationship
between IQ and outcome was actually *negative*.[4]

And this is why 'failure week' at Wimbledon High School was
such an enlightened idea. Heather Hanbury was trying to give her
high-achieving students a lesson that would help them not merely at
school or university but in later life. She was taking them outside
their comfort zone and helping them to develop the psychological
tools that are so vital in the real world.

'Our pupils are hugely successful in their exams, but they can overreact when things go wrong,' she said. 'We want them to be courageous. It sounds paradoxical, but we dare them to fail.'

II

Let us move beyond the classroom and consider some of the differences in attitudes to failure that exist in the real world. Specifically, let us take the issue of entrepreneurship, something that is widely regarded as crucial to success in the global economy.

In the United States the culture is one where entrepreneurs take risks and rarely give up if their first venture fails. Henry Ford, the car entrepreneur, is a case in point. His first enterprise, the Detroit Automobile Company, collapsed, as did his involvement with the second, the Henry Ford Company. But these failures taught him vital lessons about pricing and quality. The Ford Motor Company, his third venture, changed the world. 'Failure is simply the opportunity to begin again, this time more intelligently,' he said.

In Japan, on the other hand, the culture is very different. For complex reasons of social and economic history,[5] failure is more stigmatising. The basic attitude is that if you mess up you have brought shame on yourself and your family. Failure is regarded not as an opportunity to learn, but as a demonstration that you do not have what it takes. These are classic Fixed Mindset attitudes. Blame for business failure is common and, often, intense.

Now take a look at the data on entrepreneurship. According to the World Bank, Japan has the lowest annual entry rate for new enterprises among the OECD nations. As of 2013 it had slumped to only a third of that in the United States. On the OECD Science, Technology, and Industry Scoreboard in 2008, Japan had the lowest quantity of venture capital invested: American investment was twenty times higher as a percentage of GDP.

Other studies reveal similar findings. According to the Global Entrepreneurship Monitor only 1.9 per cent of adults between the ages of eighteen and sixty-four are working actively to establish new businesses in Japan. In the United States, the figure is more than 250 per cent higher. According to the Kauffman Foundation, nearly one in every eight American adults (11.9 per cent) is currently engaged in 'entrepreneurial activity'. This is near the top of the developed world.

It goes without saying that these differences have real effects, not only on entrepreneurs, but on the wider economy. As a paper for the Wharton Business School put it: 'In Japan, the relative dearth of opportunity-driven entrepreneurship has contributed to the nation's economic malaise over the past two decades.' As for America, entrepreneurs are considered a cornerstone of the nation's success: 'empirical research has shown that "opportunity-driven" entrepreneurship is the wellspring of growth in the modern market economy'.[6]

But can these differences in the hard data really hinge on something as soft and intangible as differing conceptions of failure? In 2009, the Global Entrepreneurship Monitor carried out a major survey to find out. They looked at attitudes towards entrepreneurship in twenty innovation-based advanced economies. The results were emphatic. Japanese citizens demonstrated the highest fear of failure. Americans, meanwhile, displayed one of the lowest levels.[7]

Five years later the same attitudes prevailed. In a survey of seventy different countries, at different stages of development, and facing different challenges, Japan had the highest fear of failure of all of them with the exception of Greece, which was going through the trauma of an externally imposed fiscal consolidation. The United States remained among the lowest.[8] In a 2013 survey Japan was rated the lowest in the world in terms of believing that the skills associated with entrepreneurship can be improved over time.

Fear of failure is not an inherently bad thing. It is smart to consider the risks and to exercise caution if they are deemed severe. Fear can also spark great creative energy, a point that the entrepreneur Richard Branson has made.[9] The problem arises when opportunities exist, but it remains psychologically impossible to even engage with them. The problem is when setbacks lead not to learning, but to recrimination and defeatism.

This isn't just about entrepreneurship, it is about life. Let us take a different example that reveals the same underlying truth, but in the opposite direction. In mathematics, China and Japan rank amongst the best in the world. In the Programme for International Student Assessment (PISA) league table, which measures attainment among fifteen-year olds, China rates first and Japan seventh in maths. The United Kingdom and the United States lag well behind, in twenty-sixth and thirty-sixth positions respectively.[10]

Now, consider the differing attitudes towards mathematics between these nations. In the UK and the United States, maths is widely considered to be something you either can or can't do. When children struggle they assume they are not cut out for it. At schools up and down these nations, you hear youngsters say things like: 'I just don't have a brain for numbers.' As the Stanford academic Jo Boaler put it: 'The idea that only some people can do math is deep in the American and British psyche. Math is special in this way, and people have ideas about math that they don't have about any other subject.'[11]

In China and Japan the attitude is radically different. Maths is thought of as a bit like a language: as you persevere you become more articulate. Mistakes are held up not as evidence of a fixed inferiority, or as showing that you have 'the wrong kind of brain', but as evidence of learning. Some individuals are better than others at maths, but there is a presumption that everyone has the capacity to master basic mathematical concepts with perseverance and application.

Boaler talks of a visit to Shanghai, the area of China and the world that scores highest in maths. 'The teacher gave the students . . . problems to work on and then called on students for their answers. As the students happily shared their work the interpreter leaned across to me and told me that that the teacher was choosing students who had made mistakes. The students were proud to share their mistakes as mistakes were valued by the teacher.'[12]

Again and again, differences in mindset explain why some individuals and organisations grow faster than others. Evolution, as we noted in Chapter 7, is driven by failure. But if we give up when we fail, or if we edit out our mistakes, we halt our progress no matter how smart we are. It is the Growth Mindset fused with an enlightened evolutionary system that helps to unlock our potential; it is the framework that drives personal and organisational adaptation.

III

For one final insight into how our misguided attitudes can undermine progress, let us take one of the most astonishing behaviours of all: self-handicapping. This has been studied in businesses, in schools and in family life. It reveals just how far people are prepared to go to protect their ego at the expense of their own long-term success.

I first saw self-handicapping in action during my final year at Oxford University. We were about to take our final exams and we had all prepared well for the big day. Most of us were apprehensive, but also relieved that the waiting was finally over. Over the previous twenty-four hours the majority of us spent our time going through our revision notes for a final time.

But one group of students did something very different. They sat outside in the garden area frolicking and drinking cocktails, didn't take a single look at their notes, and made sure that everyone knew that they were going to a nightclub later that evening. They all looked pretty relaxed, joking about the coming exams.

To me, it didn't make sense. Why jeopardise three years of work for the sake of a night on the town? What could they possibly hope to gain by arriving at the first exam, one of the most important days of their lives, with a hangover? The most surprising thing of all was that many were among the brightest students, who had worked diligently for the preceding three years.

It was only years later, when reading about cognitive dissonance and the Fixed Mindset, that the pieces fell into place: they were so terrified of underperforming, so worried that the exam might reveal that they were not very clever, that they needed an alternative explanation for possible failure. They effectively sabotaged their own chances in order to gain one.

Excuses in life are typically created retrospectively. We have all pointed to a bad night's sleep, or a cold, or the dog being sick, to justify a poor performance. But these excuses are so obvious and self-serving that people see through them. We see through our own excuses too. They don't reduce dissonance because they are too blatant.

But self-handicapping is more sophisticated. This is where the excuse is not cobbled together after the event, but actively engineered beforehand. It is, in effect, a pre-emptive dissonance-reducing strategy. If these students flunked their crucial exam, they could say: 'It wasn't me who messed up, it was the booze!' It served another purpose, too: if they *did* pass the exam, they could still point to alcohol in mitigation for why they didn't get an even higher grade.

The phenomenon of self-handicapping seems, on the surface, perplexing: young sportspeople who stop training hard in the crucial few weeks before a big event; executives who breeze into a vital sales pitch without reading the relevant material; brilliant university students who suddenly decide to get drunk before a crucial exam.

But viewed through the prism of the Fixed Mindset it makes perfect sense. It is precisely because the project really matters that failure is so threatening – and why they desperately need an alternative explanation for messing up. As one psychologist put it: 'One can admit to a minor flaw [drinking] in order to avoid admitting to a much more threatening one [I am not as bright as I like to think].'[13]

In a seminal 1978 study into self-handicapping by psychologists Steven Berglas and Edward Jones, students were given an exam.[14] Before taking the exam students were asked whether they would like to take a drug that would inhibit their performance. This wasn't really a choice at all. After all, why would anyone wish to actively undermine their chances of success? But, in the event, a large proportion chose to take it.

To some observers it seemed crazy, but to Dr Berglas it made perfect sense. He had himself experimented with drugs for the first time just before he took the crucial SAT examinations in high school. He was expected to get a perfect score. His self-image was bound up in the performance. The drug-taking gave him the perfect cover story if things went wrong.[15]

Some psychologists have argued that self-handicapping can have short-term benefits. If you can pin a particular failure on, say, drinking too much, it cushions your self-esteem in the event of a poor result. But this misses the real lesson in all this. What is the point of preserving self-esteem that is so brittle that it can't cope with failure?

Think back to the surgeons earlier in the book. They had healthy egos. They had enjoyed expensive educations and owned impressive certificates. They were widely revered by colleagues and patients. But this is precisely why the culture was so dangerous. Surgeons are often so keen to protect their self-esteem that they can't admit their fallibility.

Self-esteem, in short, is a vastly overvalued psychological trait. It can cause us to jeopardise learning if we think it might risk us looking anything less than perfect. What we really need is resilience: the capacity to face up to failure, and to learn from it. Ultimately, that is what growth is all about.

On the afternoon of 30 June 1998, David Beckham's life changed forever. He was twenty-three years old and playing for England in his first World Cup in Saint-Etienne in central France. It was a crucial knockout match against Argentina for a place in the quarter-finals.

The score was level at 2–2. More than 20 million of his countrymen were tuning in on television back home and tens of thousands more were watching in the stadium. For Beckham it was a dream to be out on the field of play representing his country.

Two minutes into the second half, Beckham was in the middle of the pitch when he was hit hard from behind by Diego Simeone, an Argentinian player. He felt a knee go into his back and he was knocked flat. As Simeone got up, he tugged Beckham's hair, and then patted him on the head.

Beckham reacted immediately, flicking his leg towards his opponent. His foot travelled less than two feet, and made minimal contact with Simeone, but the Argentinian went down, clutching his thigh. Beckham instantly knew he had made a terrible mistake, and prepared for the worst. His stomach turned to ice as the referee raised a red card into the air.

England would go on to lose the match on penalties. Beckham, who had been sent off and spent the rest of the game in the dressing room, knew that he would be in the line of fire from the British press.

But nothing prepared him for the storm that was about to engulf him and his family.

When the team arrived back at Heathrow Airport the next day, the twenty-three-year old was pursued relentlessly by cameras and journalists. He received bullets in the post, his effigy was burned from a lamppost, and one national newspaper turned his face into a dartboard.

The first match of the following season, he had to be escorted into the ground under police guard. Every time he touched the ball for Manchester United, opposition fans erupted in booing. He had made a small mistake in reacting to a poor challenge from an opponent at the World Cup, but he was treated almost like a criminal. Many commentators doubted he would last the season. As one journalist put it: 'You have to fear for Beckham's career. Nobody can expect him to come back from something like this.'

In the event Beckham had the finest season of his career. Manchester United won the Treble (the Premier League, the FA Cup and the Champions League), the first, and so far only, English club to achieve that feat. Beckham played in almost every game. At the end of the season he was voted second in the FIFA World Player of the Year awards behind Rivaldo of Brazil and Barcelona, and ahead of Batistuta, Zidane, Vieri, Figo, Shevchenko, and Raúl.

His contributions were remarkable. He made sixteen assists in the league and seven in the Champions League. He scored vital goals, not least the opening strike in the historic FA Cup semi-final reply against Arsenal and an equaliser in the final game of the Premier League season against Spurs. He also took both corners when United scored twice during extra time to clinch the Champions League title from under the noses of Bayern Munich. It was a superb set of performances.

But let us rewind to the very first game of that season, against Leicester. United were trailing 2–1 when they were awarded a free kick, just outside the area. It was a huge moment given what had happened just a few weeks earlier at Saint-Etienne. Beckham had been booed throughout the game by opposition fans. He would later say that his stomach tightened as he strode over to place the ball. But as he walked back to take the shot, he felt everything change. He said:

> It was only as I stepped up to take the free kick that I felt my will-power hardening. It would have been easy to be negative, to worry about the consequences, but I just felt that little bit of steel inside. Partly, it was the extraordinary support I had received [from United fans]. But it was also all the practice over the years: the thousands of free kicks I had taken in rain, sleet and snow. It gave me confidence.

Adversity rarely comes in as public a form as that endured by Beckham in Saint-Etienne. But responding to adversity, coming back from failure, absolutely depends on how we regard the setback. Is it evidence that we lack what it takes? Does it mean we are not up to the job? This is the kind of response offered by those in a Fixed Mindset. They are sapped by impediments, and often lose willpower. They try to avoid feedback, even when they can learn from it.

But when you regard failure as a learning opportunity, when you trust in the power of practice to help you grow through difficulties, your motivation and self-belief are not threatened in anything like the same way. Indeed, you embrace failure as an opportunity to learn, whether about improving a vacuum cleaner, creating a new scientific theory, or developing a promising football career.

'It was tough to get sent off, but I learned a valuable lesson,' Beckham told me. 'Isn't that what life is about?'

Coda: The Big Picture

I

Almost every society studied by historians has had its own ideas about the way the world works, often in the form of myths, religions and superstitions. Primitive societies usually viewed these ideas as sacrosanct and often punished those who disagreed with death. Those in power didn't want to be confronted with any evidence that they might be wrong.

As the philosopher Bryan Magee put it: 'The truth is to be kept inviolate and handed on unsullied from generation to generation. For this purpose, institutions develop – mysteries, priesthoods, and at an advanced stage, schools.'[1] Schools of this kind never admitted to new ideas and expelled anyone who attempted to change the doctrine.[2]

But at some point in human history this changed. Criticism was tolerated and even encouraged. According to the philosopher Karl Popper, this first occurred in the days of the Ancient Greeks, but the precise historical claim is less important than what it meant in practice. The change ended the dogmatic tradition. It was, he says, the most important moment in intellectual progress since the discovery of language.

And he is surely right. For centuries before the Greeks the entire weight of intellectual history was about preserving and defending established ideas: religious, practical and tribal. This defensive tendency, seemingly so universal in human history, has been a subject of speculation for anthropologists over many years.

But the answer, surely, is that ancient tribes were trapped in a Fixed Mindset. They thought that the truth had been revealed by a god or god-like ancestor and did not feel any need to build new knowledge. New evidence was regarded not as an opportunity to learn fresh truths, but as a threat to the established worldview.

Indeed, those who questioned traditional assumptions were often met with violence. History is full of episodes where ideas were tested not rationally but militarily. According to *Encyclopaedia of Wars* by Charles Phillips and Alan Axelrod, 123 conflicts in human history can be traced directly to differences in opinion, whether religious, ideological or doctrinal.[3]

Think back to cognitive dissonance. This is where dissenting evidence is reframed or ignored. Wars of ideology can be seen as an extreme form of dissonant reduction: instead of shutting your ears to inconvenient evidence, you murder the dissenters. This is a sure-fire way to guarantee that religious and traditional assumptions are not challenged, but it also torpedoes any possibility of progress.

But the Greek period challenged all this. As the philosopher Bryan Magee put it: 'It spelt the end of the dogmatic tradition of passing on an unsullied truth, and the beginning of a new rational tradition of subjecting speculations to critical discussion. It was the inauguration of scientific method. Error was turned from disaster to advantage.'[4]

It is difficult to exaggerate the significance of that last sentence. Error, under the Greeks, was no longer catastrophic, or threatening, or worth killing over. On the contrary, if someone had persuasive evidence revealing the flaws in your beliefs, it was an opportunity to learn, to revise your model of the world. Scientific knowledge was seen as dynamic rather than static; something that grows through critical investigation, rather than handed down by authorities. As Xenophanes wrote:

> The gods did not reveal, from the beginning,
>> All things to us, but in the course of time,
>> Through seeking we may learn and know things better.

This subtle shift had truly staggering effects. The Greek period inspired the greatest flowering of knowledge in human history, producing the forefathers of the entire Western intellectual tradition, including Socrates, Plato, Aristotle, Pythagoras and Euclid. It changed the world in ways both subtle and profound. As Benjamin Farrington, former professor of classics at Swansea University, put it:

> With astonishment we find ourselves on the threshold of modern science. Nor should it be supposed that by some trick of translation the extracts [from ancient Greek manuscripts] have been given an air of modernity. Far from it. The vocabulary of these writings and their style are the source from which our own vocabulary and style have been derived.

But this period was tragically not to last. Looking back from our vantage point, it is astonishing just how suddenly the advance in human knowledge ground to a halt. For much of the time between the Greeks and the seventeenth century, western science remained in a cul-de-sac, a point that has been powerfully made by the philosopher, scientist and politician Francis Bacon.

As Bacon wrote in *Novum Organum*, his masterpiece, in 1620: 'The sciences which we possess come for the most part from the Greeks. [But] from all these systems of the Greeks, and their ramifications through particular sciences, there can hardly after the lapse of so many years be adduced a single experiment which tends to relieve and benefit the condition of man.'[5]

This was a truly devastating assessment. The key argument here is that science had come up with almost *nothing* to 'benefit the condition of man'. To us, accustomed to the way science transforms human life, this seems remarkable. But in Bacon's time, this was the way it had been for generations. Scientific progress just didn't happen.

Why this halt in progress? The answer is not difficult to identify: the world drifted back into the old mindset. The teachings of the early church were brought together with the philosophy of Aristotle (who had been elevated to a revered authority) to create a new, sacrosanct worldview. Anything that contradicted Christian teaching was considered blasphemous. Dissenters were punished. Error had, once again, become disastrous.

Perhaps the most extraordinary example of how inconvenient evidence was ignored or reframed relates to the Judeo-Christian idea that women have one more rib than men, drawn from the scriptural passage in Genesis that Eve was created from Adam's rib. This could have been disproven at any time by doing something very simple: counting. The fact that men and women have the same number of ribs is just obvious.

And yet this 'truth' was generally accepted all the way until 1543, until contradicted by the Flemish anatomist, Andreas Vesalius. This shows, once again, that when we are fearful of being wrong, when the desire to protect the status quo is particularly strong, mistakes can persist in plain sight almost indefinitely.

Bacon's towering achievement was to challenge the dogmatic conception of knowledge that had restrained mankind for centuries. Like the Greeks he argued that science was not about defending truths, but challenging them. It was about having the courage to experiment and learn. 'The true and lawful goal of sciences is none other than this: that human life be endowed with new discoveries and powers,' he wrote.[6]

He also warned against the dangers of confirmation bias:

The human understanding when it has once adopted an opinion (either as being the received opinion or as being agreeable to itself) draws all things else to support and agree with it. And though there be a greater number and weight of instances to be found on the other side, yet these it either neglects and despises, or else by some distinction sets aside and rejects, in order that by this great and pernicious predetermination the authority of its former conclusions may remain inviolate.[7]

Bacon's work, along with other great thinkers such as Galileo, set the stage for a second scientific revolution. Theories were subjected to experimental criticism. Creativity, as a direct consequence, flourished. Testing the ideas of authority figures thoroughly was not considered disrespectful, but obligatory. Error had once again been transformed from disaster to advantage.

The point here is not that the ideas and theories of our forebears are not worth having; quite the reverse. Theories that have been through a process of selection, rigorously tested rules of thumb, practical knowledge honed through long trial and error and countless failures, are of priceless importance.

We are the beneficiaries of a rich intellectual legacy and, if the slate were wiped clean, if all the cumulative knowledge gained by our ancestors were to somehow disappear, we would be lost. As Karl Popper put it: 'If we started with Adam [i.e. with the relatively small amount of knowledge of early mankind], we wouldn't get any further than Adam did.'[8]

But theories that claim to furnish knowledge about the world that have never failed, which have been held in place by authority alone, are a different matter. It is these ideas, and the underlying belief that they are sacrosanct, that is so destructive. The scientific method is about pushing out the frontiers of our knowledge through a willingness to embrace error.

Think back to Galileo's disproof of Aristotle's theory about heavier objects falling faster than lighter ones (perhaps apocryphally he did this by dropping balls from the Leaning Tower of Pisa). This was a crucial discovery, but it also symbolised the beautifully disrupting power of failure. A single controlled experiment had refuted the ideas of one of the most respected intellectual giants in history, setting the stage for new answers, new problems and new discoveries.[9]

But the battle between these two conceptions of the world – one revealed from above, the other discovered from below – continued to rage. When Galileo saw the phases of Venus and the mountains of the moon through his newly invented telescope, he proposed that the sun rather than the earth was the centre of the universe.

At the time, the theory that the earth moved around the sun was believed to contradict scripture. Psalm 93:1 states that 'the world is firmly established, it cannot be moved'. Psalm 104:5 says: 'the Lord set the earth on its foundations; it can never be moved'. And Ecclesiastes 1:5 says: 'And the sun rises and sets and returns to its place.'

But when Galileo invited Christian scholars to look through his telescope in order to see the new evidence, they flatly refused. They didn't want to see any data that might count against the earth-centric view of the universe. It is difficult to think of a more revelatory episode of cognitive dissonance. They simply shut their eyes.

As Galileo said in a letter to the German mathematician Johannes Kepler:

> My dear Kepler, I wish that we might laugh at the remarkable stupidity of the common herd. What do you have to say about the principal philosophers of this academy who are filled with the stubbornness of an asp and do not want to look at either the planets, the moon or the telescope, even though I have freely and deliberately offered them the opportunity a thousand times? Truly, just as the asp stops its ears, so do these philosophers shut their eyes to the light of truth.

Galileo was ultimately forced to recant his views, not through rational argument, but through force. He was placed before the Inquisition and found 'vehemently suspect of heresy' and ordered to 'abjure, curse and detest' his opinions. He was sentenced to formal imprisonment and remained under house arrest for the rest of his life.

According to popular legend, as Galileo retracted his views, he muttered under his breath: 'But still it moves.'

This brief foray into the history of science shows that the basic analysis of this book is reflected in some of the most significant trends in human history. Religion was fixed in its thinking about the natural world. Knowledge was revealed from above rather than discovered through a process of learning from mistakes. That is why progress was so slow for not merely decades, but centuries.

This takes us back to healthcare, where errors are also profoundly dissonant. As we have seen this has many facets, but at least one of them is the cultural insinuation that senior doctors are infallible. Is it any wonder that they find it so difficult to learn and adapt? It is noteworthy that the inability of senior doctors to embrace their flaws and weaknesses, indeed to admit that such things are even possible, is sometimes called a 'god complex'.

Similarly, the criminal justice system has long been infused with an almost religious air of infallibility, particularly when it comes to wrongful convictions. As we noted earlier, one district attorney said: 'Innocent men are never convicted. Don't worry about it. It is a physical impossibility'.[10] But if the system is already flawless, why bother to reform it?

Science at its best has a different approach, one based upon the bracing idea that there are things still to learn, truths yet to be discovered. As the philosopher Hilary Putnam put it: 'The difference between science and previous ways of trying to find out truth is, in large part, that scientists are willing to test their ideas, because they don't regard them as infallible . . . You have to put questions to nature and be willing to change your ideas if they don't work.'*[11]

II

The impasse that Bacon once identified regarding natural science in the seventeenth century echoes the situation we face today with the social world. Natural science is about material objects like billiard balls, atoms and planets (physics, chemistry and the like) while social science is about human beings (such as politics, criminal justice, business and healthcare). It is this world that needs to undergo a Baconian revolution.

Take Bacon's criticism of medieval science: that knowledge was handed down from authority figures. This tallies directly with the dogma of top-down knowledge in the social sphere today. We see this phenomenon when politicians talk about their pet ideas and

---

* Science is not without flaws, and an eye should always be kept on social and institutional obstacles to progress. Current concerns include publication bias (where only successful experiments are published in journals), the weakness of the peer review system, and the fact that many experiments do not appear to be replicable. For a good review of the issues, see: www.economist.com/news/briefing/21588057-scientists-think-self-correcting-alarming-degree-if-not-trouble.

ideologies – school uniform improves discipline, delinquents can be scared out of crime through prison visits, and so on. They don't see the need for experiments or data because they think they have reached the answer through conviction or insight.

And these habits of assumed understanding are kept in place as they once were in the natural sciences by the narrative fallacy. This is what makes us think that the world is simpler than it really is. These nice, neat, intuitive stories (think back to *Scared Straight*) delude us into thinking we have a handle on real-world complexity, when often we don't. This is not to say that narratives are not worth having; it is merely to suggest that they should be seen for what they are: rhetorical devices requiring empirical validation.

The irony is that the social world is more complex than the natural world. We have general theories predicting the movement of the planets, but no general theories of human behaviour. As we progress from physics, through chemistry and biology, out to economics, politics and business, coming up with solutions becomes more difficult. But this strengthens rather than weakens the imperative of learning from failure.

We need to come up with enlightened ways of making trial and error effective through the use of controlled trials and the like, and be more willing to iterate our way to success. As situations become more complex we will have to avoid the temptation to impose untested solutions from above and try to discover the world from below.

While we have spent the last few centuries using experimentation and data in modern science, these have been largely neglected in the social world. Until 2004 there were only a few dozen controlled experiments in education, but hundreds of thousands in physics.

And the irony is that, unlike in the medieval world, today we are fully aware of the complexity of physics. We talk about rocket science as the ultimate intellectual pursuit. We are mesmerised by Relativity and Quantum Theory. We recognise that creative people make great leaps in the natural sciences, but we also realise that this process is checked by experimentation. Scientific advance is, at least in part, precision-guided. That is Bacon's legacy.

But when it comes to the social world we often trust gut instinct. Political pundits range widely over various issues, making arguments on education one week, then criminal justice the next. The narratives are often powerful. But few journalists or commentators would feel entitled to argue about engineering or chemistry, at least without firm data. They would always subordinate narrative to evidence in these domains.

And yet often in the social world this presumption is flipped. Arguments are deemed *more* compelling when stripped of evidence. Instead, we admire conviction, which is often a synonym for gut feeling. Chris Grayling, then the Lord Chancellor and Secretary of State for Justice in the UK, once said: 'The last Government was obsessed with pilots [i.e. pilot schemes]. Sometimes you just have to believe in something and do it.' This contempt for evidence echoes the stance of the pre-scientific age.

We noted in Chapter 7 that many of the seminal thinkers of the last two centuries favoured free markets and free societies precisely because they resist the human tendency to impose untested answers from above. Free markets are successful, in large part because of their capacity to clock up thousands of useful failures. Centrally planned economies are ineffective, on the other hand, because they lack this capacity.

Markets, like other evolutionary systems, offer an antidote to our ignorance. They are not perfect, and often need government intervention to work properly. But well-functioning markets succeed because of a vital ingredient: adaptability. Different companies trying different things, with some failing and some surviving, add to the pool of knowledge. Cognitive dissonance is thwarted, in the long run, by an irrefutable failure test: bankruptcy. A company owner who runs out of money cannot pretend that his strategy was a successful one.

Liberal societies underpinned by the values of social tolerance also harness these benefits. John Stuart Mill, the British philosopher, wrote about the importance of 'experiments in living'. He based his defence of freedom not on an abstract value, but upon the recognition that civil society also needs trial and error. Social conformity, he argued, is catastrophic because it limits experimentation (it is the sociological equivalent of deference to authority). Criticism and dissent, far from being dangerous to the social order, are central to it. They drive new ideas and fire creativity.*

'Protection against the tyranny of the magistrate is not enough,' Mill wrote. '[We need protection against] the tyranny of prevailing opinion and feeling; against the tendency of society to impose, by other means than civil penalties, its own ideas and practices as rules of conduct on those who dissent from them.' Mill's notion of liberalism, like that of Popper, was largely underpinned by the insight that Bacon identified in relation to the natural sciences: the mismatch between the complexity of the world and our capacity to understand it.

But what Mill didn't say (unsurprisingly, given that RCTs had not become established in the culture) is that trial and error, on its own, is sometimes insufficient to drive rapid progress. Why? Because social complexity can play havoc with the interpretation of observational feedback.

Controlled trials, where practical and ethical, have the potential to boost learning by isolating causal relationships. And yet they are not a panacea. We have to be mindful of unintended consequences and the holistic context, which are sometimes neglected by those who perform RCTs.

Creative leaps and paradigm shifts in science, business and technology require a capacity to connect distant concepts and ideas. Once again, we can only do this by engaging with the problems and failures that fire the imagination.

This analysis seems to call for intellectual humility, the recognition that our ideas and theories will often be flawed. But how do we tally this with the observation that many of the most successful people are bold and sometimes even dogmatic? Entrepreneurs and scientists often risk a great deal to champion a theory or business idea. This doesn't seem to square with the idea that science and

---

* As the creativity researcher Charlan Nemeth has put it: 'the presence of dissenting minority views appear to stimulate more originality. . .'.

markets are guided by learning from mistakes rather than top-down knowledge.

Here it is necessary to distinguish between two different levels of analysis. If we return to Unilever and the nozzle, we described the approach by the mathematicians (who reasoned their way to an inadequate solution) as top-down and that of the biologists (who experimented their way to a brilliant solution) as bottom-up.

But suppose that the team of mathematicians that came up with a defective nozzle was but one of twenty-five teams of mathematicians employed by Unilever to come up with a new design. And suppose that each of the nozzles created by these various teams was tested, with the winning nozzle used as the starting point for the teams to go back to the drawing board, to come up with a new design, and so on. Suddenly this approach starts to look very different. This is the importance of *variation*, a concept with parallels in biological evolution.

When you have top-down approaches competing with each other, with a failure test to determine which of them is working, the system starts to exhibit the properties of bottom-up. That is what well-functioning markets do: entrepreneurs competing with each other, with the winning ideas replicated by the competition, which are then improved upon, and so on. Many scientists are also entrepreneurial, going against the status quo in the hope of discovering new truths.

To put it another way, the difference between top-down and bottom-up is not just about differences in activity, it is also about the relevant perspective. It is at the level of the system that bottom-up learning is vital because of the imperative of adaptability. And that is the story of aviation, well-functioning markets, biological evolution and, to a certain extent, the common law.

At the level of individuals the question is more open. Do individual organisations progress faster when they iterate their way to success or when they come up with bold ideas and stick to them doggedly? In high tech, as we have seen, the world is moving so fast that entrepreneurs have found it necessary to adopt rapid iteration. They may have bold ideas, but they give them a chance to fail early through the minimum viable product (MVP). And if the idea survives the verdict of early adopters, it is iterated into better shape by harnessing the feedback of end-users.

In other words, competition has favoured entrepreneurs that take bottom-up learning seriously rather than those that do not. And that is a powerful operating assumption in a rapidly changing world. If valid learning can be achieved through iteration at a fast pace and low cost, it is crazy to pass up the opportunity. Success, at the level of the individual as well as at the level of the system, will increasingly hinge on adaptability.

In other words, learning from failure.

II

Having looked at the big picture, let's narrow the focus and look at how we can wield the lessons of this book in a practical way. How can we harness the power of learning from mistakes in our jobs, our businesses and in our lives?

The first and most important issue is to create a revolution in the way we think about failure. For centuries, errors of all kinds have been considered embarrassing, morally egregious, almost dirty. The French Larousse dictionary historically defined error as 'a vagabond-age of the imagination, of the mind that is not subject to any rule'.

This conception still lingers today. It is why children don't dare to put their hands up in class to answer questions (how embarrassing to risk getting an answer wrong!), why doctors reframe mistakes, why politicians resist running rigorous tests on their policies, and why blame and scapegoating are so endemic.

As business leaders, teachers, coaches, professionals and parents, we have to transform this notion of failure. We have to conceptualise it not as dirty and embarrassing, but as bracing and educative. This is the notion we need to instil in our children: that failure is a part of life and learning, and that the desire to avoid it leads to stagnation.

We should praise each other for trying, for experimenting, for demonstrating resilience and resolve, for daring to learn through our own critical investigations, and for having the intellectual courage to see evidence for what it is rather than what we want it to be.

If we only ever praise each other for getting things right, for perfection, for flawlessness, we will insinuate, if only unintentionally, that it is possible to succeed without failing, to climb without falling. In a world that is complex, whose beauty is revealed in its intricacy and depth, this is misconceived. We have to challenge this misconception, in our lives and in our organisations.

To do so would be nothing less than revolutionary. A liberating attitude to error would change almost every aspect of our professions, schools and political institutions. It will not be easy, there will doubtless be resistance, but the battle is worth it. Instead of shying away from criticism and inconvenient evidence, we should embrace them.

As the author Bryan Magee, drawing on the work of Karl Popper, put it:

> No one can possibly give us more service than by showing us what is wrong with what we think or do; and the bigger the fault, the bigger the improvement made possible by its revelation. The man who welcomes and acts on criticism will prize it almost above friendship: the man who fights it out of concern to maintain his position is clinging to non growth. Anything like a widespread changeover in our society towards Popperian attitudes to criticism would constitute a revolution in social and interpersonal relationships – not to mention organisational practice.[12]

Once we have this new mindset, we can start to create systems that harness the power of adaptivity in our lives. What does this mean in practice? Well, let us start with how to improve our judgements and decision-making. We noted in Chapter 3 that intuitive judgement improves when it is given a chance to learn from mistakes. This is how chess masters build their skill and how paediatric nurses are able to detect illnesses that are apparently invisible.

But consider the following questions. Do you fail in your judgements? Do you ever get access to the evidence that shows where you might be going wrong? Are your decisions ever challenged by objective data? If the answer to any of these questions is 'no', you are almost certainly not learning. This is not a question of motivation or diligence, but of iron logic. You are like a golfer playing in the dark.

Think back to the example of psychotherapists from Chapter 3. They are often industrious, caring and compassionate – and yet many don't improve with time on the job. Why? The reason is simple. Most psychotherapists gauge how their clients are responding to treatment not with objective data, but by observing them in clinic. But this data is highly unreliable since patients might exaggerate how well they are to please the therapist. Moreover, psychotherapists rarely track their clients after therapy has finished. This means that they do not get any feedback on the lasting impact of the treatment.

So, how to address this problem? It is possible to see the basic contours of an answer without even knowing much about psychotherapy itself. Psychotherapists need to access the data on where they are going wrong, so they have an opportunity to reform and refine their judgements and, at a deeper level of adaptation, the models they use to make sense of the problems they are confronting.

With this in mind, consider what would happen if psychotherapists used a standardised and proven interview procedure to assess well-being in their patients. Suddenly they would have more objective information about how their clients are progressing. And if long-term outcomes were carefully tracked relative to valid historical data of similar cases, clinicians would have direct feedback on how patients were faring relative to established norms.

The stage is set for meaningful evolution. The lights have been switched on. As a landmark paper by a team of psychologists, which set out these proposals in detail, put it: 'Increasingly, there are reliable benchmarks for various disorders to which therapists can compare the progress of their clients. Therapists can use feedback about client progress to adjust therapy to achieve optimal outcomes.'[13]

But it should be clear that this is not just about psychotherapy, it is about intuitive expertise and decision-making in all its manifestations. If we are operating in an environment without meaningful feedback, we can't improve. We must institutionalise access to the 'error signal'.

This is also true of developing expertise in sport. In sport, feedback is almost always instant and obvious. We know when we have hit a ball out of bounds in golf or mistimed a forehand in tennis. But enlightened training environments maximise the quantity and quality of feedback, thus increasing the speed of adaptation.

Take football. Every time a player fails to control an incoming pass, he has learned something. Over time the central nervous system adapts, building more finesse and touch. But if a young player practises on a full-sized pitch, touching the ball infrequently, he will not improve very fast. On the other hand, if he practises on a smaller pitch, touching the ball frequently, his skill will improve more quickly.

Feedback is relevant to all the skills in football, including perceptual awareness, dribbling and passing and the integration of all of these abilities in a real-match context. Great coaches are not interested in merely creating an environment where adaptation can take place, they are focused on the 'meta' question of which training system is the most effective. They don't just want players to improve, but to do so as fast and as profoundly as possible.

In a similar way, within the healthcare there are debates about whether the Virginia Mason System creates the most effective method of reducing medical errors, just as there are discussions about whether the Toyota Production System is the best way of improving efficiency on a production line. But both models will eventually be superseded. We will learn to create more effective evolutionary systems, not just in healthcare and manufacturing, but in aviation, too.*

How, then, to select between competing evolutionary systems? A good way is to run a trial. In the case of football, for example, you could randomly divide a squad of youngsters with similar ability into two groups, then train them for a few weeks using different drills, then bring them back together and measure who has improved faster. A controlled trial of this kind, provided there is objective measurement, would establish the relative effectiveness of the drills,

---

* For a look at how the method of learning from failure has altered in aviation over the years, and with interesting thoughts on how it will continue to evolve, see Sidney Dekker lecture: https://vimeo.com/102167635

without the comparison being obscured by all other influences. In other words, the process of selecting between evolutionary systems is itself evolutionary in nature.

Another practical issue when it comes to harnessing the power of failure is to do so while minimising the costs. One way to achieve this for corporations and governments is with pilot schemes. These provide an opportunity to learn on a small scale. But it is vital that pilots are designed to test assumptions rather than confirm them. If you populate a pilot with your best staff in a prized location, you will learn virtually nothing about the challenges that are likely to occur.

As Amy Edmondson of Harvard Business School puts it:

> Managers in charge of piloting a new product or service . . . typically do whatever they can to make sure that the pilot is perfect right out of the starting gate. Ironically, this hunger to succeed can later inhibit the success of the official launch. Too often, managers in charge of pilots design optimal conditions rather than representative ones. Thus the pilot doesn't produce knowledge about what *won't* work.

Another powerful method we have looked at is randomised control trials. These are growing in the corporate world, but remain unexploited in many areas such as politics. The Behavioural Insights Team (BIT), a small organisation which started life inside Number 10 Downing Street and is now a social purpose company, was set up in 2010 to address this problem. It has already conducted more RCTs than the rest of the UK government combined in its entire history (sadly, this isn't saying much).

At a couple of meetings at their offices in central London, the team talked through some of these trials, not just in the UK but beyond. In one they tested different styles of letter (different wording, and so on) sent to Guatemalan taxpayers who had failed to declare their income tax on time. The most effective design increased payment by an astonishing 43 per cent. This is the power of testing to see what works and what doesn't. 'There is still a great deal of political resistance to running trials, in the UK and beyond,' David Halpern, the chief executive of BIT, said, 'but we are slowly making progress.'

Another 'failure based' technique, which has come into vogue in recent years, is the so-called pre-mortem. With this method a team is invited to consider why a plan has gone wrong before it has even been put into action. It is the ultimate 'fail fast' technique. The idea is to encourage people to be open about their concerns, rather than hiding them out of fear of sounding negative.

The pre-mortem is crucially different from considering what *might* go wrong. With a pre-mortem, the team is told, in effect, that 'the patient is dead': the project has failed; the objectives have not been met; the plans have bombed. Team members are then asked to generate plausible reasons why. By making the failure concrete rather than abstract, it alters the way the mind thinks about the problem.

According to the celebrated psychologist, Gary Klein, 'prospective hindsight', as it is called, increases the ability of people to correctly identify reasons for future outcomes by 30 per cent. It has also been backed by a host of leading thinkers, including Daniel Kahneman. 'The pre-mortem is a great idea,' he said. 'I mentioned it at Davos . . . and the chairman of a large corporation said it was worth coming to Davos for.'[14]

A pre-mortem typically starts with the leader asking everyone in the team to imagine that the project has gone horribly wrong and to write down the reasons why on a piece of paper. He or she then asks everyone to read a single reason from the list, starting with the project manager, before going around the table again.

Klein cites examples where issues have surfaced that would otherwise have remained buried. 'In a session held at one *Fortune* 50-size company, an executive suggested that a billion-dollar environmental sustainability project had "failed" because interest waned when the CEO retired,' he writes. 'Another pinned the failure on a dilution of the business case after a government agency revised its policies.'[15]

The purpose of the pre-mortem is not to kill off plans, but to strengthen them. It is also very easy to conduct. 'My guess is that, in general, doing a pre-mortem on a plan that is about to be adopted won't cause it to be abandoned,' Kahneman has said. 'But it will probably be tweaked in ways that everybody will recognize as beneficial. So the pre-mortem is a low-cost, high-pay-off kind of thing.'

Throughout the book we have looked at other techniques such as marginal gains and the lean start-up. But the point about all these methods is that they harness the incalcuable potency of the evolutionary mechanism. Providing they are used with an eye to context, and are fused with a growth-orientated mindset, they set the stage for an endlessly powerful process: cumulative adaptation.

IV

On a clear afternoon in early spring, I visited Martin Bromiley, the pilot whose story opened this book. He lost his wife, Elaine, during a routine operation in 2005. His two children, Adam and Victoria, were four and five at the time. At the time of writing, they are fourteen and fifteen.

North Marston is a classically beautiful English village. In the centre is a small pub called the Pilgrim. Rolling hills and green meadows surround a small, tight-knit community with a population of around eight hundred people. The sun was shining as I drove through the quiet lanes to the Bromiley family home.

As we sat in his lounge, Martin talked about his ongoing campaign to champion patient safety. Slight, quietly spoken, but determined, he continues to lead the Clinical Human Factors Group as an unpaid volunteer, and spends much of his free time encouraging the adoption of a mindset that regards adverse events not as threats but as learning opportunities.

A couple of weeks before our meeting, Martin had sent out a tweet to gauge what the campaign had achieved. His question was characteristically simple and to the point. 'Question – can you give me some specific examples of the impact of learning from my late wife's death? How has it changed things?' he wrote.

Within minutes, responses started flowing in, not just from the UK but around the world. Mark, a consultant in respiratory and intensive care medicine in Swindon, wrote: 'It has been one of the drivers for increasing simulation training. This is having a big impact on improving quality of care.'

Nick, who works in medical safety, wrote: 'We use your story at both undergraduate and postgraduate to discuss situational awareness and hierarchy/ raising concerns.' Jo Thomas, a nurse and senior lecturer in paramedic science, wrote: 'Your strength is reaching clinicians far beyond the operating and anaesthetic/ recovery rooms. [It has] challenged assumptions.'

Geoff Healy, an anaesthetist from Sydney, Australia wrote: 'Your strength and courage has educated at least two if not three or more generations of anaesthetists. The lives saved or altered because of your work are incalculable. We refer to this event everyday.'

These answers articulate the truth that hopefully underpins this book. Learning from failure may have the sound of a management cliché. It may be trotted out as a truism or a mantra lacking traction. But the quiet work of Martin Bromiley should help us to glimpse a wider vista. Learning from failure expresses a profound moral purpose. It is about saving, sustaining and enhancing human life. Martin said:

There has undoubtedly been progress in many areas of healthcare. Ten years ago, hospital-acquired infections like MRSA were dismissed as 'one of those things'. They were considered an inevitable problem that we couldn't do much about. Today, there is a real desire to confront these types of problems and figure out how to prevent harm in the future.

But that mindset is by no means universal. You only have to look at the sheer scale of preventable deaths, both in the UK and around the world, to see that there is still a profound tendency to cover up mistakes, and a fear about what independent investigations might uncover. We need to flip this attitude 180 degrees. It is the single most important issue in healthcare.

As the sun began to set over the horizon, the front door swung open: Adam and Victoria had returned from school. It happened to be Adam's fourteenth birthday and he spoke with excitement about going out for pizza that evening. I asked them what they were hoping to do with their lives. Victoria answered instantly and emphatically: 'I want to be a pilot,' she said. Adam expressed an interest in aviation, too, but leans towards meteorology.

We started to talk about the work that their father is doing to change attitudes in healthcare. 'I am really proud of Dad,' Adam said. 'He puts so much time into the group, even though he has a full-time job. If you had told him ten years ago that he would make such a big difference, he wouldn't have believed it. He gets letters and messages almost every week.'

Victoria, sitting alongside him, nodded. 'Our mother's death was very hard for all of us and we know that nothing can bring her back,' she said, her face etched with emotion. 'But I hope Dad continues with his work, and helps to spare other families from what we have had to go through.'

Victoria paused for a moment, and then her face brightened. 'I think Mum would have liked that,' she said.

Acknowledgements

I have failed quite a lot in life, particularly in my old sport of table tennis, so the subject matter of this book is close to my heart. The idea for it was triggered by a growing realisation that the common theme linking successful people, organisations and systems is a healthy and empowering attitude to failure. This is as true of David Beckham and James Dyson as it is of the aviation industry and Google.

The book has gone through a number of iterations, hopefully finding marginal gains with each change, which mirrors the argument within the pages about how improvement happens. Most of these iterations were inspired by the suggestions of friends and colleagues who read early drafts. I am hugely grateful to Danny Finkelstein, David Papineau, Chris Dillow, Max Reuter, Ben Preston, Andy Kidd, Kathy Weeks, Carl Macrae, Mark Thomas, Dilys Syed, David Honigman and James Naylor. Any defects that remain are mine and mine alone, although I hope I can learn from them too.

I would also like to thank the brilliant Nick Davies, who edited the book in the UK, Emily Angell, who edited the US edition, and Jonny Geller, my agent, who always fizzes with ideas and enthusiasm. I have also had terrific support from colleagues at *The Times*, including Tim Hallissey, Nicola Jeal and John Witherow. *The Times* is a wonderful publication to work for.

One of the most enjoyable things about writing a book of this kind is coming into contact with eye-opening books, papers and journal articles. I have tried to reference all of these in the endnotes, which provide further reading for those who wish to delve a little deeper, but I would like to acknowledge, here, some of the books that influenced me the most. These include a number of works by Karl Popper: *The Logic of Scientific Discovery*; *Conjectures and Refutations*; *The Open Society and its Enemies; The Poverty of Historicism*; and *Unended Quest*. I have also much enjoyed, and learnt from, *The Structure of Scientific Revolutions* by Thomas Kuhn and *Against Method* by Paul Feyerabend.

There are some marvellous popular books that have influenced the argument, too. These include *Just Culture* by Sidney Dekker, *Safe Patients, Smart Hospitals* by Peter Pronovost, *Human Error* by James Reason, *Being Wrong* by Kathryn Shultz, *Adapt* by Tim Harford, *Antifragile* by Nassim Nicholas Taleb, *Complications* by Atul Gawande, *Mistakes Were Made (But Not by Me!)* by Carol Tarvis and Elliot Aronson, *Uncontrolled* by Jim Manzi, *Teaming* by Amy Edmondson, *Where Good Ideas Come From* by Steven Johnson, *Creativity Inc.* by Ed Catmull, *Self Theories* by Carol Dweck, *The Decisive Moment* by Jonah Lehrer and *Philosophy and the Real World* by Bryan Magee.

I would also like to thank all of those who agreed to be interviewed, or who have read particular chapters, or helped in other ways. Many are mentioned within the pages, but I would like to separately acknowledge James Dyson, Owain Hughes, David Halpern and the Behavioural Insights Team, Jim Manzi, David Bentley, Carol Dweck, Robert Dodds, Sidney Dekker, Steve Art, Meghan Mahoney, the wonderful people at Mercedes F1 and Team Sky, Toby Ord, Mark McCarthy, Tony McHale, Rita Weeks, David Beckham, Steve Jones and Esther Duflo.

Most of all, I would like to thank Kathy, my amazing wife, Evie and Teddy, our children, and Abbas and Dilys, my parents. This is for you.

Notes

1. A Routine Operation

1 Material on Elaine Bromiley's operation based on interviews with Martin, Victoria and Adam Bromiley, the independent report by Dr Michael Harmer and other supporting documents.

2 Daniel Coyle, *The Talent Code: Greatness Isn't Born. It's Grown. Here's How.* (Random House, 2009).

3 http://www.iata.org/publications/Documents/iata-safety-report-2013.pdf

4 http://www.iata.org/pressroom/pr/Pages/2015-09-89-01.aspx

5 Members of the IATA. http://www.iata.org/pressroom/facts_figures/fact_sheets/Documents/safety-fact-sheet.pdf

6 'To Err is Human', by the Institute of Medicine: https://www.iom.edu/~/media/Files/Report%20Files/1999/To-Err-is-Human/To%20Err%20is%20Human%201999%20%20report%20brief.pdf

7 Peter I. Buerhaus, 'Lucian Leape on the Causes and Prevention of Errors and Adverse Events in Health Care', *Journal of Nursing Scholarship*, June 2007.

8 http://journals.lww.com/journalpatientsafety/Fulltext/2013/09000/A_New,_Evidence_based_Estimate_of_Patient_Harms.2.aspx

9 http://www.c-span.org/video/?320495-1/hearing-patient-safety

10 Joe Graedon and Teresa Graedon, *Top Screwups Doctors Make and How to Avoid Them* (Harmony, 2011).

11 http://www.c-span.org/video/?320495-1/hearing-patient-safety

12 http://www.c-span.org/video/?320495-1/hearing-patient-safety

13 'A Safer Place for Patients: Learning to Improve Patient Safety',

National Audit Office report, 3 November 2005.

14 Atul Gawande, *Complications: A Surgeon's Notes on an Imperfect Science* (Profile, 2008).

15 http://www.who.int/classifications/help/icdfaq/en/

16 CBS News Story, 21 April 2014, http://www.cbsnews.com/news/ferry-captains-acts-murderous-south-korean-president/

17 Sidney Dekker, lecture in Brisbane: https://vimeo.com/102167635

18 Gerry Greenstone, 'The History of Bloodletting', *British Columbia Medical Journal*, January 2010.

19 Nancy Berlinger, *After Harm: Medical Error and the Ethics of Forgiveness* (Johns Hopkins University Press, 2007).

20 Compared with similar centres nearby, it had lower compensation claims than all but seven of its competitors. But also see Dr David Studdert et al., 'Disclosure of Medical Injury to Patients' in *Health Affairs*, 2007.

21 C. A. Vincent, M. Young, A. Phillips, 'Why do people sue doctors? A study of patients and relatives taking legal action', *Lancet*, 1994; 343: 1609–13.

22 http://www.ncbi.nlm.nih.gov/pubmed/18981794

23 David Hilfiker, 'Facing Our Mistakes', *New England Journal of Medicine*, 1984.

24 James Reason, *A Life in Error: From Little Slips to Big Disasters* (Ashgate, 2013).

25 Rae M. Lamb, 'Hospital Disclosure Practices: Results of a National Survey', *Health Affairs*, 2003.

26 http://www.chron.com/news/article/Detective-work-required-to-uncover-errors-1709000.php

27 J. L. Vincent, 'Information in the ICU: Are we being honest with patients? The results of a European questionnaire', *Intensive Care Medicine*, 1998; 24(12): 1251–6.

28 http://www.ncbi.nlm.nih.gov/pubmed/21471476

29 http://www.nytimes.com/2002/10/15/us/alphonse-chapanis-dies-at-85-was-a-founder-of-ergonomics.html

30 Kim Phong L. Vu and Robert Proctor, *Handbook of Human Factors in Web Design*, Second Edition (CRC Press, 2004).

2. United Airlines 173

1 Information relating to the flight sourced from the National Transportation Safety Board Aircraft Accident Report (28 December 1978); *Focused on Failure*, episode from the Mayday TV series; various news sources; and multiple interviews with investigators, pilots and investigators.

2 http://www.eurohoc.org/task/task_docs/CAPAP2002_02.pdf

3 http://www.airdisaster.com/reports/ntsb/AAR78-08.pdf

4 http://www.airdisaster.com/reports/ntsb/AAR73-14.pdf

5 Malcolm Gladwell, *Outliers: The Story of Success* (Penguin, 2009).

6 This also hints at why so many scientific discoveries are made 'accidentally', such as penicillin, etc.

7 J. Vanden Bos et al., 'The $17.1billion problem: the annual cost of measurable medical errors', *Health Affairs*, 2011.

8 Sidney Dekker of Griffith University has lectured extensively about how the model used to understand why accidents happen has evolved over the last century and a half, in many remarkable and fascinating ways.

9 Oskar Morgenstern, Abraham Wald obituary, *Econometrica*, October 1951.

10 H. Freeman, 'Abraham Wald', in D. L. Sills (ed.), *International Encyclopedia of Social Sciences*, 16 (1968), 435–8.

11 Karl Menger, 'The Formative Years of Abraham Wald and His Work in Geometry', in *Annals of Mathematical Statistics*.

12 http://youarenotsosmart.com/tag/abraham-wald/

13 Ibid.

14 Ibid.

15 https://hbr.org/2011/04/strategies-for-learning-from-failure

16 http://cna.org/sites/default/files/research/0204320000.pdf

17 Oskar Morgenstern, Abraham Wald obituary.

3. The Paradox of Success

1 Information on United 1549 from investigation report (http://www.ntsb.gov/investigations/AccidentReports/Reports/AAR1003.pdf), two Mayday National Geographic documentaries on the flight, and various media reports.

2 http://content.time.com/time/specials/packages/article/0,28804,1894410_1894289_1894258,00.html

3 Karl Popper, from *Conjectures and Refutations: The Growth of Scientific Knowledge* (Routledge & Kegan Paul, 1963).

4 The story is a little more complex. The experiment only partially confirmed Einstein's theory. It took further experiments for scientists to universally agree that light is attracted to heavy bodies.

5 See Karl Popper, *Conjectures and Refutations*.

6 Philip H. Gosse, *Omphalos: An Attempt to Untie the Geological Knot* (Scholar's Choice, 2015).

7 Karl Popper, *Conjectures and Refutations*.

8 This example is cited in Bryan Magee's *Philosophy and the Real World: An Introduction to Karl Popper* (Open Court Publishing, 1985).

9 Nassim N. Taleb, *The Black Swan: The Impact of the Highly Improbable* (Penguin, 2008).

10 Daniel Kahneman and Gary Klein, 'Conditions for Intuitive Expertise, Failure to Disagree', *American Psychologist*, September 2009, Vol. 64, No. 6.

11 Ibid.

12 K. Anders Ericsson (ed.), *Development of Professional Expertise: Toward Measurement of Expert Performance and Design of Optimal Learning Environments* (Cambridge University Press, 2009).

13 Such a system has been recommended by K. Anders Ericsson in *Development of Professional Expertise: Toward Measurement of Expert Performance and Design of Optimal Learning Environments* (Cambridge University Press, 2009). A similar system driven by objective feedback has been proposed for psychotherapists by Terence Tracey of Arizona State University and colleagues. See Tracey et al., 'Expertise in Psychotherapy: An Elusive Goal?', *American Psychologist*, January 2014.

14 http://www.telegraph.co.uk/news/nhs/10940874/Can-the-Japanese-car-factory-methods-that-transformed-a-Seattle-hospital-work-on-the-NHS.html?mobile=basic

15 Ibid.

16 Ibid.

17 Charles Kenney, *Transforming Health Care: Virginia Mason Medical Center's Pursuit of the Perfect Patient Experience*, (Productivity Press, 2010).

18 http://www.nytimes.com/2008/05/18/us/18apology. html?pagewanted=all

19 http://www.nytimes.com/2008/05/18/us/18apology. html?pagewanted=print&_r=0

20 Peter Pronovost, lecture on System Safety at Johns Hopkins University.

21 http://www.nytimes.com/2010/03/09/science/09conv.html

22 Peter Pronovost, *Safe Patients, Smart Hospitals: How One Doctor's Checklist Can Help Us Change Healthcare from the Inside Out* (Plume, 2004).

23 Atul Gawande, *Complications*.

24 The Francis Report: http://www.midstaffspublicinquiry.com/sites/ default/files/report/Executive%20summary.pdf

25 The Kirkup Report: https://www.gov.uk/government/uploads/ system/uploads/attachment_data/file/408480/47487_MBI_Accessible_ v0.1.pdf

26 Select Committee Report: http://www.publications.parliament.uk/ pa/cm201415/cmselect/cmpubadm/886/88602.htm

27 http://www.deadbymistake.com/

28 Michael Gillam et al., 'The Healthcare Singularity and the Age of Semantic Medicine' in *The Fourth Paradigm: Data-Intensive Scientific Discovery* (Microsoft, 2009).

29 Atul Gawande, *The Checklist Manifesto: How To Get Things Right* (Profile, 2010).

30 Atul Gawande, *Complications*.

31 http://www.nytimes.com/2009/05/26/health/26autopsy. html?pagewanted=all&_r=0

32 Atul Gawande, *Complications*.

33 http://www.pbs.org/wgbh/pages/frontline/criminal-justice/ post-mortem/more-deaths-go-unchecked-as-autopsy-rate-falls- to-miserably-low-levels/

34 James Reason, *A Life in Error: From Little Slips to Big Disasters* (Ashgate, 2013).

35 http://www.chfg.org/resources/07_qrt04/Anonymous_Report_
Verdict_and_Corrected_Timeline_Oct_07.pdf

4. Wrongful Convictions

1 William Blackstone, *Commentaries on the Laws of England*
(Forgotten Books, 2012).
2 Edwin M. Borchard, *Convicting the Innocent and State Indemnity for
Errors of Criminal Justice* (Justice Institute, 2013).
3 Ibid.
4 Carole McCartney, 'Building Institutions to Address Miscarriages of
Justice in England and Wales: "Mission Accomplished"?', *University of
Cincinnati Law Review*.
5 For more on DNA in criminal justice see Jim Dwyer, Barry Scheck
and Peter Neufeld, *Actual Innocence: When Justice Goes Wrong and
How to Make it Right* (New American Library, 2003); and David Lazer
et al., *DNA and the Criminal Justice System: The Technology of Justice*
(MIT Press, 2004).
6 http://www.nhs.uk/Conditions/Blood-groups/Pages/Introductions.
aspx
7 Quote taken from Jim Dwyer, Barry Scheck and Peter Neufeld,
Actual Innocence.
8 For an analysis of some of the pitfalls of interpreting very small
fragments of DNA see David Bentley QC, 'DNA and Case Preparation',
Law Society Gazette, January 2015.
9 Information on wrongful convictions from the Innocence Project,
state databases and various interviews.
10 Information on Michael Shirley taken from court documents,
reports and two author interviews with his solicitor, Anita Bromley.
11 Innocence Project.
12 Samuel R. Gross et al., 'Exonerations in the United States, 1989
through 2003', *Journal of Criminal Law and Criminology*, vol. 95, no. 2,
2005.
13 Dwyer, Scheck and Neufeld, *Actual Innocence*.
14 Leon Festinger, Henry Riecken and Stanley Schachter, *When
Prophecy Fails* (Martino Fine Books, 2009).
15 Poll cited in Carol Tavris and Elliot Aronson, *Mistakes Were Made*

(but Not by Me): Why We Justify Foolish Beliefs, Bad Decisions and Hurtful Acts (Pinter & Martin, 2013).

16 Elliot Aronson and Judson Mills, 'The Effect of Severity of Initiation on Liking for a Group', *Journal of Abnormal and Social Psychology*, September 1959, Vol. 59.

17 Carol Tavris and Elliot Aronson, *Mistakes Were Made (but Not by Me)*.

18 Charles Lord, Lee Ross and Mark Lepper, 'Biased Assimilation and Attitude Polarisation: The Effects of Poor Theories on Subsequently Considered Evidence', *Journal of Personality and Social Psychology*, 1979, Vol. 37.

19 Innocence Project website.

20 Kathryn Schulz, *Being Wrong: Adventures in the Margin of Error* (Portobello Books, 2011).

21 Quoted in Tavris and Aronson, *Mistakes were Made (by Not by Me)*.

22 Schulz, *Being Wrong*.

23 http://www.nytimes.com/2011/11/27/magazine/dna-evidence-lake-county.html?_r=0

24 http://www.nytimes.com/2011/11/27/magazine/dna-evidence-lake-county.html

25 https://www.youtube.com/watch?v=wPtaYIvGxqn

26 Dwyer, Scheck and Neufeld, *Actual Innocence*.

27 Ibid.

28 Innocence Project.

29 Dwyer, Scheck and Neufeld, *Actual Innocence*.

5. Intellectual Contortions

1 Tavris and Aronson, *Mistakes were Made (but Not by Me)*.

2 John Banja, *Medical Errors and Medical Narcissism* (Jones & Bartlett, 2005).

3 Ibid.

4 Ibid.

5 Jeff Stone and Nicholas C. Fernandez, 'How Behaviour Shapes Attitudes: Cognitive Dissonance Processes', in William D. Crano and Radmila Prislin (ed.), *Attitudes and Attitude Change* (Psychology Press, 2013).

6 http://www.tonyblairoffice.org/news/entry/iraq-syria-and-the-middle-east-an-essay-by-tony-blair/

7 http://blogs.wsj.com/economics/2010/11/15/open-letter-to-ben-bernanke/

8 http://www.bloomberg.com/news/articles/2014-10-02/fed-critics-say-10-letter-warning-inflation-still-right

9 http://www.bloomberg.com/news/articles/2014-10-02/fed-critics-say-10-letter-warning-inflation-still-right

10 Philip E. Tetlock, *Expert Political Judgement: How Good Is It? How Can We Know?* (Princeton University Press, 2006).

11 Sydney Finkelstein, *Why Smart Executives Fail: And What You Can Learn from Their Mistakes* (Portfolio Penguin, 2013).

12 Terrance Odean, 'Are Investors Reluctant to Admit their Losses?', *The Journal of Finance*, October 1998.

13 Paul J. H. Schoemaker, *Brilliant Mistakes: Finding Success on the Far Side of Failure* (Wharton Digital Press, 2011).

14 Karl Popper, *The Poverty of Historicism* (Routledge, 2002).

15 As recounted in *Safe Patients, Smart Hospitals* by Peter Pronovost.

16 David Hilfiker, 'Facing Our Mistakes', *New England Journal of Medicine*, 12 January 1984.

17 C. E. Milch et al., 'Voluntary electronic reporting of medical errors and adverse events: An analysis of 92,547 reports from 26 acute care hospitals', *Journal of General Internal Medicine*.

18 Peter Pronovost, *Safe Patients, Smart Hospitals*.

6. Reforming Criminal Justice

1 The Lysenko story is covered in dozens of articles and books, including *Lysenko and the Tragedy of Soviet Science* (Rutgers University Press, 2006), by Valery N. Soyfer and *The Lysenko Effect: The Politics of Science* (Prometheus Books, 2004) by Nils Roll-Hansen.

2 http://tauruspet.med.yale.edu/staff/edm42/IUPUI-website/emorris.tar/emorris/emorris/Ethics%20Course%2009/Journal%20articles/lysenko-nature-rev-genetics2001-nrg0901_723a.pdf

3 Jasper Becker, *Hungry Ghosts, Mao's Secret Famine* (Simon & Schuster, 1997).

4 http://www.haydenplanetarium.org/tyson/watch/2008/06/19/
george-bush-and-star-names

5 http://thefederalist.com/2014/09/16/
another-day-another-quote-fabricated-by-neil-degrasse-tyson/

6 http://thefederalist.com/2014/10/02/
neil-tysons-final-words-on-his-quote-fabrications-my-bad/

7 Giuliana Mazzoni and Amina Memon, 'Imagination Can Create
False Autobiographical Memories', *Psychological Science*, September
2010.

8 Elizabeth F. Loftus and John C. Palmer, 'Reconstruction of automobile destruction: An example of the interaction between language and
memory', *Journal of Verbal Learning and Verbal Behavior*, 13, (1974),
585–9.

9 http://news.bbc.co.uk/1/hi/uk/4177082.stm

10 Innocence Project website.

11 Gary L. Wells, Nancy K. Steblay and Jennifer E. Dysart, 'A Test of
the Simultaneous vs Sequential Lineup Methods: An Initial Report of
the AJS National Eyewitness Identification Field Studies', American
Judicature Society. It is worth noting that the cost of implementation
of these reforms is relatively small.

12 Innocence Project website.

13 http://articles.chicagotribune.com/2002-09-29/
news/0209290340_1_jogger-case-jogger-attack-matias-reyes

14 Dwyer, Scheck and Neufeld, *Actual Innocence*.

15 http://www.miamiherald.com/incoming/article1953372.html

16 'Strengthening Forensic Science in the United States', report,
2009.

17 http://www.nytimes.com/2014/12/02/opinion/why-our-memory-
fails-us.html

18 Shai Danziger, Jonathan Levav and Liora Avnaim-Pesso,
'Extraneous factors in judicial decisions', Proceedings of the National
Academy of Sciences.

19 http://blogs.discovermagazine.com/notrocketscience/2011/04/11/
justice-is-served-but-more-so-after-lunch-how-food-breaks-sway-the-
decisions-of-judges/#.VYaU8oYk-So

20 http://articles.chicagotribune.com/2014-06-10/news/
chi-dna-links-murder-and-rape-of-holly-staker-11-to-second-murder-
8-years-later-20140610_1_holly-staker-dna-evidence-dna-match

21 Interview with author.

22 http://www.chicagotribune.com/news/local/breaking/ct-juan-rive-
ra-shoes-met-20141210-story.html#page=1

7. The Nozzle Paradox

1 See Steve Jones lecture: https://www.youtube.com/watch?v=for_
WIKgdWg. See also Owen Barder: http://www.owen.org/blog/4018

2 Including Karl Popper and Friedrich Hayek.

3 Tim Harford, *Adapt: Why Success Always Starts with Failure*
(Abacus, 2012).

4 Paul Omerod, quoted in Ibid.

5 Terence Kealey, *The Economic Laws of Scientific Research* (Palgrave
Macmillan, 1996).

6 Nassim Nicholas Taleb, *Antifragile: Things that Gain from Disorder*
(Penguin, 2013).

7 See Jonah Lehrer, *The Decisive Moment* (Canongate, 2007), p. 47.

8 Daniel Kahneman, *Thinking, Fast and Slow* (Penguin, 2012).

9 http://www.bbc.co.uk/news/business-27579790

10 Peter Sims, *Little Bets: How Breakthrough Ideas Emerge from Small
Discoveries* (Random House Business, 2012).

11 Ibid.

12 Ryan Babineaux and John Krumboltz, *Fail Fast, Fail Often: How
Losing Can Help You Win* (Tarcher, 2014).

13 David Bayles and Ted Orland, *Art and Fear: Observations on the
Perils (and Rewards) of Artmaking* (Image Continuum Press, 2001).

14 https://www.youtube.com/watch?v=vY3OtMBCEKY

15 Eric Ries, *The Lean Startup: How Constant Innovation Creates
Radically Successful Businesses* (Portfolio Penguin, 2011).

16 Ibid.

17 Ibid.

18 Jim Collins and Morten T. Hansen, *Great by Choice: Uncertainty,
Chaos and Luck – Why Some Thrive Despite Them All* (Random House
Business, 2011).

19 Peter Sims, *Little Bets: How Breakthrough Ideas Emerge from Small Discoveries* (Random House Business, 2012).

20 http://www.bbc.co.uk/news/business-27579790

21 Interview with author.

22 http://www.ncbi.nlm.nih.gov/pmc/articles/PMC1470513/

23 As measured by Disability Adjusted Life Years, a conventional measure in development.

24 Toby Ord, 'The Moral Imperative toward Cost-Effectiveness in Global Health', Center for Global Development, March 2013.

25 http://lesswrong.com/lw/h6c/taking_charity_seriously_toby_ord_talk_on_charity/

26 https://www.givingwhatwecan.org/

8. Scared Straight?

1 *Scared Straight!*, documentary directed by Arnold Shapiro, 1978.

2 *Scared Straight!*, commentary by Peter Falk.

3 See James Finckenauer, *Scared Straight: The Panacea Phenomenon Revisited* (Waveland Pv Inc, 1998).

4 Peter W. Greenwood, *Changing Lives: Delinquency Prevention as Crime Control Policy* (University of Chicago Press, 2007).

5 Quoted in documentary *Scared Straight!*

6 Diagrams have been amended from 'Test, Learn Adapt' © Crown copyright June 2012, licensed under the terms of the Open Government Licence. Reproduced with permission.

7 Ben Goldacre, *Bad Science* (Harper Perennial, 2009).

8 Mark Henderson, *The Geek Manifesto: Why Science Matters* (Bantam Press, 2012).

9 See Ben Goldacre's excellent book *Bad Pharma: How Drug Companies Mislead Doctors and Harm Patients* (Faber & Faber, 2014).

10 I am grateful to Jim Manzi for making these points so clearly in his excellent book *Uncontrolled* (Basic Books, 2012).

11 Jonathan Sheperd, 'The Production and Management of Evidence for Public Service Reform in Evidence and Policy'.

12 Interview with author.

13 James Finckenauer, *Scared Straight*.

14 Interview with author.

15 Ibid.

16 Ibid.

17 See James Finckenauer; Scott O. Lilienfeld, 'Scientifically Unsupported and Supported Interventions for Childhood Psychopathology: A Summary', *Pediatrics*, 115; 761–4; and Daniel P. Mears, 'Towards Rational and Evidence-based Crime Policy', *Journal of Criminal Justice* (2007), Vol. 35; Issue 6, 667–82.

18 Silverman Prize.

19 http://reclaimingfutures.org/juvenile-justice-reform-scared-straight-facts-vs-hype

20 A. Petrosino, C. Turpin-Petrosino, M. E. Hollis-Peel and J. G. Lavenberg, 'Scared Straight and Other Juvenile Awareness Programs for Preventing Juvenile Delinquency: a Systematic Review'.

21 http://www.nytimes.com/2007/03/23/nyregion/23solve.html

22 http://www.northjersey.com/news/neighbor-sentenced-in-decades-old-ridgefield-park-murder-1.1238173

9. Marginal Gains

1 Reproduced with permission of Esther Duflo.

2 https://www.ted.com/speakers/esther_duflo

3 Jeffrey Sachs, *The End of Poverty: How We Can Make it Happen in Our Lifetime* (Penguin, 2005).

4 William Easterly, *The White Man's Burden: Why the West's Efforts to Aid the Rest Have Done So Much Ill and So Little Good* (Oxford University Press, 2007).

5 Tim Harford, *Adapt: Why Success Always Starts with Failure.*

6 https://www.ted.com/speakers/esther_duflo

7 Abhijit Banerjee and Esther Duflo, *Poor Economics: A Radical Rethinking of the Way to Fight Global Poverty* (Penguin, 2012).

8 Alan G. Robinson and Sam Stern, *Corporate Creativity: How Innovation and Improvement Actually Happen* (Berrett-Koehler, 1998).

9 See *Uncontrolled* by Jim Manzi.

10 https://hbr.org/2009/02/how-to-design-smart-business-experiments.

11 Interview with author.

12 Stephen J. Dubner and Steven D. Levitt, *Think Like a Freak: How to Think Smarter about Almost Everything* (Allen Lane, 2014).

13 See this excellent essay by Eric Ries: http://www.startuplesson-slearned.com/2010/04/learning-is-better-than-optimization.html

14 The tech blogger, Andrew Chen, has made this point brilliantly in a series of blog posts. See for example http://andrewchen.co/know-the-difference-between-data-informed-and-versus-data-driven/

10. How Failure Drives Innovation

1 Interview with author.

2 C. Nemeth, M. Personnaz, B. Personnaz and J. Goncalo, 'The Liberating Role of Conflict in Group Creativity: A Cross-Cultural Study'. Submitted to *European Journal of Social Psychology* (2004), 34, 365–74. See more at: http://psychology.berkeley.edu/people/charlan-jeanne-nemeth#sthash.bVcF2wGG.dpuf

3 Jonah Lehrer, *Imagine: How Creativity Works* (Houghton Mifflin Harcourt, 2012).

4 C. Nemeth and J. Kwan, 'Originality of Word Associations as a Function of Majority v Minority Influence Processes', *Social Psychology Quarterly*, 48.

5 See Jonah Lehrer, *Imagine: How Creativity Works* (Houghton Mifflin Harcourt, 2012).

6 He also integrated developments in metallurgy and high quality ink.

7 David Eagleman, *Incognito: The Secret Lives of the Brain* (Canongate, 2012).

8 Julia Cameron, *The Artist's Way: A Spiritual Path to Higher Creativity* (Pan, 1995).

9 Steven Johnson, *Where Good Ideas Come From: The Seven Patterns of Innovation* (Penguin, 2011).

10 Ibid.

11 See http://www.alfredwallace.org

12 Lorentz on Special Relativity, Hilbert on General Relativity.

13 See Ronald Cohn and Jesse Russell, *Relativity Priority Dispute* (VSD, 2012).

14 http://www.fundinguniverse.com/company-histories/hmi-industries-inc-history/

15 Jim Collins and Morten T. Hansen, *Great by Choice*.

16 Gerard J. Tellis and Peter N. Golder, *Will and Vision: How Latecomers Grow to Dominate Markets* (Figueroa Press, 2006).

17 Jim Collins and Morten T. Hansen, *Great by Choice*.

18 Jim Collins and Morten T. Hansen, *Great by Choice*.

19 Ibid.

20 Ed Catmull, *Creativity Inc* (Transworld Digital, 2014).

21 Ibid.

22 R. G. Dorman, *Dust Control and Cleaning* (Elsevier, 1973).

11. Libyan Arab Airlines Flight 114

1 Information relating to the flight sourced from Zvi Lanir, 'The Reasonable Choice of Disaster', *Journal of Strategic Studies*, 1989.

2 Major John T. Phelps, 'Aerial Intrusions by Civil and Military Aircraft in Time of Peace', *Military Law Review*, Winter 1985.

3 https://hbr.org/2011/04/strategies-for-learning-from-failure

4 Amy Edmondson, 'Learning From Mistakes is Easier Said than Done: Group and Organisation Influences on the Detection and Correction of Human Error', *Journal of Applied Behavioral Science*, 32, no. 1 (1996), 5–28.

5 Sidney Dekker, *Just Culture: Balancing Safety and Accountability* (Ashgate, 2012).

6 Interview with the author.

7 Interview with the author.

8 Sidney Dekker, *Just Culture*.

9 https://hbr.org/2011/04/strategies-for-learning-from-failure

10 Ben Dattner (with Darren Dahl), *The Blame Game* (Free Press, 2012).

11 Jean Brittain Leslie and Ellen Van Velsor, 'A Look at Derailment Today: North America and Europe', quoted in *The Blame Game* by Ben Dattner.

12 Fiona Lee, C. Peterson and L. Tiedens, 'Mea Culpa: Predicting Stock Prices From Organizational Attributions', in *Personality and Social Psychology Bulletin*, 30 (12), 2004, 1–14.

12. The Second Victim

1 *Baby P: The Untold Story*, documentary by BBC TV.

2 http://www.theguardian.com/commentisfree/2008/nov/18/comment-social-services-child-protection

3 Ray Jones, *The Story of Baby P: Setting the Record Straight* (Policy Press, 2014).

4 *Baby P: The Untold Story*.

5 Ray Jones, *The Story of Baby P*.

6 http://andrewadonis.com/2012/10/09/social-work-needs-a-teach-first-revolution/

7 http://www.dailymail.co.uk/news/article-1268433/In-hiding-mother-accused-abuse-cuddling-child.html

8 Ray Jones, *The Story of Baby P*.

9 http://www.communitycare.co.uk/2009/10/19/care-applications-to-cafcass-continue-to-soar/

10 Ray Jones, *The Story of Baby P*.

11 See Statistical Appendix to Office of National Statistics Report on Violent Crime and Sexual Offences.

12 *Baby P: The Untold Story*.

13 J. F. Christensen, W. Levinson and P. M. Dunn, 'The heart of darkness: the impact of perceived mistakes on physicians', *Journal of General Internal Medicine*, 1992, 7, 424–31.

14 T. D. Shanafelt, C. M. Balch, L. Dyrbye, et al., 'Special report: Suicide ideation among American Surgeons', *Archive of Surgeons*, 2011, 146, 54–62.

15 *Baby P: The Untold Story*.

16 Sidney Dekker, *Just Culture*.

17 Interview with Brian Leversha.

18 Stewart was found guilty of endangering the jet passengers but not guilty of endangering people and property on the ground, a contradiction that was later reported by the Law Society.

19 http://picma.org.uk/sites/default/files/Documents/Events/November%20Oscar%20article.pdf

13. The Beckham Effect

1 http://cpl.psy.msu.edu/wp-content/uploads/2011/12/Moser_
Schroder_Moran_et-al_Mind-your-errors-2011.pdf

2 Carol I. Diener and Carol S. Dweck, 'An Analysis of Learned
Helplessness: Continuous changes in performance, strategy and
achievement cognitions following failure', *Journal of Personality and
Social Psychology*, Vol. 36(5), May 1978, 451–62.

3 In press. But see: https://hbr.org/2014/11/
how-companies-can-profit-from-a-growth-mindset

4 http://www.forbes.com/forbes/2009/0824/colleges-09-
education-west-point-america-best-college.html

5 http://www.west-point.org/parent/wppc-st_louis/
Handbooks/2011ParentCadetInfo.pdf

6 Angela L. Duckworth, Christopher Peterson, M. D. Matthews and D.
R. Kelly, 'Grit: Perseverance and Passion for Long-Term Goals', revised
for resubmission to the *Journal of Personality and Social Psychology*,
2007, June 92(6), 1087–101.

7 See https://www.man.com/GB/cultivating-skill-in-a-world-lack-
ing-genius, *IQ versus RQ: Differentiating Smarts from Decision
Making Skills*, by Michael J Mauboussin and *Understanding
Overconfidence: Implicit theories, preferential attention, and distorted self-assessment*, by Joyce Ehrlinger and Carol S. Dweck (in
press).

14. Redefining Failure

1 Karl Popper, *The Logic of Scientific Discovery* (Routledge, 2002).

2 http://www.bbc.co.uk/news/magazine-26359564

3 Carol Dweck, 'The Role of Expectations and attributions in the
Alleviation of Learned Helplessness', *Journal of Personality and Social
Psychology*, Vol 31, April 1975.

4 See Barbara G. Licht and Carol S. Dweck, *Developmental
Psychology*, Vol. 20, July 1984. This links with what we learned in
Chapter 5, where those with the strongest reputations – in medicine,
in economics, in politics – were most threatened by their own mistakes, and were most likely to reframe them.

5 http://www.silicon-edge.com/blog/japan-has-problems-but-its-not-a-fear-of-failure

6 http://knowledge.wharton.upenn.edu/article/the-entrepreneurship-vacuum-in-japan-why-it-matters-and-how-to-address-it/

7 http://www.gemconsortium.org/assets/ uploads/1313079015GEM_2009_Global_Report_Rev_140410.pdf

8 http://gcmconsortium.org/docs/download/3616

9 https://www.youtube.com/watch?v=hIuoHmoibfE

10 http://www.oecd.org/pisa/keyfindings/pisa-2012-results-overview.pdf

11 Jo Boaler, *Mathematical Mindsets* (forthcoming).

12 Ibid.

13 http://mindsets-and-motivation-lab.commons.yale-nus.edu.sg/wp-content/uploads/sites/39/2014/12/OKeefe-2013.pdf

14 E. E. Jones and S. Berglas, 'Control of attribution about the self through self-handicapping strategies: The appeal of alcohol and the role of underachievement', *Personality and Social Psychology Bulletin*, 4, 200–206.

15 https://www.nytimes.com/2009/01/06/health/06mind.html?_r=0

Coda

1 Bryan Magee, *Philosophy and the Real World*.

2 See Karl Popper, *Conjectures and Refutations*.

3 But see also Karen Armstrong, *Fields of Blood: Religion and the History of Violence* (Bodley Head, 2014).

4 Bryan Magee, *Philosophy and the Real World*.

5 Francis Bacon, *Novum Organum* (Leopold Classic Library, 2015).

6 Ibid.

7 Ibid.

8 *Uncertain Truth*, TV programme in which Popper is interviewed by the art historian, Ernst Gombrich. https://www.youtube.com/watch?v=VWcSiM9ZjoU

9 Edwin M. Borchard, *Convicting the Innocent and State Indemnity for Errors of Criminal Justice* (Justice Institute, 2013).

10 Another powerful point that has been made by the thinker and entrepreneur, Jim Manzi.

11 https://www.youtube.com/watch?v=rAP4E3EpedE

12 Bryan Magee, *Philosophy and the Real World.*

13 http://www.ncbi.nlm.nih.gov/pubmed/24393136

14 http://www.mckinsey.com/insights/strategy/
strategic_decisions_when_can_you_trust_your_gut

15 https://hbr.org/2007/09/performing-a-project-premortem

Index